MODERN BISTROT
COOKERY

MODERN BISTROT
COOKERY

Antony Worrall Thompson

Illustrations by Michael Frith
Wines by Joseph Berkmann

Headline

First published in 1994 by HEADLINE BOOK PUBLISHING

10 9 8 7 6 5 4 3 2 1

British Library Cataloguing in Publication Data

Thompson, Antony Worrall
Modern Bistrot Cookery
I. Title
641.5

ISBN 0-7472-0839-5 (Hardback)
0-7472-7883-0 (Softback)

Design by Design/Section
Printed and bound in Italy by Canale & C. Spa

HEADLINE BOOK PUBLISHING
A division of Hodder Headline PLC
338 Euston Road
London NW1 3BH

CONTENTS

To Francesca

ACKNOWLEDGEMENTS

My thanks to all the special people who have enabled me to turn an idea into a cookbook. Francesca Hazard, to whom I have dedicated the book, who spent hours and hours of her spare time, often long into the night, bashing away at her word processor, and chipping in with, more often than not, invaluable comments about my use of the English language and relevancies that might occur to an amateur cook.

Fiona Lindsay, my agent, who in the last eighteen months since she took me under her wing, has managed to cajole me out of my slumbers. I hadn't written a book since *The Small and Beautiful Cookbook* in 1984, and now all of a sudden I have managed to write two more.

Michael Frith, whose watercolours for Craig Brown's restaurant column in *The Sunday Times* I have long admired. I was very excited when he agreed to produce the art work for this book; I hope he doesn't regret working with me, as I know there have been many occasions when he has found it extremely hard to pin me down. The results are superb.

Roy Ackerman, who gave me the opportunity to restart my restaurant career at One Ninety Queen's Gate and who subsequently gave me the confidence and backing to open Bistrot 190 from where many of the dishes in this book derive.

My Head Chefs at One Ninety Queen's Gate, dell'Ugo and Zoë, including Chris Millar, Troy Clayton (now back in the United States), Konrad Melling and Mark Emberton, without whose considerable talents in controlling those operations, I would not have been able to complete this project.

Luisa Alves, my PA, who kept me sane during the last few months of the book by managing my over-stretched diary, deflecting phone calls and generally making it appear as if I was in eight places at once.

Paul Reece, Managing Director of Simpson's of Cornhill plc, of which I am also a director, for allowing me the freedom in my contract to spend the time required to write *Modern Bistrot Cooking*.

Alan Brooke, Publishing Director of Headline, who gave the go-ahead for this book and must have torn his hair out waiting for the final manuscript. Susan Fleming, my editor, and Celia Kent, Managing Editor of Headline, who both showed exceptional patience and understanding when deadlines were proving to be difficult.

To all the food writers who have inspired me to produce dishes that have filled restaurants over the last fifteen years. I include Elizabeth David, Jane Grigson, Wolfgang Puck, Jeremiah Towers, Alice Waters, Lindsey Bareham, Penelope Casas, Paula Wolfert, Giuliano Bugialli, Claudia Roden, Elizabeth Luard, Madeleine Kamman, Marcella Hazan, Bert Green, Viana La Place, Darina Allen and numerous others.

To my mother, who didn't bat an eyelid when she discovered me standing on a chair at the age of five burning scrambled eggs. Subsequently she encouraged me to take a serious interest in food throughout my formative years.

To my ex-wife Militza who inspires me to work harder in order to pay her monthly maintenance.

To all the restaurant critics, including Fay Maschler, Jonathan Meades, Craig Brown, Nick Lander, Matthew Fort and Emily Green, whose columns I have read avidly for several years. They generally appeal to the 'foodie purists', but in a funny sort of way, this has inspired me to pursue my stubborn approach in providing restaurants that attract happy, fun customers.

And finally a special thank-you to Joseph Berkmann, for stepping into the breach at the last moment when I made the decision to include wines in the text. His vast knowledge and understanding of the companionship of food and wine far exceed any information that I would have been able to impart to the reader.

INTRODUCTION

What is a *bistrot*? The *Concise Oxford Dictionary* gives the following definition: 'small bar or restaurant', which is very concise and very unimaginative. Let's face facts, the boffins in Oxford haven't done their homework very well. And what is the correct spelling, *bistrot* or *bistro*? I haven't really got to the bottom of this. Most French ones seem to include the 't' whereas the Brits leave it off - another case of Franglais, I would imagine. On this subject I'm going to side with the French, so *bistrot* it is!

The general consensus of opinion about the conception of the *bistrot* is that the word derived from Russian, meaning something like 'quick' or 'hurry'. Apparently, at the turn of the nineteenth century the Russians in Paris were an impatient bunch who used to snap their fingers and shout '*bistrot*!' in the local hostelries. (Sounds like a few of our customers in today's market.) This soon got around, and the shrewd cookies of the Parisian catering industry used to put the sign '*bistrot*' outside their establishments. The Russians then knew they could get a meal in a hurry.

In my view, a *bistrot* in France generally offers good, simple, no-nonsense food of a classical nature, food that can be kept warm or reheated, casseroles such as *coq au vin*, or *boeuf bourguignonne*, good soups, a simple salad, a roast chicken, a *daube* of beef, a couple of grills including *steak frites*, etc. It is also family food, usually served in an establishment owned and run by a family, mum in the kitchen or on the cash desk, dad out front or in the kitchen, various children waiting or washing up, and probably aunts, uncles and cousins helping as well. In this way, they keep their overheads down and consequently are able to offer cheaper prices.

As a general rule, we in England don't use the family environment in our restaurants or *bistrots* as they do in other parts of Europe, more's the pity. Of all European (EC) countries, we are definitely the strangers or loners. I can't think of any other European country that has such weak family links, so far as the restaurant business goes. Empire builders, maybe, but we've got a lot to learn regarding building the family unit.

When we started Bistrot 190 in Kensington, I felt there was a need to introduce home cooking at a sensible price, in a small neighbourhood restaurant. The recession had just begun, the word *bistrot* had been out of fashion since the early 1970s, so the time seemed right for its reintroduction. It worked, the *bistrot* has been packed since it opened, but it's not exactly like a French *bistrot*. I created a wild animal that occasionally got out of control, but was full of energy, with cheerful, intelligent staff and punchy music. I wanted the customers to have fun, I wanted to do away with the stuffiness that characterised restaurants in the 1980s, those *nouvelle* temples of food. I admit I was part of it, but I knew in 1988, when I sold my restaurant Ménage à Trois in Knightsbridge, that an era was over, it was time to do a U-turn away from pretty pictures on plates, and replace blandness with an intense spectrum of flavours, with food that was not frightened of flavour. Simon Hopkinson of Bibendum and Rowley Leigh of Kensington Place had already started the trend: Bistrot 190 continued their good work and at affordable prices.

The menu included several 'classics', a surprise really as I'm not too much of a 'classics' man, relishing more the challenge of combining different flavours with a sometimes over enthusiastic degree of imagination. My philosophy towards my customers is 'don't frighten them', and that may be stating the obvious, but it is amazing how many restaurants do. Customers can be alienated by menus, not recognising a single dish; by the aggressive unfriendly approach of the *maître d'* or restaurant manager, so that he or she feels unable to ask a question without appearing to be a fool; by the overpowering enthusiasm and professionalism of the waiters, so much so that you can't drop your napkin without a waiter rushing up with a

clean one (expensive on laundry); by the *sommelier* making you feel knee-high to a grasshopper for your lack of wine knowledge, and then placing your wine so far away from the table that you stare in desperation at your ice-bucket, willing the wine to jump magically to your table (I definitely prefer to pour my own wine); by the other customers turning around to investigate who could possibly be laughing in a restaurant (you're in a temple of food, not an amusement arcade, how dare you enjoy yourself); by the waiters or *maître d'* lying through their teeth when you complain, knowing full well you are right, coming back with answers such as 'Chef says that's the way he cooks it'. So far as the latter is concerned, you're far likelier to win a friend and keep a customer by being honest, apologising and buying them a drink.

Remember this fact: an unhappy customer will tell of a miserable visit to at least ten of his friends, who in turn could each tell ten of theirs. They often write to the press and the guides, and generally will want to make the restaurateur's life hell, as their life was made hell. The happy customer may tell a few people but usually only if asked; the unhappy customer makes far more effort to spread the word. That's the nature of the beast, especially the British beast. So at Bistrot 190 and the other restaurants, customers will always find on the menu dishes that they'll recognise, whether it be *steak frites*, chargrilled spicy chicken, or a simple salad. The wines will be recognisable: you'll get your first glass poured, then it's down to you, but the bottle is always on the table or within grabbing distance. I want you to shout, not whisper, laugh, not sulk, and have a bundle of fun. I don't want miserable old sods or snobs. My waiting staff are usually friendly, sometimes lacking in professionalism and whilst they may pick up your napkin, you certainly won't get another. As well as pleasing the customer, we're in business to make money.

My restaurant philosophy is very much one of trying to create a café society, where anyone can eat out on a regular basis without breaking the bank. What alternatives do we have for meeting friends for a snack or a drink? The pub I suppose, but most are not geared towards females and still fewer can cope with children, except on the rare sunny day when they can play in the back garden. Let's get on to home entertaining. Brits tend not to be very neighbourly as a rule and so entertaining is often for special occasions or 'keeping up with the Joneses'. Cafés and *bistrots* are the friendly alternative, mutual ground, no pretensions, no one forcing you to eat a banquet, one course or more - the choice is yours, a glass or a bottle, go for it, have fun, that's life, or it certainly should be.

And that is the theme of this book, simple, fun home cooking adapted from my *bistrots*. As for the title of the book, *Modern Bistrot Cooking*, I think the average impression of a *bistrot* is that it serves old-fashioned family food. There is no reason why it should be old-fashioned though. *Bistrots* must evolve with time as does everything else, nothing stands still. Fashions exist in food, as they do in other things. I have included several traditional recipes, but they are there because in their own way they have become fashionable again and because today's market demands to eat this style of food. Other dishes are modern interpretations of classics, or dishes borrowed or stolen from my culinary travels or readings.

I was once mentioned in column inches as the 'Robin Hood of Chefs' because I was providing food for the people at affordable prices. Emily Green of the *Independent* re-named me 'Prince of Thieves', a title that I find flattering and have used in many articles and interviews since. Emily, God bless her little cotton-socks, was criticising me for stealing other people's ideas - shock, horror - *moi*? But, of course, she was right. My regular travels around the globe - in the Americas, Australasia, the East - have all given me snippets and in some cases great chunks of inspiration, which I adapt in my own little way to 'create' a dish. Nothing in cookery is written in stone, dishes are constantly evolving, and I do my fair share of the evolvement - a different herb here, a different sauce there, a different combination, a different presentation ... Very little is new in cookery.

Many chefs think alike; I thought I had created my Garlic Terrine (see page 122) when I opened Bistrot 190, and yet a few weeks later I discovered it at Jacques Maximin's restaurant in Nice. I had certainly never seen it before, never read about it, but there you are, two chefs with the same idea at the same time - who stole from whom? ESP, I reckon. Of course, I get ideas from eating out, or from reading my large library of cookbooks and from general discussions, who doesn't. I seem to have a knack for knowing what food customers enjoy, but you can't please everybody, which is why the restaurant world is such an exciting place to be. There's room for all of us who want to provide a genuine product; different interpretations of the customers' needs are what makes our world go round. 'Prince of Thieves' or not!

I have written *Modern Bistrot Cooking* for you, the real people, not for chefs or restaurateurs (there are plenty of books for them). This one is for you to use at home, not for putting on the coffee table and thinking 'Wow, that looks fabulous, but there's no way I'm attempting that dish.' I did my 'Cheffie Ego Trip', when I wrote *The Small and Beautiful Cookbook* back in 1984; it was a book trying to prove to my peers that I could cook, but it wasn't really suited for the public; every dish had 101 different ingredients, a complicated mousse or a poncey garnish - that was the 1980s. The recipes in this book are achievable by most amateur enthusiasts; some dishes are more complex than others, and some dishes require pre-preparation, but that's the essence of *bistrot* food. The dishes work, but if *you* can't make them work, you know where to find me. The menus are balanced; I have, however, made suggestions for alternatives where there may be a problem of purchase in some parts of the country. Seasonings are a very personal part of cooking, hence many recipes say 'season to taste'. Cooking times and temperatures are estimates - I am not in your kitchen so I don't know the temperature of your oven, the heat of your hob, or the size and quality of your ingredients.

You can mix and match the dishes, remember cookery is all about confidence in your own abilities. I have not written the Gospel according to Antony - as I change other people's food, so you can change mine. As I read cookery books for inspiration, so should you. Just go for it, have fun, and believe in your own abilities.

MY WINE POLICY

'A little knowledge is a dangerous thing,' or so they say, but we all have to start off with a little knowledge and from there on in we expand it or don't as the case may be. What I can't understand is people accepting without question the 'wine with food rules'. You don't need to be conventional, you can play with wine and food combinations. The main rule to follow should be: if you like the combination, that's good enough. You'll receive no end of advice if you really want to learn about wine from the wine experts in the weekend papers, but your tastebuds must make the final decision.

The rules that are in common practice at present are:

young before old
white before red
dry before sweet
white with fish
red with red meat
wine doesn't work with salad dressings, eggs, artichokes, asparagus or chocolate

According to David Rosengarten, who writes about wine at length in the USA, and whose views I respect, rules are made to be broken, and as I've broken the rules all my life I don't intend to stop now. So let's analyse these rules.

YOUNG BEFORE OLD
The idea behind this statement is that generally during a dinner you will build up to a crescendo with your masterpiece served at the end. This can be damaging: the strong

lingering tastes of fresh fruit and tannins can overpower the subtlety and complexity of an older wine rendering the last wine you drink, which is probably the best, wasted. You might like to try the following: if you are drinking fruity wines then you should drink the older vintage first and the young later; but if you are drinking tannic wines such as Bordeaux then the old rules apply, young first, old later. Think of taste not waste. You can follow the progression from light to heavy, but not necessarily youth to antiquity.

WHITE BEFORE RED

This was often the rule because fish usually precedes meat, but in today's health-conscious world we may choose fish as a main course preceded by *carpaccio* of beef or a duck salad. So you may choose a light Beaujolais or Pinot Noir with the *carpaccio*, followed by a chunky Chardonnay with the fish. Fashions change, too. Previously we may have been used to a lighter style of white from Burgundy or the Loire, but today customers often choose wines by grape varieties - Sauvignon, Chardonnay, Cabernet Sauvignon, Merlot, etc. - and a very fashionable request in restaurants nowadays is 'Can I have a glass of Chardonnay?' These tend to be real hunks, deep, oaky New World whites from California and Australia, often inappropriate to be followed by a light red such as a Beaujolais. Also one usually thinks of Sauvignons being drunk before Chardonnays, but in fact Sauvignons can easily follow Chardonnays as they will generally stand up to anything. These whites can easily stand up to meat, and lighter styles of red often have enough acidity to work with fish. Think about it.

DRY BEFORE SWEET

In most cases this rule works, but there are the exceptions. One that stands out in food fashions is the service of *foie gras*, with which it is common practice to serve a sweet wine, perhaps a Sauternes. If you have this at the start of the meal, it works well so long as the wine following is not too dry - a Mosel or Gewürztraminer would be ideal partners.

WHITE WITH FISH

It would be quite acceptable to stick to this rule without making too many mistakes, but you must establish whether the wine and fish are similar or whether they should be contrasting. The acidity of white wine tends to cut through the fats and oils and the fishy taste, similar to squeezing lemon juice over a piece of grilled fish. But many of today's white wines, as I explained earlier, are very chunky and often oaky, and wines such as some of the New World Chardonnays which are low in acidity, might overpower some fish with their sweetness and exaggerate the fishiness because they don't have the proper acidity. I think, therefore, that you need a light acidic white. Having said that, many reds are made in a light style with very little tannin and wood, so their acidity can cut through the strong taste of fish. As a general rule any red, provided it is very young, will go with fish. When deciding which colour to choose, the way in which the fish is prepared is important: the sauce, seasoning and cooking procedures. If the fish has been cooked in red wine then it would obviously be very acceptable to drink a red. Likewise, if the fish has been barbecued, then the smoky, charred flavour will stand up well to a light red, such as a Beaujolais.

RED WITH RED MEAT

White wines have long been drunk with chicken and veal, but the new rich whites of the New World - California, Australia and New Zealand - can make great partners for a red meat stew or a spicy red meat dish. If the meat dish is very rich, you want a wine that can cut through this richness, something that is tannic and well structured, so have fun playing with combinations, don't be put off by rules.

NO WINE WITH ...

The principal no-no's for wine are salad dressing, eggs, artichokes, asparagus and chocolate, which have a reputation for being lousy partners. Wine writers often shy away from making selections to go with these ingredients.

With salad dressings, remember to use a high oil ratio to vinegar or lemon juice, at least 4 parts to 1. Usually a light white wine with high acidity will match suitably as the salad dressing and the wine have similar components.

As for eggs, one wouldn't normally have wine with breakfast, but where the egg in a dish is partnered by other ingredients, a low alcohol white wine would be suitable: the fattiness of the egg contrasting with the acidity of the wine. Similarly, one or two reds go well with eggs: again these should be light and low in alcohol, especially if some of the other ingredients in the dish are known to work well with the wine. A classic, of course, is *oeufs en meurette*, a dish from Burgundy, cooked with bacon and Beaujolais, and so, not unreasonably, Beaujolais would be a good partner.

Artichokes and asparagus tend to make wines taste sweeter, but if they were prepared with an acidic component, such as lemon or tomato, then a dry white wine or a light red would relish the challenge. Artichokes *barigoule* comes to mind, where they are cooked with white wine and olive oil, thus making a partnership with a white from Provence. With asparagus I would choose a Sauvignon from the Loire, such as a Sancerre.

Chocolate has always been a problem with wine, but mainly because those served have tended to be too thin and wimpish. You need a powerhouse to survive, perhaps a Pedro Ximenez sherry, a rich young port, or a Madeira. The chocolate actually tends to make the fortified wines less rich and more quaffable. Apart from these combinations, the addition of fruits such as berries to the chocolate will help.

As with cooking, the pleasures of combining food and wine come from confidence in your own judgement. Don't be bamboozled into believing everything you read; your choice counts, so have fun experimenting.

So I have chosen to impart a little wine knowledge to you which, as I have said before, can be dangerous, but then I've never been one to flinch at a little excitement. Talking of excitement, I've asked Joseph Berkmann to write about wines to complement each menu. Joseph is an amazing character. Looking at him you would imagine him to be a charming, mature, successful businessman, but that would only be half the story. Put him on a windsurfer, or a pair of skis, and you would see a man dressed in blue wearing red underpants over his leggings and sporting a red cape ... Superman could be his middle name! He can outperform men half his age, but then he did ski for his native country, Austria.

Joseph Berkmann is one of us, a natural restaurateur, who used to run the best chain of restaurants in London. Later in his career, he turned to wines and now owns Berkmann Wine Cellars, one of the most successful wine importers in this country. Joseph is the perfect man to tell us about the wine for my menus, because as a restaurateur he understands the importance of the marriage of food and wine. Too often wine writers in our weekend newspapers tell us of wonderful wines, but how often do they try and match these wines with food? Not very frequently. Their columns would be far more readable if this was the case.

Joseph is never one to stand still. From his base in the South of France he dictates his wine policies from all over the world, travelling far and wide looking for wines that will suit the current trends in restaurants and, more importantly, the expanding supermarket trade.

I was very excited when Joseph agreed to write the wine notes. He writes in a similar vein to myself, an easy-going, amusing read, conveying his vast knowledge without sounding pompous or reverent.

You, the reader, and I, the writer, may occasionally have differing views but that's what makes the food world so interesting, everything is subjective.

EVERY DAY SHOULD BE VALENTINE'S DAY

New Potatoes with Soured Cream and Sevruga Caviar

Crudités with Dips

Native and Rock Oysters with Shallot and Chilli Vinegar

Warm Asparagus with Maltaise Sauce

Poached Lobster with Coriander Salsa

Baked Banana with Häagen-Dazs Ice Cream

Coffee and Chocolates

St Valentine's Day - why we need an excuse to be romantic is beyond me. It seems to be an overplayed commercial exercise giving an excuse for quadrupling the price of red roses. Here I've created a sexy menu for any gushing day you choose including Valentine's Day. The atmosphere must be romantic and decadent. A pervasive and evasive quality - it's difficult to capture all of it, but without all of it you have nothing.

The setting: create that special atmosphere full of romantic messages; a fusion of the spiritual and the physical that improves the excitement of passionate love.

Historically we come laden with roses and chocolates because they both contain PEA, Phenyl-ethylamine Adrenalin type substances that are known to slow down the breakdown of beta endorphin which is one of the happiest of our hormones; sexes float along on a stream of enkephalins.

Apart from the romantic idea of aphrodisiacs, most column inches written lack credibility. Several foods however have flavours, textures and physical characteristics which hint of sexual pleasure either at the time of eating or several hours later when they have been absorbed and reappear as a body odour. Curry is definitely out; black truffles are the parents of some of the higher flights of aphrodisiac fantasy, producing a musky note with a faint whiff of garlic.

Our menu should be a sexy sharing affair which can be hand-fed to your partner: one plate for each course, shared and savoured by one for the other. Everything should be suggestive: don't hold back, self-denial is a wasteful skill. The menu needs planning; you don't want to spend half your evening in the kitchen and yet you don't really want to be interrupted by waiting staff.

To start, a little iced vodka straight from the freezer or set in a craggy ice block, or some pink champagne served before a crackling fire in chilled silver goblets with crudités and dips, the vegetables covered in newly fallen snow. Create a dish of new potatoes topped with soured cream and caviar.

After languishing slowly over champagne or vodka (never be in a hurry), suggest to your partner that it's time for dinner. The scene must be dramatic, designed for the occasion - a low table with cushions or a classic candle-lit affair with beautiful crystal. Don't confuse colours, no garish crockery, just plain white; beautiful flowers or the table scattered with red rose petals, little gifts or chocolates, love messages or poems.

First, a tray of oysters (half rock, half native) set high on a stand of crushed ice and seaweed. I always associate the erratic course of love with fish, as each taste gives a new experience, my reactions virginal. Oysters, with some justification, due to their smell, appearance and trace minerals such as zinc, have long been regarded as the food of love, but forget the aphrodisiacal qualities, enjoy them for their suggestions. Pour them one by one down your partner's throat or let them be sucked from their battered shells: a great start, simply accompanied by hot brown rolls, Echire butter and some chilli and shallot vinegar. Melted butter (forget the cholesterol for one day) is also very sexy and it recurs throughout my menu, so an alternative starter (depending on your bank balance) would be a large amount of caviar set in a solid ice stand with just warm blinis and melted butter and, if you must, chopped egg but definitely no onion. As you feed your partner allow a little melted butter to dribble down his or her chin, very suggestive...

The next course should involve asparagus, cooked to retain a little crunch to avoid the droop; asparagus should be proud, standing up to be counted, hand-fed to your partner with nothing more than a little nut butter (*beurre noisette*) or orange-flavoured hollandaise (maltaise sauce). If you really wanted to pull out all the stops, this could be accompanied by a whole truffle *en croûte* - the *croûte* being a light casing of golden filo pastry. A finger bowl is not a necessity on this occasion as your partner is at this time in a sharing, licking frame of mind, so what better than the natural juices for sanitising one's grubby paws?

For the main course, I would avoid red wine and red meat which are too heavy for

love. They're perfect for the cuddle in front of a black and white movie after Sunday lunch, but not when we want to improve the sexual appetite or the excitement at table. I'm staying with shellfish which leaves plenty of room for the heart to swoon a little. Lobster, on this occasion not a snob food, is a luxury that needs no special atmosphere for an introduction. Lobster is expensive because of its rarity; perfect for the occasions when we go 'OTT' about love; a symbol of expensive nights out, but enjoyed at home where you can really get to grips with it - every bit is devoured (avoiding the harder parts of the shell), munched, scrunched, sucked, each tiny claw investigated, penetrated and eviscerated. What more do you need apart from two large lobsters cooked in salted water, cut into chunks (don't be prissy) and accompanied by hot melted butter or a salsa based on coriander? Lobster could be replaced by langoustine or crab. Drink a good Fumé - either Pouilly or a Californian Fumé Blanc (Champagne throughout can be a little dehydrating) - reflecting your thoughts ... billowing white sheets, shards of sunlight, scent of the sea, breaking waves.

For pud, go for small amounts of baked banana served with a chunky sauce made from mashed bananas, soft brown sugar and clotted cream and a scoop of Häagen-Dazs ice cream. Spoon-fed, this is guaranteed to break down the last barriers of resistance - the night is yours.

Suggest coffee and chocolates on the sofa by the fire with a glass of cognac or Calvados which finalises your evening of romance and decadence. Don't they say the road to romance is paved with chocolate?

Stretch romance to the next morning. Provide your partner with a wonderful breakfast - flowers, exotic fruits, creamy yogurts, fresh juices and of course, champagne. Champagne for laughing, a stab of defiance with which to start the new day - a luxury for an unluxurious moment.

Serves 2

NEW POTATOES WITH SOURED CREAM AND SEVRUGA CAVIAR

6 new potatoes, cooked until tender in salted water
6 teaspoons soured cream
1 teaspoon finely sliced spring onion
freshly ground black pepper
1 oz (25g) caviar, preferably Sevruga or Beluga

Make a cross in the new potatoes and push open with your fingers. Mix the soured cream with the spring onion and black pepper. Pop a small dollop on top of each potato and follow that with 1 teaspoon caviar. Arrange on a dish scattered with rose petals.

CRUDITES WITH DIPS

Choose from the following raw prepared vegetables, all cut into bite-size pieces: carrots, cauliflower florets, Jerusalem artichokes, red cabbage, celery, celeriac, chicory, cucumber, fennel, kohlrabi, button mushrooms, spring onions, red and yellow peppers, radishes, sea kale, tomatoes, baby turnips.

To these could be added the following blanched vegetables: French beans, broccoli florets, baby leeks, mangetouts, new potatoes, asparagus, salsify.

And perhaps hard-boiled quails' or gulls' eggs.

The selection of vegetables does not need to be wide. Arrange them in a large colourful bowl on crushed ice (or newly driven snow, if you live in the country and it has recently snowed). Serve with a selection of dips which could include Anchoïade Rémoulade Sauce (page 51), Tapénade (page 49), Hummous (page 104), Aubergine Caviar (page 104), Soured Cream Dressing (page 86) or Rouille (see below).

Rouille
3 hard-boiled egg yolks
2 raw egg yolks
3 cloves garlic, peeled and mashed with a little salt
1 teaspoon tomato purée
1 dessertspoon harissa (chilli paste)
juice of 1 lemon
a pinch of saffron stamens, soaked in 1 tablespoon warm water
1½ teaspoons Dijon mustard
freshly ground white pepper
6fl oz (175ml) extra virgin olive oil

Combine all the ingredients except the olive oil in a food processor and blend until smooth. With the machine running, add the oil in a continuous trickle and process as for mayonnaise.

NATIVE AND ROCK OYSTERS WITH SHALLOT AND CHILLI VINEGAR

6 rock oysters
6 native oysters
crushed ice
1 lemon, halved
Shallot and chilli vinegar
5fl oz (150ml) red wine
10fl oz (300ml) red wine vinegar
4 shallots, peeled and finely diced
2 red chillies, seeded and finely diced

Make the vinegar first. Over a medium heat, boil the wine, vinegar, half the shallots and all the chilli for 15 minutes. Strain and bottle. When you want to serve add the remaining shallots.

Open the oysters, or easier still, get your fishmonger to open them for you as late as possible in the day. Serve on a bed of crushed ice with the lemon halves. Serve with the vinegar, warm brown rolls and Echire butter.

WARM ASPARAGUS WITH MALTAISE SAUCE

1lb (450g) asparagus, woody ends removed, stems peeled
salt
Maltaise sauce
10fl oz (300ml) Hollandaise Sauce (see page 110)
juice of 2 blood oranges, reduced by boiling to 1 tablespoon
1 teaspoon Orange Curaçao liqueur

Plunge the asparagus into a large pan of boiling salted water and cook for approximately 12-15 minutes, depending on the thickness of the stems. The asparagus can be tied in bundles for easy removal. It can also be cooked ahead, plunged into icy water and then reheated in boiling salted water when serving. Drain the asparagus on kitchen paper and serve on a long platter, with melted butter or Maltaise sauce. For the latter, simply add the orange juice and liqueur at the end of cooking the hollandaise.

POACHED LOBSTER WITH CORIANDER SALSA

2 x 2lb (900g) lobsters, live
salt and freshly ground black pepper
Coriander salsa
2oz (50g) coriander leaves
½oz (15g) parsley leaves
3 spring onions, finely chopped
I clove garlic, peeled
2fl oz (60ml) extra virgin olive oil
2fl oz (60ml) water
2 green chillies, finely chopped
2 tablespoons lime juice
grated rind of I lime

Have the fishmonger kill the lobsters (a sharp stab between the eyes on the crown of the head). Place in cold water salted enough to float a raw egg in and bring to the boil; remove from the heat and leave in the water for 20 minutes. Don't muck about putting different aromatics, such as vegetables and herbs, in the water; you want to taste the fresh unadulterated flavour of the sea.

Meanwhile, make the salsa. Combine all the ingredients in a food processor, retaining some texture until ingredients are emulsified; season to taste with salt and black pepper.

Drain the lobsters well, and cut the flesh into bite-size pieces; remove the gritty sac from the head and discard. Serve with a leaf salad if required, accompanied by the salsa.

BAKED BANANA WITH HAAGEN DAZS ICE CREAM

I tub Häagen-Dazs ice cream
Baked bananas
2 bananas, peeled
2 tablespoons dark rum
2 tablespoons soft dark brown sugar
zest and juice of I orange
Mashed bananas
2 bananas, peeled
3 tablespoons clotted cream
I tablespoon soft brown sugar
a squeeze of lemon juice
Caramel sauce
3oz (75g) sugar
water
2fl oz (60ml) double cream

Preheat the oven to 350°F/180°C/Gas 4. Place the bananas for baking on cooking foil. Cover with the rum, sugar, orange juice and zest and wrap in the foil. Bake for 12 minutes in the oven.

For the mashed bananas, mash all the ingredients together.

For the caramel sauce, cover the sugar with water in a clean copper pan and bring to the boil. Boil to the caramel stage and slowly add the cream. Bring back to the boil, stirring.

To serve, place the mashed bananas and ice cream in separate ramekins on the serving plate with the baked bananas in the centre. Pour over the caramel sauce.

WINE NOTES

A great American comic once said that 'wine is fine, but liquor is quicker'. I suppose there will be partisans of vodka, that tasteless slugger, but is that really a drink for romance and Valentine's Day? I should have thought pink Champagne was obligatory, Taittinger's Rosé, light and elegant.

If there are but two of you (which AWT must have had in mind, not having been married for twenty years or more, like the rest of us), then the pink Champagne will take you through spuds, dip and oysters. It is always difficult to follow Champagne with a Chardonnay, however illustrious, so my usual recommendation for great white Burgundy with lobster wouldn't work here, especially not with asparagus. Stronger flavours are needed, and the ideal, indeed the perfect, wine would be a special reserve of aged Pouilly-Fumé (not Fuissé), a wine made from old vines, about two or three years in bottle and usually labelled Prestige or something fancy like that. If you cannot find it, the next best thing would be an exotic Sauvignon from New Zealand's Hawkes Bay, or a really top Californian Fumé Blanc.

No sweet wine with bananas, you'd go to sleep before time's up. All the same I should recommend something a bit more appropriate than male Cognac or Calvados: Green Chartreuse - the greatest aphrodisiac known to woman.

A DEDICATION TO FOOD CRITICS

Duck Livers, Goat's Cheese and Spinach
A Stew of Fishes in a Saffron Broth, Clam Crostini
Walnut Tart with Crisp Apples

A menu uniting some of my favourite flavour combinations. The starter incorporates pan-fried duck livers with wilted spinach leaves and goat's cheese. At dell'Ugo this has proved to be one of our most popular starters, despite a well known food critic who hated the combination. I do not cater for purists in my restaurants, I don't need to as there are the Marco Pierre Whites, the Roux Brothers and others who will. My repertoire tries to please those who want off-the-wall creative dishes. There's a place in the restaurant world for all of us.

This brings me on to food critics. We all have a role to play in life and the role of the food critic is no less important than any other. Well-written restaurant reviews sell copy and help to fill restaurants; some might say they also empty restaurants, but I'm one of those who feel all publicity is good publicity. When you imagine how many restaurants open each year, then to feature in column inches is a 'result', whatever anyone else argues. We need critics, critics need restaurants. Restaurant criticism is very subjective. I can't tell a critic that he or she is wrong if they say they don't like one of my dishes. What *does* upset me is when food critics get their facts wrong, when they write about dishes that don't even appear on my menu, when they make a booking and turn up 45 minutes late and then write how they had their wrists slapped; they sometimes forget we're in business to make money, and time is money. They may quote the wrong opening hours or the wrong phone number (probably the fault of the sub-editors), and these are problems restaurateurs can do without.

We the restaurateurs also need a certain understanding of the psychology of a food critic: one critic used to be accompanied by a particularly tiresome partner and the reviews tended to be bad; the partner has now changed and the critic is easier to please. Another critic gave bad reviews when accompanied by his wife and generally good reviews when accompanied by his girlfriend. It's often judging their moods that is most important, and if they're having fun, then often you're halfway to enjoying a good review. It is not just the critics, the same goes for the public. Couples can often mean bad news: either they're in love, in which case they are staring into each other's eyes and the food is hardly noticed or touched; or they're arguing, in which case they'll probably still be in love in the morning but the restaurant will be the culprit who ruined the night before. One particular critic story keeps coming to mind. He booked a limo for the day, picked up a few friends, had a few bevvies, went to the rugby sevens, had a few more bevvies, then went down to one of my friend's restaurants in Kent with the same mates, all rather the worse for wear. The critic proceeded to throw up between the first and main courses and then the following week his column said the food didn't taste quite right. Not surprising really! It sometimes makes our job quite hard.

I've digressed from the menu. Following this delicious starter I serve a slightly Oriental broth filled with all manner of delicious goodies. The broth is made with clam and mussel juices, white wine and hints of saffron. The fishes include mussels, clams, monkfish and red mullet. The flavourings are made up with coriander, chilli, garlic and ginger. I finish the broth with some brightly coloured vegetables, sugar snap peas, spring onions, courgettes, spinach and cherry tomatoes. I serve the dish with crostini topped with chopped clams mixed with finely chopped orange and lemon rind, grated ginger, chopped coriander and red chilli.

For pud I serve a small portion of very rich walnut tart which is based on a favourite recipe from Madeleine Kamman's book on Savoie cooking. This is delicious served with some slices of crisp apple.

Serves 4

Duck Livers, Goat's Cheese and Spinach

3oz (75g) unsalted butter
4 tablespoons olive oil
16 duck livers (remove any sinew and green stains)
salt and freshly ground black pepper
2 tablespoons balsamic vinegar
4 tablespoons red wine
2 shallots, peeled and finely diced
1 clove garlic, peeled and finely diced
1 teaspoon soft thyme leaves
12oz (350g) spinach, washed, stems removed and thoroughly dried
6oz (175g) goat's cheese, cut into ½in (1cm) cubes

Heat half the butter in a frying pan with 1 tablespoon of the olive oil. Season the duck livers with salt and black pepper. Place the livers in the hot pan and fry quickly until all sides are browned, but the centres are still rosy. This takes about 5 minutes. Remove the livers and keep warm. Deglaze the pan with balsamic vinegar, scraping any coagulated bits from the bottom of the pan, and add the red wine; boil aggressively to reduce a little and fold in the remaining butter. Return the livers to the pan and keep warm.

Into another pan pour the remainder of the olive oil. Over a medium heat cook the shallots, garlic and thyme leaves until soft but not brown. Add the spinach and, stirring constantly, cook until the spinach has wilted. When the spinach has wilted and released some of its liquids, drain and discard the liquid and add the goat's cheese. By stirring with a wooden spoon, combine the spinach and the goat's cheese until the cheese starts to melt. Season with salt and black pepper to taste.

Place a spoonful of the spinach-cheese mixture on the centre of four warm plates and top with the warm duck livers and their sauce.

A Stew of Fishes in a Saffron Broth, Clam Crostini

1 pint (600ml) dashi (see page 43) or water and a pinch of saffron strands
4 tablespoons olive oil
4 teaspoons sesame oil
1 teaspoon chilli oil
2 shallots, peeled and finely diced
2 cloves garlic, peeled, crushed with a little salt
2 tablespoons chopped coriander root or stems
2in (5cm) piece of fresh ginger, peeled and grated
1 red chilli, seeded and diced
½ bottle dry white wine
2 bay leaves
2 strips dried orange peel
2lb (900g) baby clams, cleaned
2lb (900g) small mussels, cleaned
8oz (225g) monkfish fillet, cut into 1in (2.5cm) cubes
2 x 8oz (225g) red mullet, scaled, cleaned and filleted
3oz (75g) sugar snap peas, topped and tailed
8 spring onions, washed and cut into 1in (2.5cm) pieces
1 courgette, washed and cut into thin slices
12 cherry tomatoes, peeled
salt and freshly ground black pepper
8 Clam Crostini (see below)

Place the *dashi* and saffron in a saucepan and heat gently. Meanwhile heat the three oils in a separate large saucepan. Add the shallots, garlic, coriander root, ginger and chilli to the oils and cook until soft but not brown. Add the white wine, bay leaves and orange peel and bring to the boil. Simmer for 10 minutes and add the clams. Cover the pan and cook for 5 minutes. Add the mussels and cook for a further 5 minutes until the shells open. Discard any mussels or clams which stay closed. Remove the clams and mussels and set aside to cool.

Pass the cooking liquor through muslin or a rinsed out clean tea towel into the saffron broth. Remove the mussels and clams from their shells and finely chop the clams; these will be used for the crostini. Set aside the mussels.

Bring the fish broth to a simmer and add the monkfish. Cook for 2 minutes then add the red mullet, the sugar snap peas and the spring onions; cook for a further 2 minutes. Add the courgettes, cherry tomatoes and mussel flesh and cook for 1 minute. Season to taste with salt and black pepper. Pour into a large soup tureen and serve with a separate plate of clam crostini.

CLAM CROSTINI
Roast 16 cloves of garlic in a preheated oven (400°F/200°C/Gas 6) for 20 minutes with a drizzle of olive oil. Bake 8 slices of baguette for the Crostini (see page 166). When the garlic is

cooked, squeeze the flesh out to produce a purée. Spread the purée on to the crostini. Mix the chopped flesh of 2lb (900g) baby clams (see above) with 1 teaspoon each of chopped orange rind, lemon rind and ginger, 2 tablespoons finely chopped fresh coriander and 1 red chilli, seeded and finely chopped. Season with 1 tablespoon lemon juice, 2 tablespoons extra virgin olive oil, salt and freshly ground black pepper. Pile the clam mix on top of the crostini.

WALNUT TART WITH CRISP APPLES

Pastry crust

4½oz (125g) unsalted butter, cut into pieces
a pinch of salt
4 tablespoons soft brown sugar
5oz (150g) plain flour, sifted
1 tablespoon dark rum
1 whole egg
1 egg yolk
1 dessertspoon fresh lemon juice

Filling

4oz (100g) unsalted butter at room temperature
4oz (100g) chopped walnuts
3oz (75g) soft brown sugar
2 eggs
2 tablespoons espresso strength cold coffee
2 tablespoons dark rum

Topping and garnish

40 walnut halves
1 tablespoon walnut oil
2 crisp green apples

To make the pastry, combine 4oz (100g) of the butter, the salt and the sugar in a food processor. Add the flour and process with several short pulses. Remember the more you work the pastry the tougher it becomes. Add the rum, the egg, egg yolk and the lemon juice. Process until blended into a smooth ball; add a little more flour if the dough is too sticky. Cover the dough with cling film and refrigerate for 30 minutes.

Preheat the oven to 350°F/180°C/Gas 4 and grease a 9in (23cm) spring-form tart pan with the remaining butter. Blend all the filling ingredients in a food processor until a smoothish paste.

Roll the pastry into a circle about ⅙in (4mm) thickness and line the spring-form tart pan. Crimp the edges and pour in the filling. Arrange the walnut halves on top of the filling and brush them lightly with walnut oil. Bake on the lowest shelf of the oven for 20 minutes and then another 25 minutes on the top shelf. Remove from the oven and cool completely before removing the spring-form pan.

Present the tart, then cut three thin slivers per person. Garnish with apples cut in thin slices and then into julienne.

WINE NOTES

There are quite a few restaurant critics that deserve goat's cheese followed by a fish dish that contains garlic and chilli. Indeed, given half a chance I might add a dash of potassium cyanide to improve the sauce, but maybe I should just recommend a disgusting wine to show my deep affection for restaurant critics.

Warm goat's cheese is a killer of white wines. What you need here is a lively fresh Beaujolais-Villages or a young Brouilly, served chilled, to take you through the fish stew. Then, with the walnut tart (and providing no restaurant critic is anywhere near), you can go to town and produce that great bottle of Sauternes or Barsac you have been hoarding (from one of the greater vintages of course, '86, '88, '89). True bliss, and a happy ending to a thoroughly bad idea.

Buffalo Mozzarella with Pan-fried Cornmeal Tomatoes
Roast Cod on a Stew of Mushrooms, Leek and Potato Rösti
Belgian Endive Salad
Pear Crisp with Toffee Sauce

Simple country fare. The starter begins with a classic combination - a popular starter with the ladies - tomatoes and Mozzarella, with a twist. Instead of raw tomatoes, I dust slices of beefsteak tomatoes in cornmeal or polenta and pan-fry until crusty. I serve them hot with the cold slices of buffalo Mozzarella, some extra virgin olive oil and ripped basil. There was a time not long ago when the only Mozzarella you could buy resembled the texture of a rubber tyre; most of it had never even seen Italian shores, usually emanating from Denmark. However, times are changing, now you can and must buy buffalo Mozzarella, a totally different kettle of fish; you haven't lived until you've had the real thing.

For the main course I serve cod, a wonderful example of our British heritage. We used to knock the cod as a poor man's fish but it is an outstanding example of a cold water fish - meaty, juicy and, more to the point, still good value. When very fresh it can take on the world in terms of taste and quality. In this dish, I bake the cod and serve it on a rich stew of field mushrooms. If you have the inclination and the money, this stew is made more remarkable by the addition of dried *cèpes*. I say more remarkable because this dish is really something else, requiring not a little forethought. The mushrooms, for instance, are cooked with all sorts of goodies such as garlic, red wine, a pig's trotter and pancetta and, instead of covering with silver foil, the whole is topped with pork rind which imparts a silky richness to the stew. Once cooked, the mushrooms are allowed to cool slightly, the pig's trotter is removed and boned, blended with half the mushrooms and returned to the stew. Such intensity of peasant flavours, earthiness at its best. For a variation of textures, I serve a rösti with a centre of creamed leeks and a side salad of Belgian endive or chicory.

For pudding, I serve a pear crisp which is an American version of a crumble, slightly spiced slices of pear with hints of lemon rind topped with a crumble of rolled oats, brown sugar, butter and cinnamon. Serve with clotted cream or a toffee sauce.

Serves 4

BUFFALO MOZZARELLA WITH PAN-FRIED CORNMEAL TOMATOES

12 thin slices buffalo Mozzarella cheese
Maldon rock salt and freshly ground black pepper
3 tablespoons extra virgin olive oil
1 tablespoon aged balsamic vinegar
1 clove garlic, peeled and crushed with a little salt
1 tablespoon finely chopped red onion

Tomatoes

2 beefsteak tomatoes, preferably green, each cut horizontally into 4 thick slices
seasoned cornmeal or polenta for dredging
6 tablespoons olive oil
3oz (75g) unsalted butter
1 garlic clove, peeled and cut in 4
4fl oz (150ml) double cream
4 tablespoons grated Parmesan cheese
2 tablespoons snipped chives

To serve

2 tablespoons ripped basil leaves

About an hour before you wish to serve, arrange the Mozzarella slices in a dish. Sprinkle with coarse salt and black pepper. Mix the olive oil, vinegar, garlic and red onions together and pour over the Mozzarella. Leave to marinate.

About 20 minutes before you want to serve, dredge the tomato slices in seasoned cornmeal or polenta. In a large frying pan, heat the olive oil and fry half the tomatoes (so they don't overlap). After 3 minutes, turn the tomatoes and cook for a further 3 minutes. The tomatoes should be golden brown on both sides. Remove them from the pan on to kitchen paper and repeat the procedure with the second batch.

Wipe the pan clean and melt the butter over a medium heat. Add the garlic and pan-fry until it is golden and the butter is turning nutty brown. Remove and discard the garlic. Add the cream and boil vigorously for 5 minutes to thicken slightly.

Add the Parmesan and chives and season to taste. Keep warm.

FINAL PREPARATION AND PRESENTATION

FINAL PREPARATION AND PRESENTATION

Take four plates. On one side of each plate arrange 3 slices of Mozzarella with the marinade. Sprinkle the Mozzarella with the basil leaves. On the other side of the plate pour a spoonful of the sauce and arrange 2 slices of tomato on top.

ROAST COD ON A STEW OF MUSHROOMS, LEEK AND POTATO ROSTI, BELGIAN ENDIVE SALAD

	Stew of Mushrooms
4 x 6oz (175g) fillets of cod	3oz (75g) dried cèpes
plain flour for dredging	4oz (100g) duck fat
1 tablespoon cracked black peppercorns	1 onion, peeled and finely diced
2oz (50g) unsalted butter	2 cloves garlic, peeled
1 teaspoon olive oil	1lb (450g) field mushrooms, sliced
salt	1 sprig thyme
Stew of Mushrooms (see below)	3oz (75g) pancetta or streaky bacon, cut into lardons
Leek and Potato Rösti (see below)	1 pint (600ml) gutsy red wine (Cahors or Zinfandel)
Belgian Endive Salad (see below)	1lb (450g) plum tomatoes, skinned, seeded and chopped
	3 x 4in (10cm) beef marrow bones
	1 pig's trotter
	1lb (450g) strip of pork rind, rolled up and tied with string
	salt and freshly ground black pepper
	2 tablespoons Gremolata (see page 134)

Make the stew of mushrooms the day before and heat through well. Have ready the rösti, warm.

Dredge the cod in flour and coat in the cracked black peppercorns. Cook skin-side down in butter and olive oil over a fierce flame for 2 minutes. Place in a hot oven (400°F/200°C/Gas 6) for 8 minutes. Remove from the oven and season with salt.

FINAL PREPARATION AND PRESENTATION

Place the stew of mushrooms in the bottom of a serving dish. Top with the baked cod, dribbled with a little olive oil.

Place a bowl of Belgian endive salad on the table and serve with the leek and potato rösti straight from the pan.

Soak the cèpes in hot water for 30 minutes. In a large pan suitable for the oven, heat the duck fat over a medium heat. Add the onion and garlic and cook gently until soft but not brown. Drain the cèpes and rinse under cold water, retaining their soaking liquor. Add the cèpes and their liquor to the garlic and onion and cook until the liquid has all but evaporated. Add the field mushrooms and thyme and cook until the mushrooms have released most of their juices. Add the pancetta or streaky bacon and the red wine. Cook for 10 minutes. Add the tomatoes, marrow bones, pig's trotter and pork rind. Cover with a circle of greaseproof paper and a lid hermetically sealed with a paste of flour and water. Pop in a low oven (300°F/150°C/Gas 2) for at least 4 hours or preferably overnight.

When cooked, remove the marrow bones, pig's trotter and pork rind. Extract the bone marrow, discard the bones and return the marrow to the mushrooms. Cut up the pork rind and place in a food processor. Bone out the pig's trotter, carefully removing all the small bones; place the meat in the food processor with half the mushrooms. Blend the contents to a smooth paste. Return this paste to the mushrooms and fold together. Season with salt and black pepper. Add the gremolata and keep warm. This casserole can be made ahead and reheated. If the casserole is too fatty for your liking, omit the pork rind or add a handful of soft breadcrumbs when reheating.

Leek and Potato Rösti

4 large waxy potatoes, peeled
salt and freshly ground black pepper
1oz (25g) Clarified Butter (see page 86)
2oz (50g) unsalted butter

Braised leeks

8oz (225g) leeks, washed and finely sliced (remove 2in/5cm of the green part)
1 clove garlic, peeled and crushed
1 shallot, peeled and finely diced
1 dessertspoon soft thyme leaves
2oz (50g) unsalted butter
4fl oz (120ml) double cream
salt and freshly ground black pepper

Braise the leeks first. Place the leeks, garlic, shallot and thyme in a small saucepan

with the butter and cook gently until soft but not brown. Raise the heat and cook until all the cooking juices have evaporated. Add the double cream and boil to thicken. Season with salt and black pepper to taste. May be prepared ahead to this stage.

Place the potatoes in a pan of salted water. Bring to the boil, reduce the heat and simmer for 10 minutes. Remove the potatoes and cool until you can handle them. Grate the potatoes on the coarsest side of the grater. Mix with the clarified butter.

Take a medium non-stick frying pan and melt the unsalted butter over a medium heat. Add half the potatoes, pushing them down with your fingers. Season with a little salt and black pepper. Top the potatoes with the leeks leaving a 1in (2.5cm) border all round. Top with the remaining potatoes, pushing down firmly. Place the pan over a medium heat and cook for approximately 6 minutes or until the bottom is golden brown. Slide the potato cake on to a large plate, place another plate on top and invert the plates; remove the top plate and slide the rösti back into the frying pan. Cook for a further 10 minutes. Serve from the pan, cut into wedges.

BELGIAN ENDIVE SALAD

One hour before serving, combine in a salad bowl 2 finely chopped anchovy fillets, 2 tablespoons finely chopped shallots, grated rind of 1 orange, 1 clove garlic, peeled and crushed with a little salt, ½ teaspoon finely ground black pepper, 1 tablespoon aged sherry vinegar and 2 tablespoons each of walnut oil and extra virgin olive oil. Just before serving, core 5 heads chicory, pull off the leaves and set aside 8 whole leaves. Rip the remaining leaves into bite-size pieces and toss with the dressing. Garnish with the whole leaves, arranged around the bowl in 'soldiers'.

PEAR CRISP WITH TOFFEE SAUCE

8 Conference pears, peeled, cored and sliced
1 dessertspoon grated lemon rind
1 tablespoon caster sugar
a pinch of grated nutmeg
3½fl oz (90ml) water
1oz (25g) powdered milk
¾oz (20g) rolled oats
8 tablespoons plain flour
7oz (200g) soft brown sugar
4oz (100g) unsalted butter
1 teaspoon ground cinnamon
¼ teaspoon salt
Toffee Sauce (see below)

Toffee Sauce
7oz (200g) caster sugar
5fl oz (150ml) water
4oz (100g) unsalted butter
6fl oz (175ml) double cream
1 teaspoon vanilla essence

Grease a deep baking dish with extra butter. Mix the pears with the lemon rind, caster sugar, nutmeg and water and place in the bottom of the dish. Work together the remaining ingredients by rubbing through your fingers until crumbly. Spread this mix over the pears, pushing down gently. Bake in a moderately hot oven (400°F/200°C/Gas 6) until the pears are tender and the crisp is crunchy and small pockets of delicious liquid are trying to push themselves through the crust. Serve hot with clotted cream or toffee sauce.

In a medium saucepan combine the sugar and half the water. Bring to the boil to dissolve the sugar, stirring occasionally. When the sugar has dissolved, stop stirring and continue to boil until the mixture turns golden brown. Brush the pan with cold water just above edge of the sugar mix to stop sugar crystals forming. Wrap your stirring hand in a tea towel, remove the pan from the heat and add the remaining water. It will probably go crazy, spitting and hissing like a mad cat - have no fear, it's meant to. When its temper has calmed down, add the butter and return to the heat stirring until smooth. Add the cream and vanilla essence and whisk again until smooth. Keep warm.

WINE NOTES

Friday in the country sounds delicious. Here is a menu to please a serious wine-drinking man, giving him a chance to display a firework of the world's most fashionable wine: Chardonnay.

For apéritif and with the Mozzarella and tomato dish, a decent Mâconnais, ideally a St-Véran, which has just the right weight and will prepare you for the next wine: an old-fashioned

rich Meursault or a slightly over-the-top Chardonnay from Australia, like Petaluma, or a classy Chardonnay from Marlborough in New Zealand, even a blowsy one from California's Edna Valley.

No sweet wine is needed, the rich Chardonnay will take care of you.

Spicy Pork in Stout
Slow-cooked Broad Beans, Olive Oil Mash
Roasted Pear with Roquefort

A simple, no-fuss menu, easily prepared, using a cut of meat that is very inexpensive. The public often forget we have an alternative white meat. Week after week, chicken hits the top or near the top of meat sales and yet the pig produces a wonderful meat and at a bargain price. In France pork is high on the list of priorities and there is a culinary use for absolutely every conceivable part of the animal, nothing is wasted. *Rillettes* from the belly, *petit salé* from the belly and ribs, *galantine* and *fromage de tête* from the head, *pâté* from the liver, *jambon* from the leg, various dried *saucissons*, *museau* from the snout (more commonly from the ox), *oreilles de porc* using pig's ear cooked in jelly; *pieds de porc*, trotters split in half and breadcrumbed, *queues de porc*, tails coated in breadcrumbs and cooked, *andouillettes*, sausages made from the tripe, *boudins blanc et noir*, white sausages from chicken and pork meat, black from the fats and blood and *crépinettes*, small cakes of minced pork encased in caul fat. The list goes on, and it sounds gruesome, I know. But most, in fact, are delicious. One has to say, however, that the French will eat anything. Have you ever noticed the absence of bird life in France? Birds definitely give France a miss on their migratory travels, otherwise, bang, they end up as some culinary creation. They even cook blackbirds and thrushes ...

Moi, I'm offering you a simple casseroled dish of pork using the bit of the pork that treads in all the muddy bits, the hand, the joint at the end of the shoulder or front leg. Very cheap, and lots of meat for the price. This pork dish was inspired by Frances Bissell's *Real Meat Cookbook* and I cooked it on the BBC's 'Hot Chefs' where it engendered great fan mail.

The hands are stuffed with prunes, anchovies, sage and black olives, marinated in a paste of black pepper, oregano, thyme, garlic, soft brown sugar, olive oil and vinegar. It's cooked in Guinness and served with young broad beans casseroled in their pods, and the alternative mashed potato using olive oil instead of butter. Home cooking at its best.

You don't really need a starter or if you do, make it very light. A savoury ending goes down well. I bake some pears with sugar, wine and spices, allow them to cool, then dip them in melted butter and roll them in finely chopped walnuts. With the pears I serve a small leaf salad and some Roquefort. This is a good alternative to the Poached Red Wine Pears with Creamy Gorgonzola (see page 112).

Serves 4

SPICY PORK IN STOUT, SLOW-COOKED BROAD BEANS AND OLIVE OIL MASH

Meat preparation
2 x 2½lb (1.1kg) pork hands, cut from the shoulder
6 stoned black olives
6 sage leaves
6 stoned prunes
6 tinned anchovy fillets
3oz (75g) unsalted butter
1 onion, peeled and finely sliced
2 tablespoons olive oil
1 bottle (33cl, or about 11fl oz) Guinness
10fl oz (300ml) Chicken Stock (see page 91)
Marinade
2 teaspoons finely crushed black peppercorns
2 teaspoons salt
2 teaspoons dried oregano
1 teaspoon soft thyme leaves

7 cloves garlic, peeled
3 tablespoons soft brown sugar
2 tablespoons olive oil
2 tablespoons red wine vinegar
To serve
Slow-Cooked Broad Beans (see below)
Olive Oil Mash (see below)

THE DAY BEFORE
Cut away the rind from each pork hand and set aside. Make 6 deep incisions in each joint and press 3 olives wrapped in sage leaves and 3 prunes stuffed with an anchovy into each piece of pork. Put all the marinade ingredients into a food processor and blend to a smoothish paste. Rub the joints all over with the marinade and

leave to marinate in the refrigerator overnight. Wrap the pork skins in cling film and refrigerate as well.

About 3½ hours before sit-down

Preheat the oven to 300°F/150°C/Gas 2. Melt the butter in a casserole and cook the onion over a medium heat until golden brown. Remove the onion from the pan, set aside and replace with the joints of pork. Add a little oil, raise the heat and brown the meat on all sides. Return the onions to the pan, with any excess marinade. Deglaze the pan with the stout, scraping up any coagulated bits from the bottom, then add the chicken stock. Cover each piece of meat with the reserved rind and cover the casserole. Place in the oven and cook for approximately 3 hours or until the meat is particularly tender. Remove the joints from the pan, discard the pork rind and take the meat off the bone in largish chunks.

Pour all the residue ingredients from the casserole into a liquidiser and process until smooth. Combine the meat with this sauce, and keep warm. The sauce should just coat the pork without being runny. If it is too thin, return it to the pan and reduce over a high heat until the required consistency.

Presentation

Present the pork on a serving platter, the broad beans in their cooking casserole and the potatoes in a glazed earthenware dish. Allow your guests to help themselves.

Slow-Cooked Broad Beans

Top, tail and string 2lb (900g) young broad beans, and cut them into 1in (2.5cm) pieces between the inner beans. Heat 4 tablespoons good olive oil in a saucepan over a moderate heat and cook 1 onion, peeled and sliced, and 2 cloves garlic, peeled and finely diced until soft but not brown. Add 4oz (100g) pancetta, cut into ¼in (5mm) dice, 2 tablespoons chopped parsley, 1 bay leaf, 1 sprig thyme and 1lb (450g) plum tomatoes, skinned, seeded and roughly chopped. Cook for 10 minutes until the tomatoes have released their liquid, then add the broad beans, 5fl oz (150ml) white wine and 10fl oz (300ml) water. Cover and stew gently for 1½ hours over a slow heat. Season with salt, freshly ground black pepper and 1 dessertspoon caster sugar. Remove the bay leaf and thyme. The dish can be prepared ahead to this point.

The oven is already hot from the pork recipe. Pour the bean stew into a casserole. Cover the top with a thin layer of fresh breadcrumbs - about 4 tablespoons - mixed with 1 tablespoon soft thyme leaves and bake in the oven until bubbling and golden, about 30 minutes.

Olive Oil Mash

Peel 2lb (900g) floury potatoes and cut them into 1in (2.5cm) cubes. Place the potatoes into a large pan of cold salted water. Bring to the boil and simmer for about 15-20 minutes or until the potatoes are tender without breaking up. Drain the potatoes and return to the saucepan over a low heat to dry. Pass the potatoes through a food mill or ricer. Do not be tempted to blend in a food processor as this can make the resulting purée very elastic and gluey. While the potatoes are cooking heat 5 tablespoons extra virgin olive oil in a frying pan and pan fry 3 tablespoons finely sliced spring onions for 3 minutes. Add 3 tablespoons chopped green olives. Fold this mix including the oil into the potatoes and season with salt and white pepper. The mash can be prepared ahead and slowly reheated towards the end of the pork cooking time.

ROASTED PEAR WITH ROQUEFORT

*4 ripe Conference or Anjou pears, peeled,
cored and halved top to bottom*

2 tablespoons caster sugar

*5fl oz (150ml) sweet white wine
(Orange Muscat or Beaumes de Venise)*

freshly ground black pepper

a pinch of grated nutmeg

a pinch of ground cinnamon

3oz (75g) unsalted butter, at room temperature

4 tablespoons Clarified Butter (see page 86)

5 tablespoons finely chopped walnuts

*4oz (100g) mixed salad leaves (see page 90),
washed and dried*

2 tablespoons Salad Dressing (see page 90)

8oz (225g) Roquefort cheese

Preheat the oven to 375°F/190°C/Gas 5. Place the pears, cut side down, in a buttered baking dish. Sprinkle in the sugar, dribble with the white wine and dust with the spices. Dot with the butter and bake for approximately 20 minutes until cooked, but not mushy. During the cooking baste the pears with the juices. Remove the pears from the oven, and allow to cool. Save the juices in a separate container. The pears can be prepared ahead to this point.

Paint the round sides of the pear with clarified butter. Allow the butter to set on the pear then roll the buttered area in chopped walnuts, pressing in firmly. Return the pears to the oven and dribble with the reserved juices. Warm the pears through for a few minutes. Serve with some of their juices, dressed salad leaves, and a wedge of Roquefort. Roquefort is often eaten with a chilled, sweet Sauternes wine so the flavours in the pears combine to make a perfect pairing ('scuse the pun) with the cheese.

WINE NOTES

The marriage of pork and garlic is most successful in Burgundy, so what better than local wine, a Pinot Noir? To counter-balance this rich dish, a lightish and lively Côte de Beaune or Hautes-Côtes de Nuits, ideally from a decent vintage like the 1990 (the knowledgeable wine drinker buys great wines of lesser vintages, and lesser wines of great vintages). An alternative to Burgundy would be one of the fresh Pinot Noirs from the New World, like Coldstream Hills or Australia's Yarra Valley or Palliser and Waipara Springs of New Zealand.

With the roasted pears a glass of port: vintage if you are rich, late bottled vintage character if you just like it rich, tawny if you make up for richness in style and elegance.

ALTERNATIVE SCALLOPS

Two Scallop Salads
A Fish Broth with Coral Parcels
Scallop and Nori Beignets with Hot Sweet and Sour Sauce
Roast Scallops, Carrot Juice and Coriander Sauce
Pan-fried Chinese Greens
Carpaccio of Pineapple with Cherries in Kirsch

An occasion of textures and sensations. I prepared this lunch for a scallop promotion a few years ago. On the surface, you might think it's all a bit too much, but it does work. Start with the scallop salads which have two different taste sensations; one is a ceviche of the mini queen scallops where lime is the predominant flavour. The ceviche originates from Mexico and while the scallop is raw because no heat is applied, it does in fact become 'cooked' by a reaction with the acid marinade. The marinade contains lime juice, chilli, red onion, coriander, tomato and avocado. The longer you marinate, the more you 'cook'. I prefer a short marination of approximately 30 minutes, but up to 3 hours is still satisfactory, any more and in my opinion the scallop becomes rubbery. The second salad is large diver-caught scallops, prepared and thinly sliced horizontally. The roe is cooked and diced and mixed with a fine dice of carrot, courgette, celery and turnip, mixed with a little powdered coriander, olive oil, soy and other seasonings and scattered over the raw scallops. So the ceviche has a soft 'cooked' texture and the raw diver-caught scallop has a wonderful natural sweetness with the crunch of raw diced vegetables.

WHY 'DIVER-CAUGHT'?
Scallops are either diver-caught or dredged. Dredged ones are much cheaper but the very nature of dredging tends to damage the scallop and often fills the shell cavity with mud or sand, making the cleaning operation much more tricky. Diver-caught scallops have been respected, handled with care and as such, have a much sweeter, untarnished taste.

Where possible buy scallops in the shell. I explain below how to clean them, but, failing that, your fishmonger will do it for you. Beware the frozen or pre-prepared scallop, there's a lot of rubbish on the market. The cooking result of these scallops tends to be rubbery and boiled because the frozen varieties can have an ice-glaze of up to 40 per cent of their weight, and the prepared 'fresh' are often soaked in water which can almost double their weight by absorption. You pay more for scallop in the shell, but it's well worth it.

HOW TO CLEAN AND PREPARE A SCALLOP

The first rule is don't be scared. For some strange reason the general public panics when it comes to preparing fish and shellfish. Place the round shell of the scallop on a tea-towel on top of a chopping board. The tea-towel will stop it slipping. Insert the blade of a flexible filleting knife between the top and the bottom shells at the front of the shell, running it flat against the top shell until you find and cut the muscle that holds the scallop to the shell. Remove and discard the flat shell.

Cut through a similar muscle on the lower half of the shell following the curve of the shell with a flexible knife if possible. Lift the scallop and gently ease away the 'skirt' that surrounds the plump white part of the scallop. With a knife or pair of scissors, snip off the dark stomach section which is attached to the orange coral. You should now be left with the creamy flesh of the main section of the scallop attached to the orange coral. Wash these quickly to remove any possible grit or sand but *don't soak*. Finally remove the white sinewy muscle which is attached to the side of the creamy part. Dry your scallop well and refrigerate until required.

BACK TO THE MENU

With the fish broth I have drawn on Oriental influences by using *dashi* as my soup base. *Dashi* is a basic stock made in Japan from kelp and dried bonito flakes, but do not fear, packets of *dashi* in powder form are available from Oriental grocers. To the *dashi* I add a little dried seaweed, some spring onion, soy sauce and lemon rind and, of course, a couple of coral parcels which are made with the scallop coral, some chilli, garlic, spring onion, *nam pla*, ginger and coriander. *Won-ton* wrappers are used for enclosing the filling. The parcels are then poached in the broth. The coral parcels come from an idea of Frances Bissell's in her cookbook *Oriental Flavours*.

Scallop and *nori* beignets display more Oriental influences, mainly from the *nori* seaweed which is wrapped around the scallops before they are fried. The batter could have been a tempura, I suppose, but it isn't. It's a brazen, boozy, beer batter made with yeast. I use it for all my 'fish and chips' - it's brill and what's more it produces the crispest batter. The scallop and *nori* is dipped in batter and deep-fried, but don't cook for too long - the batter should be crisp and golden and the centre of the scallop still a little raw. Wonderful hot and cold, crisp and moist taste contrasts. I serve these fritters with a sweet and sour dipping sauce taught to me at the Thai Cooking School in The Oriental Hotel, Bangkok.

Roast scallops is another dish inspired by visits to Thailand. 'Roast' is one of those words that sounds a bit dumb when applied to scallops. Roast it ain't, but the word does have a pleasant ring to it. Really the scallops are seared in a very hot pan and then popped in the oven for a couple of minutes to warm through. Our restaurant kitchens always have the oven on so it's easy for us. Perhaps in the domestic kitchen in the interest of economy, the scallops can be finished under the grill or allowed to continue cooking in the pan. The sauce is a light reduction of carrot juices (not puréed carrots), which are flavour-infused with lime, ginger, lemongrass and coriander.

The scallops are served with one of my favourite veg, *bok choy* or Chinese greens, which is now becoming available in supermarkets. The greens are blanched and then dribbled with olive oil and chargrilled. At home you could finish these in the pan with a few flaked almonds.

I finish with carpaccio of pineapple with cherries pickled in Kirsch. Pickled may be the wrong word, but I'd be pickled if I'd spent three months languishing in a bottle of Kirsch and sugar. I was inspired to call this dish carpaccio by Indian markets where you see beautifully prepared pineapple, thinly sliced and sold in see-through bags. Such care and patience, why can't our supermarkets do the same? It's such a pain preparing pineapple at home, and removing all the little 'eyes' can make your pineapple look as if it's been dragged through a battlefield.

The slices are laid over the bottom of a dish and scattered with the cherries and Kirsch - delicious, colourful simplicity.

Serves 4

TWO SCALLOP SALADS

Ceviche (see below)
Oriental Salad (see below)
6 iceberg lettuce leaves

Make the two salads about 30 minutes before you want to serve them.

Place a lettuce leaf on one side of each plate and put a large spoonful of ceviche in the lettuce leaf. Arrange 6 raw overlapping slices of the jumbo scallop on the other side of the plate. Spoon a quantity of the herb and vegetable dressing over the slices of jumbo scallop.

Ceviche
24 queen scallops, shucked and cleaned
juice of 2 limes
2 plum tomatoes, seeded and diced
1 avocado, peeled, halved, stoned and diced
4 spring onions, washed and thinly sliced
1 tablespoon finely chopped coriander leaves
1 red chilli, seeded and finely diced
4 tablespoons extra virgin olive oil
salt and freshly ground black pepper

Combine all the ingredients in a non-reactive bowl, except for the salt and pepper, and marinate together for at least 30 minutes. Season to taste before serving.

Oriental Salad

6 jumbo scallops, shucked and cleaned
I courgette, finely diced
I celery stalk, stringed and finely diced
I dessertspoon chopped coriander leaves
½ red chilli, seeded and finely diced
I spring onion, finely diced
I carrot, peeled and finely diced
I clove garlic, peeled and finely diced
½in (1cm) fresh ginger, peeled and grated
I teaspoon liquid honey
2 tablespoons white wine vinegar
4 tablespoons katchap manis or soy sauce
I tablespoon sesame oil
3 tablespoons corn oil
freshly ground black pepper

Remove the orange coral from the side of each scallop. Pop the corals in a small saucepan of boiling salted water and cook for 3 minutes. Drain and plunge into iced water. Cut the corals into fine dice. Slice each scallop horizontally in 4 with a sharp knife. Set aside.

Combine all the vegetables, herbs and spices in a glass bowl. In another bowl whisk together all the wet ingredients. Add the vegetable mix to the dressing and allow to marinate for 15 minutes. Just before serving season to taste with black pepper and add the diced scallop coral. Alternatively, you can keep the coral for the soup course.

A FISH BROTH WITH CORAL PARCELS

Dashi (fish broth base)

2 pints (1.1 litres) cold water
I oz (25g) kelp (kombu)
I oz (25g) dried bonito flakes (hana-katsuo)

Fish broth

I teaspoon Maldon sea salt
I tablespoon light soy sauce
4 asparagus tips, cooked
2 scallops, shucked, cleaned and sliced raw, horizontally, in 4
4 sprigs coriander
2 spring onions, finely sliced
4 small pieces wakame seaweed (optional), soaked for 20 minutes
4 twists of lemon peel, blanched
12 Coral Parcels, cooked and warm (see below)

Make the *dashi* first. Put the kelp in a medium saucepan with the water and heat over a medium flame. Do not allow the liquid to boil as kelp gives off an unpleasant odour when boiled. Simmer until the kelp is soft and the stock is strong enough; the kelp can then be discarded. Bring the temperature down by adding a further 5fl oz (150ml) cold water. Add the bonito flakes and bring to the boil. Once it reaches boiling point remove from the heat. Taste the stock and if it has enough flavour, strain it through a fine sieve lined with muslin or a washed-out tea-towel. Alternatively, packets of *dashi* powder are available from Oriental supermarkets.

FINAL PREPARATION AND PRESENTATION

Heat the *dashi*, and add the salt and soy sauce. Just before serving, attractively divide the other ingredients between four bowls. Pour the soup over the garnishing ingredients in front of your guests.

Coral Parcels

corals from 8 scallops
1 teaspoon nam pla or fish sauce
2oz (50g) tofu
1in (2.5cm) fresh ginger, peeled and grated
3 cloves garlic, peeled and chopped
1 teaspoon katchap manis or soy sauce
12 won-ton wrappers
1 red chilli, seeded and finely sliced
1 spring onion, finely sliced
12 coriander leaves

Work the first 6 ingredients in a food processor or mortar until smooth. Place ½ teaspoon of the filling on the centre of each of the 12 *won-ton* wrappers. On top of the mix place a slice of chilli, a couple of slices of spring onion and a coriander leaf. Wet the edges of the dough and gather them together pinching the top to seal. You can either make a purse shape or simply fold the *won-ton* wrapper over and seal the edges.

When ready to serve poach in boiling salted water or fish broth for approximately 3 minutes or until cooked.

SCALLOP AND NORI BEIGNETS, WITH HOT SWEET AND SOUR SAUCE

8 scallops, corals removed
1 sheet of nori seaweed, cut into 8 strips
oil for deep frying
Hot Sweet and Sour Sauce (see below)

Beer batter

11fl oz (325ml) lager beer
1½ oz (40g) fresh yeast
4oz (100g) flour
a good pinch of salt

Wrap a strip of *nori* seaweed around each scallop. Make the batter by combining the lager and yeast until smooth, then adding the flour little by little until the consistency of thick cream is achieved. Season with salt and allow to rest in a warm place for approximately an hour. As the yeast gets to work the batter will bubble up.

Heat the oil to its hottest temperature if you have a domestic deep-fryer. Dip the *nori*-wrapped scallops in batter and deep-fry for approximately 3 minutes. Remove from the oil and drain on kitchen paper. Cut each scallop in 2 horizontally and serve 4 halves per person with the dipping sauce.

Hot Sweet and Sour Sauce

10fl oz (300ml) rice wine vinegar
2oz (50g) soft brown sugar
2oz (50g) caster sugar
1 tablespoon salt
1 tablespoon diced red chilli
1 teaspoon chopped garlic
1 teaspoon finely chopped coriander stalks or root
5fl oz (150ml) water
½ cucumber, seeded and finely diced
1 tablespoon finely chopped coriander leaves

Heat the first 8 ingredients gently until the sugar has dissolved. Allow to cool, then mix in the diced cucumber and the coriander leaves.

ROAST SCALLOPS, CARROT JUICE AND CORIANDER SAUCE WITH PAN-FRIED CHINESE GREENS

8 scallops, shucked and washed, roe intact
10fl oz (300ml) Carrot Juice and Coriander Sauce (see below)
Pan-Fried Chinese Greens (see below)
a little olive oil

Prepare the sauce and the Chinese greens. Preheat the oven to 475°F/240°C/Gas 9.

Pan-fry the scallops in a very hot pan with a splash of olive oil. After 30 seconds, turn the scallops and cook the other side. The faces should be golden brown and slightly crusty. Pop the scallops in the hot oven for 2 minutes.

Arrange some of the sauce on four warm plates. Place the Chinese greens in the centre, and a large scallop on each side.

Carrot Juice and Coriander Sauce
makes 10fl oz (300ml)
1 pint (600ml) carrot juice, made or purchased
½ tablespoon finely sliced fresh lemongrass
½ tablespoon fresh lime juice
½ teaspoon grated lime peel
¼ red chilli, seeded and finely diced
¾in (1.75cm) fresh ginger, peeled and grated
salt and freshly ground white pepper
½ tablespoon chopped coriander leaves
1 teaspoon chopped mint leaves
2 carrots, peeled, finely diced and blanched

Place the first 6 ingredients in a saucepan and bring to the boil; reduce by half and pass through a fine sieve. Return the juices to the saucepan and return to the boil. Season to taste and fold in the chopped herbs and diced carrots. The sauce will be quite thin.

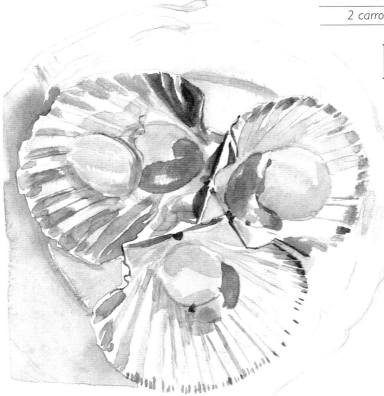

Pan-Fried Chinese Greens
2½oz (60g) flaked almonds
8 heads bok choy or Chinese greens (if unavailable use spring greens or broccoli tips)
salt and freshly ground black pepper
4 tablespoons extra virgin olive oil
I clove garlic, peeled

To toast the almonds, scatter them into a flat roasting tray and toast under the grill until golden. Shake frequently.

Boil a saucepan of salted water. Blanch the *bok choy* for 2 minutes. Remove and plunge into cold water. Drain and dry. Split each head in 2 lengthways.

Heat the olive oil in a large frying pan and add the garlic clove. Cook until the garlic is golden and then discard it. Add the *bok choy* to the flavoured oil and pan-fry quickly until golden on each side. If you have a chargrill the *bok choy* takes on a marvellous flavour. Sprinkle with the toasted flaked almonds and season to taste.

CARPACCIO OF PINEAPPLE WITH CHERRIES IN KIRSCH

I pineapple, tough outer skin and eyes removed, thinly sliced horizontally
I lb (450g) Cherries in Kirsch (see below)

Cherries in Kirsch
2lb (900g) black or morello cherries, stone in
I lb (450g) caster sugar
2 cinnamon sticks, broken into small pieces
I 6fl oz (475ml) Kirsch

Arrange several thin slices of pineapple on four large plates. Scatter the pineapple with some cherries and some of the alcoholic juices.

Discard any imperfect cherries, rinse them and mix them with the sugar and crumbled cinnamon. Pack them into jars and seal. Leave to macerate for at least a week, turning the jars each day. After a week open the jars and add the Kirsch. Re-seal and macerate for a further 3 weeks.

WINE NOTES

This meal calls for alternative Alsace wines: a Pinot Blanc before the meal and the glass carried to the table to finish off with the scallop salad and the ceviche.

Far East spices demand assertive flavours in wine, and here I should propose serving two wines side by side, a Muscat Grand Cru of a really good vintage (ordinary Muscat d'Alsace being generally a bit disappointing) and a Gewürztraminer.

Pineapple and Kirsch might suggest another eau de vie from Alsace, but it would be too much of a good thing. This is the rare moment for an aged (vieille) Prune (pronounced prünn and not proon!), the best of which comes from the Gascogne, Armagnac country. Its softness will becalm the aggressive acidity of pineapple and Kirsch.

A SPRING LUNCH FOR SIX

Brandade with Green Beans and Tapenade Crostini

Poached Fillet of Beef in Cèpe Broth with Spring Vegetables

Lemon and Lime Tart

A menu of powerful flavours - garlic and olives in the first course, the earthy flavours and aromas of *cèpes* with the fillet of beef in the main, and heady citrus of the pudding.

The salt cod in the brandade is well used in the Mediterranean, which might seem odd as few cod are found there. Cod hunts in colder waters, especially around our coasts, but apparently the Scandinavians fell in love with Mediterranean products such as olive oil, olives and fruits, so they would exchange dried cod for them. Hence the wide use of salt cod in Provence and surrounding areas. Salt cod is also used extensively in Portugal and Spain in casseroles with tomatoes, onions, peppers and other goodies. In brandade we produce a creamy mousse by blending the salt cod with potatoes, garlic, warm milk and extra virgin olive oil. This is served on a salad of lightly blanched French beans tossed with oil and aged sherry vinegar, some tapenade (a purée of black olives) and crostini. Very earthy, very Mediterranean.

The important thing here is the de-salting of the cod which takes between 24 and 36 hours in several changes of cold water. When buying salt cod, you will possibly be offered two varieties - salted or salted and dried. The plain salted will have more of the texture of fresh cod, whereas the salted and dried has the texture of leather, very unattractive, but is very tasty when used correctly. Obviously the dried variety takes longer in the soaking process.

Brandade was one of the first sophisticated dishes I learnt to cook. In my youth, many years ago, I would cycle from Kings School, Canterbury, on a Sunday after church to a pub/restaurant run by some friends called the Laings. John Laing used to run the Guinea in Bruton Place, married a Swedish doll called Ulla, and went off to run this wonderful thirteenth-century pub called the Duck Inn at Pett Bottom near Bridge in Kent. John used to run the drink side and Ulla the cooking ... a perfect partnership. To a thirteen-year-old, 5½ stone wimp, John was a frightening character, very large and very jowly with bright red cheeks and a rather jocular Dickensian manner, a country gent in all ways - open top 1920s racing Bentley, pair of shooting dogs, pretty blonde wife, all the trimmings one needs to run a welcoming countryside pub geared towards the landed gentry.

Unfortunately, he hadn't taken into account that Ulla had other plans. She turned out to be a brilliant cook and quickly earned a Michelin star, quite an achievement for a pub in the mid-sixties. It was Ulla who inspired me to take up cooking, so from my washing-up duties I would keep an eagle eye on how she prepared the food. Brandade was one of her dishes. She made it with ordinary fresh cod, but I remember it as eye-opening - very garlicky, very delicious and very revealing. I was breaking school rules by working in this pub and when I returned each Sunday for evensong in the Cathedral, I was given a wide berth ... being in the choir with strong garlic breath was not 'playing cricket'.

The poached fillet of beef in *cèpe* broth with spring vegetables is inspired by the classic *boeuf à la ficelle* where the meat to be poached is tied with string and attached to the pan handle to prevent it touching the bottom of the pan. The broth is a vegetable stock perfumed with dried *cèpes* giving it an earthy gutsiness. The meat is accompanied by small spring vegetables - leeks, carrots, turnips and new potatoes - which are also cooked in the broth. One might think poaching beef would produce a bland greyish lump. You would be right about the colour on the outside, but lurking beneath this deceptive greyness is rosy-red beef, more tender than fillet cooked by any other method and more tasty as the pungent flavour of the *cèpes* permeates the flesh.

Accompaniments for the ambitious cook could include home-pickled *cornichons* (baby gherkins), pickled baby onions, rémoulade sauce and a herby tomato sauce. This dish is best served in a flat soup bowl with the tray of accompaniments which would also include a good mustard and some rock salt. I always think that it is the accompaniments which make the dish. Use your imagination for a variety of goodies that can go with poached meat. An alternative to the spring vegetables would be a light leafy salad with a truffle oil dressing or a waxy potato salad.

For the pud, I've adapted a classic lemon tart recipe that was popularised by the Roux brothers and subsequently Marco Pierre White. Whenever I put this tart on the menu, it outsells any other pudding. As a variation to the normal shortbread tart base, I add some ground toasted almonds and some grated citrus rind. The addition of lime juice to the custardy filling makes the tart that little bit extra special. If you're feeling a little more ambitious, glaze the top of the filling with caster sugar. The modern chef tends to glaze tarts and *brûlées* with a blow-torch. Clever really, what will chefs get up to next?

Serves 6

BRANDADE WITH GREEN BEANS AND TAPENADE CROSTINI

1lb (450g) salt cod, soaked for up to 48 hours in several changes of cold water
15fl oz (450ml) milk
½ onion, peeled and stuck with 1 clove and 1 bay leaf
2 sprigs parsley
5fl oz (150ml) double cream plus 2 tablespoons
5fl oz (150ml) extra virgin olive oil
8oz (225g) floury potatoes, peeled and boiled
1 tablespoon finely chopped garlic
2 pinches grated nutmeg
2 pinches cayenne pepper
freshly ground white pepper
lemon juice
To serve
12 Crostini (see page 166)
about 3oz (75g) Tapénade (see below)
Green Bean Salad (see below)
2oz (50g) pitted black olives, diced

To make the brandade, place the cod in a mixture of water and 5fl oz (150ml) of the milk with the onion and parsley sprigs. The liquid should just cover the cod. Bring to the boil and simmer for 3 minutes. Allow the fish to cool in the liquor.

When the cod is cool, remove it and discard the liquor. Remove any skin or bone from the fish and flake it into a stainless steel bowl.

Heat the remaining milk and the 5fl oz (150ml) cream together in one saucepan and the olive oil in another, until hand-hot.

Mash the potatoes with the garlic and beat this mixture into the cod; continue beating until you have a smooth combination of fish

and potato. If you're feeling lazy, feel free to use a food processor, but don't overwork the mix or it will become over-elastic.

While beating, alternately add the oil and the creamy milk until you have a smooth mousse-like concoction. Finally season the mix with nutmeg, cayenne and white pepper to taste. The addition of a little lemon juice at this stage may suit some palates.

The brandade should be served warm and can be prepared ahead to this point. When you want to serve, add the remaining double cream and cook over a gentle flame, stirring constantly.

FINAL PREPARATION AND PRESENTATION

Spread the warm crostini with tapénade. Place a circle of the green bean salad around the edge of the plate and a dollop or quenelle of the warm brandade in the centre. Position 2 tapenade crostini to the side and scatter with a dice of black olives.

Tapénade
makes about 1½lb (675g)
3oz (75g) capers, drained and rinsed
2oz (50g) tinned anchovy fillets, drained and diced
1 dessertspoon Dijon mustard
12 basil leaves, ripped
4fl oz (120ml) extra virgin olive oil
1lb (450g) black olives, marinated in olive oil, pitted
1 teaspoon freshly ground black pepper
1 tablespoon aged red wine vinegar
3 tablespoons chopped parsley
3 tablespoons finely diced sun-dried tomatoes

ombine the first 8 ingredients in a food processor and blend until smoothish, but allowing some texture to remain. Then fold in the parsley and sun-dried tomatoes. Check the seasoning and adjust accordingly.

I have made the tapénade in a fairly large quantity as it keeps well and is a useful standby for pre-dinner drink nibbles.

GREEN BEAN SALAD

Wash 1lb (450g) French green beans, choosing the extra fine variety if possible. Top and tail and plunge them into plenty of boiling salted water (approximately 1 level teaspoon of salt for each pint/600ml). The basic rule for cooking vegetables is 'those grown under the ground, cook from cold and cover the saucepan with a lid; those grown above ground, cook in plenty of boiling water with no lid (this helps to retain the vibrant colours)'. It is important that you cook the vegetables in as much water as you can fit comfortably in the pan; in this way, when you plunge in the vegetables, the water temperature does not drop dramatically and returns quickly to the boil, speeding the cooking process and not damaging the colour.

Cook the beans for approximately 5 minutes, depending on their size. To be sure they are cooked, remove one and test by the biting method. If it is cooked to your satisfaction, strain the beans and immerse in iced water. This arrests the cooking and sets the bright green colour. When the beans are cold, drain and dry. Place the beans in a bowl and mix with ½ red onion, finely diced, 1fl oz (30ml) extra virgin olive oil, a dash of aged sherry vinegar and 4 ripped basil leaves. Season to taste with freshly ground black pepper and Maldon sea salt.

POACHED FILLET OF BEEF IN CEPE BROTH WITH SPRING VEGETABLES

4lb (1.8kg) fillet of beef, fat removed and tied
Poaching liquor
1lb (450g) leeks, washed and left whole
8oz (225g) carrots, peeled and left whole
8oz (225g) turnips, peeled and left whole
½ head celery, washed and cut vertically in 2
1 head garlic, cut horizontally in 2
¼ Savoy cabbage, washed and left in one piece
1lb (450g) tomatoes, peeled, quartered and seeded
1 onion, peeled and stuck with 2 bay leaves and 2 cloves
3 sprigs thyme
½ bunch chervil
½ oz (15g) Maldon salt
12 white peppercorns

5 pints (2.75 litres) Chicken Stock (see page 91) or water
Vegetables
2oz (50g) best quality dried cèpes
12 baby leeks, washed and left whole
12 asparagus tips
12 baby turnips, scraped, leave 1in (2.5cm) of green top
12 baby carrots, scraped, leave 1in (2.5cm) of green top
12 Jersey Royal potatoes, scraped and left whole

3 HOURS BEFORE SIT-DOWN

Simmer the poaching liquor ingredients very gently for 2 hours, barely raising a burp. Strain the liquor and discard the vegetables, herbs and spices. Pour the liquor back into a clean deep saucepan and return to the heat.

Halfway through the stock simmering time, soak the dried *cèpes* in warm water for at least an hour. When they have reconstituted, remove them and squeeze out the juices into the rich brown soaking liquor. Strain this liquor through muslin if possible (failing that, a rinsed-out tea-towel) into the stock. Rinse the mushrooms under a cold tap to remove any grit and add them to the stock as well. Gently simmer the stock for a further hour, topping up with cold water as necessary.

During this period, prepare the remaining vegetables. Heat a pan of boiling salted water and cook each vegetable separately, removing when cooked and plunging into ice-cold water. When the vegetables are cold, drain them and set aside. If you want to be a perfectionist, then ideally each vegetable should be cooked in different water, but the difference in taste is not worth the hassle. If you want, you could add the vegetable cooking water to the stock. Avoid this step if the vegetable liquor is cloudy. The vegetables can be prepared ahead.

The poaching liquor will, if you follow the method carefully and don't cook it too fast, be quite clear without being sparkly. If you want that sparkle, then you would have to clarify the broth consommé-style, but this is a little complicated and, to me, removes a great deal of the flavour.

30 MINUTES BEFORE SIT-DOWN
Place the meat into the simmering stock, having first tied its string to the handle of the pan to keep it from resting on the bottom. Allow 8-10 minutes per lb (450g) for a wonderfully rosy interior. When the meat is cooked to your satisfaction, remove and set aside to rest for 10 minutes.

FINAL PREPARATION AND PRESENTATION
About 2 minutes before service, add the vegetables to the broth to reheat. Serve the meat on a large platter surrounded by the vegetables. Serve with grain mustard, a herby tomato sauce or a rémoulade sauce, a jug of the cooking broth, some rock salt and a few pickled onions.

HERBY TOMATO SAUCE
In a liquidiser or food processor blend 12oz (350g) skinned, seeded and diced tomatoes with 4 tablespoons each of soured cream and balsamic vinegar, 1 dessertspoon finely chopped shallots, 1 teaspoon Dijon mustard and 1 dessertspoon dry sherry. Just before serving, add 3 tablespoons diced tomato (skin on), 1 tablespoon chopped tarragon and 1 tablespoon finely chopped shallot. Season to taste with Maldon sea salt and freshly ground black pepper.

ANCHOIADE REMOULADE SAUCE
A classic rémoulade in an anchovy flavoured mayonnaise finished with capers, gherkins and some chopped herbs including parsley, chervil, tarragon and chives. Blend 2 egg yolks in a food processor with 1 heaped teaspoon Dijon mustard, 2 tablespoons finely chopped basil, 8 anchovy fillets (rinsed) and 1oz (25g) capers (rinsed) until smooth. Add 15fl oz (450ml) extra virgin olive oil, little by little as for mayonnaise. Add 3 tablespoons fresh lemon juice and plenty of freshly ground black pepper. Finish with 1 tablespoon chopped capers, 1 tablespoon chopped gherkin and 1 dessertspoon ripped basil.

SWEET BROWN PICKLED ONIONS
(See page 167.)

LEMON AND LIME TART

Pastry

6oz (175g) unsalted butter

2 tablespoons caster sugar

a pinch of salt

1 dessertspoon mixed grated lemon and lime rind

1 large egg

2oz (50g) toasted almonds, finely ground

4oz (100g) plain white flour

1 egg yolk

Filling

8 eggs

1lb (450g) caster sugar

10fl oz (300 ml) double cream

juice and grated zest of 2 lemons

juice and grated zest of 4 limes

caster sugar for glazing (optional)

To make the pastry, in a food processor cream the butter, sugar, salt, citrus rinds and egg. With the machine on, pour in the ground almonds and then the flour; don't overwork the mix, blend only until the dough works itself into a loose ball. Wrap the ball in cling film and allow to rest for an hour in the refrigerator. If the ball is too hard when you try to roll it out, allow it to soften at room temperature until workable.

Preheat the oven to 325°F/160°C/Gas 3. Roll the pastry into a circle, ⅙in (4mm) thick. Butter a 9 x 2in (23 x 5cm) flan ring and a baking sheet. Line the flan ring with the pastry circle, pinching the top rim of the pastry. Prick the base with a fork in several places. Line the pastry with a circle of greaseproof paper and fill with dried beans or special pastry weights. Blind-bake the base in the preheated oven for 10 minutes, remove from the oven and take out the beans and greaseproof paper. Brush the bottom with beaten egg yolk and return to the oven for a further 7 minutes. Lower the oven temperature to 300°F/150°C/Gas 2.

To make the filling, beat the eggs and sugar together until well blended. Fold in the double cream and then the citrus juices and zest.

Pour the citrus filling into the pastry crust, place in the oven and bake for 35-45 minutes. Make sure the filling is set before removing from the oven. Allow to cool. The tart can be prepared to this stage up to 48 hours in advance. If you're feeling particular, just before serving, dust the surface of the tart with caster sugar and glaze under the grill or with a blow-torch to a golden crisp.

A small slice with a few raspberries or some crème fraîche makes an excellent end to a flavoursome meal.

WINE NOTES

Spring where? In Provence, on the terrace, slurping rosé to prepare for a serious Bandol Rouge like an '89 Château de Pibarnon? Or spring in Primrose Hill, London, watching the rain streaming down your windows?

Whatever the clime, brandade was made for Rosé de Provence, the younger the better, the stronger the better, in other words '93. No substitute will do, brandade with Mateus Rosé is like roast beef with German mustard.

For the poached fillet of beef, a full-blooded but soft red Bordeaux of the '90 vintage, muted flavours so as not to defeat the delicacy of the boeuf à la ficelle, in short a decent Cru Bourgeois from the Médoc, along the lines of Château Coufran or Château Phélan-Ségur, both champions in that year. Or a red Graves, especially 1990 Château Bouscaut, piled high in my own cellar. Such wines might relegate la tarte to tea, so that it would not get in the way of wine and spring lunch conversation.

A GARDENING LUNCH

Celeriac Vichyssoise
Jellied Daube of Beef with Roasted Red Peppers
Potato Salad with Bacon
A Collection of Cherries

It's a day when you know you want to do the garden, but you also know that your partner has taken it upon him or herself to invite a couple of guests to lunch - the last thing you need. So you must think ahead; everything on this menu can be prepared a day or two before. I start off with celeriac vichyssoise which I experienced at a lunch in the Hamptons, America, and I thought, that's different. The original vichyssoise is made from leeks, potato and cream and was created at the Ritz-Carlton hotel in New York at the turn of the century by a famous French chef called Louis Diat. Why he called it vichyssoise I've never really found out, but like so much in cookery it was probably created by accident. Anyway, it was good and has retained its place in cookery history as one of the most popular chilled soups. The addition of celeriac makes an interesting change. Celeriac is one of those vegetables that finds a regular spot in my culinary repertoire whether cold in celeriac rémoulade, roasted or made into a velvety purée with apples and cream. Another of my favourite snacking foods is celeriac crisps with anchoïade.

Jellied *daube* (dish) of beef might strike feelings of horror and disgust in the hearts of the reader - anything jellied often does - but you should try it, as its gelatinous quality is not produced through processed gelatine or aspic but through all its natural qualities. A mixture of beef chuck, rump and shin are marinated overnight in red wine, brandy, herbs, garlic and juniper berries and then cooked for 5 hours in a sealed *daube* (the name given to an oval earthenware terrine) with root vegetables, a calf's foot or a couple of pig's trotters and herbs. The *daube* (dish) is washed and the meat is layered in it with summer vegetables; I've changed these from the norm by the summery additions of spinach, courgettes, plum tomatoes and black olives. I serve the meat with a salad of roast peppers, scattered with anchovies, capers and hard-boiled egg, and a new potato salad which has crispy bacon and soured cream instead of the normal mayonnaise.

I finish with a collection of cherries. Fresh cherries on ice, poached cherries in Kirsch and a cherry ice cream. Impressive stuff with a variety of cherry tastes.

Serves 6

CELERIAC VICHYSSOISE

2 tablespoons vegetable oil
2 onions, peeled and diced
1 teaspoon soft thyme leaves
1 bay leaf
1 clove garlic, peeled and finely diced
1lb (450g) floury potatoes, peeled and cut in ½in (1cm) dice
1lb (450g) celeriac, peeled and cut in ½in (1cm) dice
1 tablespoon lemon juice
salt and freshly ground black pepper
1½ pint (850ml) Vegetable Stock (see page 148) or water
1 pint (600ml) milk
1 pint (600ml) double cream
snipped chives or celery leaves to garnish

Heat the oil in a saucepan, add the onion, thyme, bay leaf and garlic, and cook slowly until soft but not brown. Add the potatoes, the celeriac and the lemon juice and combine all the ingredients. Season with salt and black pepper. Add the stock, bring to the boil and simmer for 30 minutes.

Fill the jug of a liquidiser half full with the soup ingredients and purée until smooth. Pass through a fine sieve into a saucepan and repeat until all is liquidised.

Add the milk and cream and simmer for 10 minutes. Allow to cool and refrigerate. Garnish the cold soup with snipped chives or celery leaves.

JELLIED DAUBE OF BEEF WITH ROASTED RED PEPPERS AND POTATO SALAD WITH BACON

4lb (1.8kg) beef chuck, rump and shin, fat and gristle removed	8oz (225g) lean salt pork or lean bacon, cut into small lardons
8oz (225g) hard pork fat	5 cloves garlic, peeled and crushed with a little salt
1 teaspoon fresh thyme leaves	3 bay leaves
1 teaspoon finely chopped parsley	1 sprig thyme
a pinch of grated nutmeg	1 piece dried orange rind
a pinch of powdered bay leaf	1lb (450g) tomatoes, skinned, seeded and diced
salt and freshly ground black pepper	1 carrot, peeled and roughly chopped
Marinade (see page 57)	1 pint (600ml) Chicken Stock (see page 91)
Cooking the meat	flour and water paste
1 calf's foot, boned (chop the bones into small pieces)	2-3 sheets gelatine, soaked in cold water to soften (optional)
4oz (100g) pork rind, in one piece	
2oz (50g) unsalted butter or duck fat	
2 onions, peeled and roughly chopped	

Garnishing the meat
3 bay leaves
4 tablespoons chopped parsley
4 plum tomatoes, skinned, seeded and diced
2 courgettes, thinly sliced and blanched for 2 minutes
8oz (225g) spinach, cooked and chopped
4 tablespoons chopped black olives
24 baby pickling onions, peeled and cooked in salted water for 15 minutes

2 DAYS AHEAD

Cut the meat into 3oz (75g) cubes. Cut the pork fat into ¼ x 2in (5mm x 5cm) strips and toss the fat with the herbs and spices. Lard each piece of the rump and chuck with 2 pieces of fat, using a larding needle. It's a bit like sewing really. At the end of the larding needle is a hole into which you insert the fat. Clamp the fat with the little spike found at the top and push the needle through the meat. When the needle comes through the other side lift the spike and leave the fat behind. Larding has the effect of basting the meat during its slow cooking process.

Toss the meat in the marinade and rest overnight in the fridge.

1 DAY AHEAD

Preheat the oven to 300°F/150°C/Gas 2. Blanch the calf's foot and pork rind in salted water for 5 minutes. Drain and set aside. Drain the meat from the marinade and dry well. Add the butter to a large casserole and over a medium heat brown the meat on all sides. Remove from the casserole and set aside. Add the onion, salt pork and garlic to the casserole and brown lightly. Add the bay leaves, thyme and orange rind. Strain the marinade and deglaze the casserole with the liquid. Return the meat to the casserole and add the tomatoes, carrot, calf's foot, bones from the foot and pork rind. Cover with stock and bring to a simmer; season with

salt and pepper. Place a lid on the casserole and seal with a paste made from flour and water. Cook in the oven for 5 hours. Remove from the oven and allow to cool; break the paste and remove the lid. Degrease the surface of the liquor. Check the seasoning. Remove the beef and the calf's foot from the pot and set aside.

Strain the liquor without pressing the ingredients. You want the liquor to be as clear as possible. Test a spoonful of liquor on a very cold plate to see whether the jelly will set properly. It should be firm without being too rubbery. If it is not strong enough, fold in 2-3 sheets of pre-soaked gelatine which has dissolved in a little of the liquor.

Pour a little of the liquor into the bottom of a large charlotte mould or other straight sided mould. Allow to set and arrange the bay leaves, a sprinkling of parsley and tomatoes and some courgette slices artistically on top of the thin jelly. Do not allow any ingredients to touch the sides of the mould. Add some beef and layer alternately with diced calf's feet, spinach, onions, olives, tomatoes and parsley, seasoning between each layer. When the mould is full, pour in the jelly, tapping the mould to make sure the liquid gets between all the ingredients. Refrigerate the mould and allow to set overnight.

FINAL PREPARATION AND PRESENTATION

To serve, dip the mould briefly in hot water and turn upside down on a large platter. Surround with the roasted pepper salad, and serve with the potato salad.

Beef Marinade
2 tablespoons red wine vinegar
1 bottle red Burgundy
5fl oz (150ml) brandy
2 tablespoons olive oil

2 sprigs fresh thyme
I onion, peeled and finely sliced
I carrot, peeled and finely sliced
2 cloves garlic, peeled and finely chopped
2 bay leaves
I 2 roasted juniper berries

Simply mix together in a suitable dish.

ROASTED RED PEPPERS

Preheat the oven to 375°F/190°C/Gas 5. Cut 5 red peppers in half, remove the seeds and place the halves skin-side up on a baking tray. Brush the peppers with olive oil and bake in the oven until the pepper skins have blackened and blistered, about 10-15 minutes. Transfer the peppers to a paper or polythene bag. Seal the ends and allow the peppers to steam in their own heat for approximately 10 minutes. Remove them from the bag and peel off their skins. Retain any juices and cut each piece of pepper in half lengthways. Mix the peppers and their juices with 6 tinned anchovies, mashed, 18 ripped basil leaves, 4 tablespoons extra virgin olive oil, 1 red chilli, seeded and diced, 1 clove garlic, peeled and finely diced, and 1 tablespoon aged sherry vinegar. Allow to marinate overnight.

Arrange the peppers around the daube and scatter with 24 tiny capers and 2 finely chopped hard-boiled eggs.

Potato Salad with Bacon

I½lb (675g) Jersey Mids, scrubbed but not peeled
6oz (175g) Crispy Bacon (see page 86)
I red onion, peeled and finely diced
4 tablespoons snipped chives
4 tablespoons finely chopped parsley
I 5fl oz (450ml) soured cream
salt and freshly ground black pepper

Cook the Jersey Mids in salted water until tender, then drain and allow to cool. Combine with the remaining ingredients and season to taste.

A COLLECTION OF CHERRIES

Cherry Ice Cream (see below)
Poached Cherries in Kirsch (see below)
I lb (450g) sweet black cherries, washed and laid on crushed ice

To serve, place the ice cream in one bowl, the poached cherries in another and top with a few fresh cherries. Place all the dishes on the table and allow your guests to help themselves.

Cherry Ice Cream

I lb (450g) ripe sweet black cherries, washed and stoned
3 egg yolks
4oz (100g) caster sugar
I 5 fl oz (450ml) double cream
4 tablespoons Kirsch

Cook the cherries over a low heat for 25 minutes with 3 tablespoons water, stirring from time to time. Place three-quarters of the cherries in a food processor and blend until a fairly smooth purée. Whisk the egg yolks with the sugar. Heat the cream. Pour the cream on to the eggs and sugar, then return to the heat or cook over hot water, stirring continuously until the custard coats the spoon. Strain on to the cherry purée. Fold in the remaining cherries and the Kirsch. Allow to cool. Pour into an ice cream machine and process according to the manufacturer's instructions.

Poached Cherries in Kirsch

2lb (900g) sweet black cherries, washed and stoned
2oz (50g) unsalted butter
a pinch of grated nutmeg
a pinch of ground cinnamon
4oz (100g) caster sugar
½ bottle Zinfandel red wine
4 tablespoons Kirsch
1 tablespoon cornflour
1 tablespoon chopped mint

Cook the cherries in the melted butter for 5 minutes, then add the nutmeg, cinnamon and sugar; cook for a further 5 minutes. Add the wine and cook for a further 5 minutes. Add the Kirsch.

Dissolve the cornflour in 1 tablespoon of cold water. Strain the cherries and fold the cornflour into the liquid. Thicken over a low heat. Return the cherries to the sauce to warm. Fold in the chopped mint and serve.

WINE NOTES

Gardening is thirsty work, not least for the people who watch. Champagne seems a bit ostentatious among the weeds, so let's refresh with that Austrian drink known as 'Gespritzer', quite simply white wine with added soda water or Perrier. The Austrians use Grüner Veltliner for this, but the once again reasonably priced Muscadet of France or an Italian Soave will do just as well.

Then, after the vichyssoise, a cellar-cool red from Beaujolais, ideally a Fleurie, or a Juliénas or

Moulin-à-Vent. If you are without a cellar, put the wine in the refrigerator the day before, then place it on the table at the same time as you serve the vichyssoise and its temperature will be perfect by the time you tackle the jellied daube. If the gardening hut/gazebo/summer pavilion has no refrigeration, just wrap a wet towel around the bottle and place it in a draught between two doors. The water's evaporation from the towel will cool the wine.

THE DAY AFTER THE DAY BEFORE

Smoked Duck with Rocket Salad and Ratatouille Chutney

Roast Monkfish with Pancetta and Herbs
Cooked Spinach Salad and Skordalia

Chocolate Terrine with Prunes, Raspberry and Red Wine Sauce

A supper menu easily prepared ahead, starting with a simple smoked duck which can be bought from most supermarkets. This is thinly sliced and served with a rocket salad dressed with olive oil and a lovely chutney made with the normal ratatouille ingredients: tomatoes, onions, aubergines, red and green peppers, but with the addition of sugar, chilli powder and malt vinegar. If you want to do your own thing, I have included a recipe for smoking the duck without a smoker - ingenious, well read on.

The main course uses one of my favourite fish, monkfish. An ugly fish, rarely seen in the shops with its head intact, it used to be dirt cheap but like everything else, once discovered by restaurant chefs, the price goes up. Monkfish has a wonderful meaty texture similar to lobster; in fact, it was said a few years ago that certain frozen-food manufacturers were cutting monkfish to the shape of scampi and passing it off as such ... shock horror! The funny thing is that with the price of monkfish today, the manufacturers could easily sell it breaded in its own right. Take a largish tail of monkfish, remove all but 1in (2.5cm) of the bone, leaving it attached at the tail, and stuff the fillets with a mixture of herbs, spinach and garlic. The fish retains its original shape by wrapping the fillets in pancetta, the Italian bacon, tying with string and roasting. This can be done ahead. Then, just prior to your dinner, the fish can be cut into steaks and popped in the oven while you're eating the starter.

I serve the fish with a cooked spinach salad tossed with lemon juice and extra virgin olive oil, and skordalia, a Greek garlicky purée served at room temperature which includes lemon, olive oil, ground almonds and plenty of garlic and pepper.

Finish off the supper with a frozen chocolaty pudding which can be prepared well in advance. It's been a favourite of mine since my days at Ménage à Trois. An AWT health warning follows: don't attempt to prepare this dish, let alone eat it, if you're on a diet or if you have heart problems because it's jam-packed full of delicious calories and cholesterol. It's a frozen chocolate terrine made with the best chocolate, butter, egg yolks and cream and it is served with a little healthy aside of puréed raspberries and red wine.

Serves 6

SMOKED DUCK WITH ROCKET SALAD AND RATATOUILLE CHUTNEY

3 breasts of smoked duck, bought or home-smoked (see below)
4oz (100g) rocket leaves, washed and dried
1 fl oz (30ml) extra virgin olive oil
juice of ½ lemon
salt and freshly ground black pepper
Ratatouille Chutney (see below)

Marinade
6 tablespoons soy sauce
3 tablespoons hoisin sauce
3 tablespoons dry white wine
1 teaspoon chopped red chillies
1 onion, peeled and finely chopped
3 teaspoons soft brown sugar
3 teaspoons minced fresh ginger
1 teaspoon Liquid Smoke (see page 188)

Slice the smoked duck breasts thinly and arrange evenly between six plates. Dress the rocket leaves with the extra virgin olive oil and the lemon juice. Season with a little salt and ground black pepper. Place a handful of rocket leaves on each plate and serve the ratatouille chutney separately.

Home-Smoked Duck without a smoker
3 duck breasts, half chargrilled

Combine all the marinade ingredients and marinate the duck for at least 8 hours, turning regularly. Have ready three greased foil or roasting bags. Preheat the oven to 350°F/180°C/Gas 4.

Place one duck breast and one-third of the marinade in each greased foil or roasting bag, seal well, and cut two slits in the top. Bake in the oven until cooked, about 15 minutes. Allow to cool in the cooking juices.

Ratatouille Chutney

2lb (900g) plum tomatoes, skinned, seeded and roughly chopped
1lb (450g) onions, peeled and roughly chopped
1lb (450g) aubergine, cut into ½in (1cm) cubes and salted for ½ hour
1lb (450g) courgettes, cut in ½in (1cm) slices
2 red peppers, seeded and cut in ½in (1cm) squares
1 green pepper, seeded and cut in ½in (1cm) squares
2 green chillies, seeded and finely diced
6 cloves garlic, peeled and finely diced
2 sprigs thyme
1 tablespoon oregano leaves
1 teaspoon cayenne pepper (less if you don't like the fire)
1 tablespoon salt
15fl oz (450ml) white wine vinegar
1lb (450g) caster sugar

Place all the vegetables in a large non-reactive saucepan. Add the garlic, thyme, oregano, cayenne and salt. Cook over a low heat until some of the juices are extracted from the vegetables. Increase the heat and cook for a further 25 minutes, stirring, after which most of the liquid should have evaporated and the vegetables are soft but still whole. Add the vinegar and sugar and combine. Reduce the heat to moderate and cook for a further hour, when the chutney should be quite thick. Spoon into hot Kilner jars and seal. Best left for 2 months if possible.

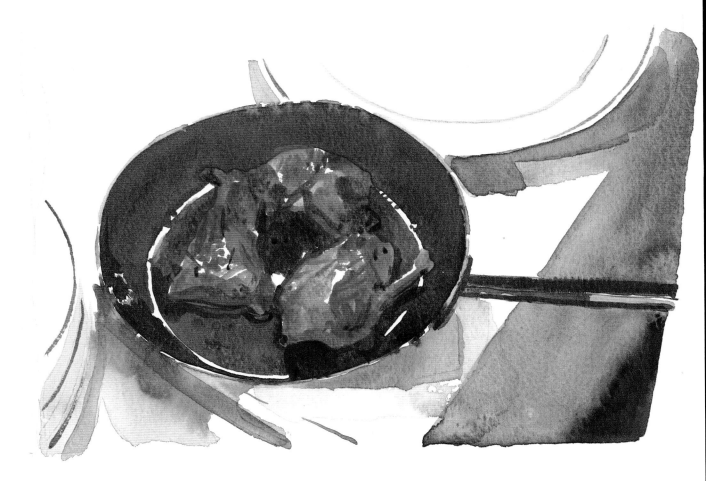

ROAST MONKFISH WITH PANCETTA AND HERBS, COOKED SPINACH SALAD AND SKORDALIA

1 x 5lb (2.25kg) monkfish tail
8oz (225g) pancetta or speck, thinly sliced
salt and freshly ground black pepper
8oz (225g) Cooked Herb Mix (see below)
6 cloves Garlic Confit (optional, see page 117)
extra virgin olive oil
Cooked Spinach Salad (see below)
Skordalia (see below)

Ask your fishmonger to remove the cartilaginous bone but leaving 2in (5cm) attached to the flesh at the end of the tail. Lay the pancetta out on a flat surface, slightly overlapping and covering the length of the tail. Season the tail inside and out with salt and ground black pepper. Arrange the herb mix and the garlic confit along the length of the tail and bring the two halves of the tail together sandwiching the herbs. Lay the tail on the pancetta and wrap it around the fish. Tie the tail with butcher's string at 1in (2.5cm) intervals. Leave the tail to rest in the fridge for about an hour to allow the flavours to develop.

Preheat the oven to 375°F/190°C/Gas 5. Place the tail on a roasting tray, dribble with olive oil and roast for 25-35 minutes. The fish should feel firm to the touch. Allow to cool.

Just prior to service, cut the tail into 6 large steaks and pan-fry in about 2 tablespoons of olive oil, turning once so that both faces of the steaks have a nice golden crust. This will take about 5 minutes on each side.

FINAL PREPARATION AND PRESENTATION

Have ready the spinach salad and the skordalia.

Serve a slice of monkfish on each of six warm plates with a portion of spinach salad. Dribble the fish with extra virgin olive oil. Serve the skordalia in a separate bowl and, if you are a nice person, warn your guests about the garlic content!

COOKED HERB MIX

Sweat 2 very finely chopped onions in about 2fl oz (60ml) olive oil until soft. Roughly chop a large bunch of parsley and a small bunch of tarragon. Blanch the herbs in boiling water for seconds only, then refresh in cold water. Drain well then purée in a blender with the onion and 1 tablespoon freshly ground white pepper.

Cooked Spinach Salad
2lb (900g) fresh spinach, stems removed and washed thoroughly
salt and freshly ground black pepper
6 tablespoons extra virgin olive oil
2 cloves garlic, peeled
lemon juice to taste

Cook the spinach in a covered pan with 1 tablespoon salt and just the water that clings to the leaves after washing for approximately 10 minutes until tender. Drain the spinach well. Heat the olive oil in a pan and add the garlic, cook gently until golden brown; remove the garlic and discard. Add the spinach and cook at a high heat to evaporate more of the spinach liquor. Season with black pepper and lemon juice. Allow to cool to room temperature. Add more olive oil and lemon juice as necessary.

Skordalia
8 cloves garlic, peeled and finely chopped
2 teaspoons salt
10oz (300g) mashed potato or soft breadcrumbs
6 tablespoons hot water
4oz (100g) ground almonds
15fl oz (450ml) extra virgin olive oil
4fl oz (120ml) fresh lemon juice
freshly ground white pepper

Blend and pulverise the garlic and the salt in a mortar and pestle or food processor if feeling lazy. The mortar and pestle give the best results. Add the potato, the water and the ground almonds and mix to combine. Gradually add the olive oil as you would for mayonnaise, and add lemon juice to taste. Season with white pepper.

CHOCOLATE TERRINE WITH PRUNES, RASPBERRY AND RED WINE SAUCE

20 dried prunes
7fl oz (200ml) freshly made tea
2fl oz (60ml) brandy
17fl oz (500ml) double cream
6oz (175g) dark chocolate, broken into pieces
3oz (75g) unsalted butter
3 eggs, separated
1½oz (40g) caster sugar
¾oz (20g) cocoa powder
To serve
Raspberry and Red Wine Sauce (see below)

Soak the prunes in the tea and brandy overnight until they are plump. Drain thoroughly and chop roughly.

Line a 2lb (900g) loaf tin with oiled cling film. Whip 10fl oz (300ml) of the cream until stiff and carefully spread it on to the base and sides of the loaf tin. Freeze until firm.

Melt the chocolate with half the butter in a bowl set over a saucepan of simmering water. Leave to cool slightly. Beat the egg yolks with the sugar until light and fluffy. Beat the remaining butter and cocoa powder together until light and fluffy. Fold the chocolate butter into the egg mixture, then fold this into the cocoa butter. Fold in the chopped prunes.

Whisk the remaining cream until it forms soft peaks. Whisk the egg whites until they form soft peaks. Fold the cream and then the egg whites into the chocolate and prune mixture until evenly combined. Pour the mixture into the cream-lined loaf tin. Cover with foil or cling film and freeze for 4-6 hours or preferably overnight, until solid.

Cut in thin slices and serve with the sauce.

Raspberry and Red Wine Sauce
1lb (450g) raspberries
2 tablespoons lemon juice
5oz (150g) caster sugar
1 bottle red wine
10fl oz (300ml) orange juice
2 strips fresh orange peel, each studded with 1 clove
½ vanilla pod
1 bay leaf

Liquidise the raspberries with the lemon juice and sugar, then pass through a fine sieve.

Place the red wine, orange juice, orange peel, vanilla pod and bay leaf in a wide, shallow sauce-pan and bring to the boil. Add the raspberry purée.

Bring the liquid to a fast boil and boil until it has reduced to a generous 10fl oz (300ml). Allow to cool, then refrigerate.

WINE NOTES

The word 'Greek' must have sparked me off, because no sooner did I read the recipes than I began to fancy a glass of retsina. People often ask me 'How can a wine expert like retsina?' I like it, especially with such outlandish ingredients as ratatouille chutney and spinach flavoured with garlic. There is of course retsina and retsina: Demestica (frequently referred to by some friends as Domestos) is not my favourite, but there are others, like the delicately flavoured Retsina Boutari, or Tsantalis.

For those who hate the very idea of resinated wine, I'd suggest truly Mediterranean white, like Clos Nicrosi from Patrimonio in Corsica, or a Regaleali Bianco from Sicily, or a dry old Vernaccia from Sardinia. If you can't find any of those at your usual wine merchant, try a barrel-fermented Sémillon from Bordeaux. Exaggerated wine by all accounts, but perfect with exaggerated food.

THE ARRIVAL OF SUMMER

Chilled Tomato Soup with Frozen Extra Virgin Olive Oil

Grilled Salmon with Lime Butter

Aubergine and Wilted Greens with Risotto Cake

Lemon Syllabub with Red Fruits

A summery menu with bright colours and refreshing tastes. I start with a chilled tomato soup based on the gazpacho theory, using bread, vinegar, garlic, olive oil, cucumber, tomatoes and peppers. With traditional gazpacho, you might float a few ice cubes on the surface of the soup. I have taken a more Italian route by freezing extra virgin olive oil in ice-cube trays (half-fill each section) and floating *those* on top.

Use only ripe tomatoes, preferably vine-ripened. Hot-house tomatoes from Holland or other countries tend to be tasteless. It's time that public demand put a stop to countries growing vegetables purely for their looks. I want to find real flavour, not just a uniform sized nothing looking up at me from the plate. Holland and California are probably the worst offenders for producing marvellous-looking, but tasteless, clones of the real thing. Time was when we had seasons, but demand in the 1980s changed all that: the public then clamoured for year-round strawberries, asparagus and the like, and the growers responded. I want the return of the seasons. Fairly recently we discovered plum tomatoes, not in a tin, but sun-ripened flavoursome beauties, short of season, but well worth looking forward to. Now trendy, they are going the fateful path of the Canary or Dutch special. I could scream ... they used to have blemishes, now they're perfect. I'm not perfect, and I certainly don't want perfect tomatoes. I want them to have struggled for survival, fought against the elements, ripened with the sun, built up craggy character and taste ... enough said.

On to the main course. My principles for tomatoes should stretch to salmon as now, through clever farming methods, we can buy cheap salmon all year. Obviously it is preferential to eat wild salmon, but I have a twinge of remorse when I see these magnificent fish leaping up waterfalls in Scotland only to land as a steak on someone's plate. Wildlife is worth preserving, so if we can farm salmon and other fish that is of a similar quality to the wild, then I say let's go for it. Vegetables are grown to be eaten as are cattle, pigs and sheep, so there seems no reason why we shouldn't farm fish for the same purpose. It's the farming methods that are

important. There are now lakes with wave machines, similar to the ones they have at the local swimming pool, and so the fish are made to use their muscles. Lazy farmed fish produce fatty limp flesh, so check out the quality before buying.

Salmon is an excellent fish for grilling. I serve it with wilted greens and a spicy butter made with limes, chilli and ginger. The greens are tossed in the flavoured butter until they release some of their own juices and wilt. They are seasoned and wrapped in sliced, chargrilled aubergine. For the carbohydrate, a cooked risotto cake which is half-cooked risotto, set in a mould and finished off in the oven with spinach and Parmesan. Equally good served cold as part of a picnic.

The pudding is a favourite of mine. I love the refreshing taste of lemon acidity contrasting with the rich sweetness of the red fruits tossed in Cassis and sugar. For the syllabub, I use a variation of Jane Grigson's in her book *English Food*. It works every time and if something is good, why change for the sake of change. Be careful not to overbeat as the cream can curdle and separate with the reaction of the lemon.

Serves 4

CHILLED TOMATO SOUP WITH FROZEN EXTRA VIRGIN OLIVE OIL

2 slices white country bread, crusts removed, broken into large crumbs
1 tablespoon sherry vinegar
1 clove garlic, peeled and finely chopped
2 teaspoons caster sugar
1 red chilli, seeded and finely diced
2fl oz (60ml) extra virgin olive oil
1lb (450g) plum tomatoes, peeled and seeded
1 tablespoon Heinz tomato ketchup (only the best)
15fl oz (450ml) good tomato juice
4 spring onions, finely sliced
1 red pepper, roasted or grilled, peeled, seeded and diced
½ large cucumber, peeled, seeded and roughly diced
1 tablespoon Pesto (see below)
salt and freshly ground black pepper
8 cubes frozen extra virgin olive oil
8 basil leaves, ripped

Place the bread in a food processor or blender. With the machine running add the vinegar, garlic, sugar and chilli, and blend until smooth. Add the extra virgin olive oil until the bread will absorb no more, then, a little at a time, add the tomatoes, tomato ketchup, tomato juice, spring onions, red pepper, cucumber and pesto. Continue to blend to form a smooth emulsion. Season to taste with salt and black pepper, and chill.

Pour into a brightly coloured Portuguese or Spanish terracotta bowl and garnish, just before serving, with frozen olive oil and ripped basil leaves.

PESTO

makes about 10oz (300g)
4oz (100g) basil leaves
2 large garlic cloves, peeled
4oz (100g) Parmesan cheese, grated
1oz (25g) pine nuts
extra virgin olive oil

Blend the first four ingredients together in a food processor, although I prefer to chop them finely together. Add enough oil to make a smooth purée.

Keep in the fridge for up to a month if need be, but cover it with a little oil to retain the colour.

GRILLED SALMON WITH LIME BUTTER, AUBERGINE AND WILTED GREENS WITH RISOTTO CAKE

4 x 6oz (175g) Scottish salmon fillets, skin on but scaled
salt and freshly ground black pepper
olive oil
½ quantity Lime Butter (see below), at room temperature
Aubergine and Wilted Greens (see below)
Risotto Cake (see below)
grated zest of 2 limes

Preheat the grill or chargrill. Season the salmon fillets with salt and ground black pepper. Dip in olive oil and place flesh-side down on the chargrill at an angle to the grill bars. Grill for 1 minute and turn at right angles leaving the same side down; this will give the salmon stylish grid-like markings. Turn the salmon over and cook skin side down until the salmon is cooked through (approximately 4 minutes) and the skin is charred and crispy. Do the same if cooking under an ordinary grill. Remove from the grill and keep warm.

FINAL PREPARATION AND PRESENTATION

Have ready the aubergine and greens, the lime butter and the risotto cake. Place a salmon fillet on each of four warm plates with 2 'rolls' of the aubergine and greens. Place a spoonful of the butter on top of the salmon and sprinkle with the lime zest. Serve the risotto cake separately in wedges.

Aubergine and Wilted Greens
2 aubergines, each cut into 4 slices lengthways
salt and freshly ground black pepper
extra virgin olive oil
1 lb (450g) mixed greens (beetroot, carrot or turnip tops, sorrel, chard, mustard greens) or spinach, washed
½ quantity Lime Butter (see below), at room temperature

Salt the aubergine slices lightly and leave for half an hour. This extracts any bitter

69

juices. Rinse the slices, pat dry and season with black pepper. Dip the slices in olive oil and grill or chargrill for 3 minutes each side. Remove from the grill.

Place the washed mixed greens in a saucepan with the lime butter and 1fl oz (30ml) extra virgin olive oil. Place over a medium heat and cook, turning regularly, until the greens start to release their liquid and wilt. Season to taste with salt and black pepper. Drain slightly.

Place the aubergine slices on a flat surface and spoon the wilted greens on each slice. Roll up and keep warm.

LIME BUTTER

Chop 1 spring onion finely with 1 clove garlic and cook gently in ½oz (15g) unsalted butter until soft but not brown. Allow to cool. In a food processor place 6oz (175g) softened unsalted butter, the spring onion/garlic mix, 1 tablespoon finely diced medium hot green chilli, 1 teaspoon grated fresh ginger, 1 tablespoon fresh lime juice, 1 dessertspoon grated lime zest and ½ teaspoon each of salt and freshly ground white pepper. Blend until well combined and smooth. Refrigerate overnight to allow flavours to develop. Bring to room temperature before using in the cooking.

RISOTTO CAKE

Preheat the oven to 375°F/190°C/Gas 5. Bring 2 pints (1.1 litres) of chicken stock to the boil. In another saucepan melt 2oz (50g) unsalted butter, add a finely diced onion, a diced clove of garlic and a teaspoon of soft thyme leaves. Cook until the onion is soft but not brown. Add 4 handfuls of Arborio rice (about 10oz/300g) to the pan and stir thoroughly until combined with the onions and butter. Cook for a further 2 minutes, then add about 5fl oz (150ml) of white wine. When that has been absorbed by the rice add a ladleful of the hot stock. Stir until the rice has absorbed the liquor and repeat, adding a small amount of stock at a time. The risotto should cook for about 15-20 minutes until the rice is nearly tender with a little bite. Five minutes before the end of cooking, add 2 handfuls washed young spinach leaves, and let them wilt. Stir in 3oz (75g) grated Parmesan cheese and another 2oz (50g) butter. Season to taste with salt and black pepper.

Butter an ovenproof pudding dish and sprinkle with equal parts toasted breadcrumbs and grated Parmesan. Pour the risotto into the dish and press the rice firmly down. Bake in the preheated oven for 15-20 minutes. Remove the dish from the oven and allow to stand for 10 minutes. Invert the dish on to a plate and tap the dish to release the cake. Serve immediately.

LEMON SYLLABUB WITH RED FRUITS

4fl oz (120ml) dry white wine
2fl oz (60ml) brandy
1 teaspoon grated lemon rind
juice of 1 lemon
1 tablespoon clear honey
10fl oz (300ml) double cream
a pinch of grated nutmeg
Red fruits
1 punnet strawberries, hulled and quartered
1 punnet raspberries, picked over
1 punnet blackberries, berries removed from their stems
1 punnet redcurrants, berries removed from their stems
4fl oz (120ml) Crème de Cassis
3oz (75g) caster sugar
1 tablespoon lemon juice

Place the first 5 ingredients in a non-reactive bowl and leave overnight for the flavours to mingle and develop. Next day, add the cream and nutmeg and beat with a whisk until the syllabub holds its shape. Pour into a glass bowl and refrigerate.

In another glass bowl combine all the fruits gently with the Cassis, sugar and lemon juice. Allow to macerate for approximately 3 hours, turning the fruits from time to time.

To serve, offer the bowl of fruits with the bowl of syllabub and allow your guests to combine or eat separately as they wish. A refreshing combination.

WINE NOTES

Salmon offers an opportunity to rediscover German Riesling from the Moselle where the wines are less broad and have rather more acidity than flat Palatinate wines or the big wines of the Rheingau. Now it is very important to note here that commercial Bernkasteler and Piesporter were not the kind of wines I had in mind, even if it says 'Qualitätswein' on the label. Rarely have any wines been further from Qualität than those sugar-water concoctions sold by the British off-licence trade. There is of course drinkable Bernkasteler, but it comes with a second name like Doktor or Bratenhöfchen; this is unfortunately not so in the case of Piesporter where 'Michelsberg' is, if anything, worse than

plain Piesporter. So to avoid confusion, look out for other names: Erdener Treppchen, Urziger Würzgarten, Kaseler Nieschen, Wehlener Sonnenuhr, Maximin Herrenberg, Ockfener Bockstein - to name just a few of the best-known, rich finds at bargain prices, to be rediscovered. Their fall in prices is the result of the very poor image of German wines, plus the snobs' dictum that 'classy' wine has to be dry. Nonsense! Just try the new wave of dry German Rieslings, about as attractive as a skinny fashion model in bed.

Could Antony's exotic cookery give old-fashioned German Rieslings a new lease of life?

Seared Peppered Tuna Sashimi with Spicy Lentil Salad
Marinated Duck Breast with Chargrilled Chinese Greens
Aubergine Compote
Star Anise Crème Brûlée

My continued love affair with the East influences this menu. Tuna is a very fashionable fish. We've obviously known it for decades in its tinned form and very good it is too, but worlds apart from the fresh fish. Much has been written about the fishing of tuna, most of it to do with the fact that dolphins get trapped in the nets, so we always insist on line-caught fish. As the dish is raw, I'm also looking for prime quality and by using line-caught fish, I don't encounter the bruising that is often apparent with those caught in nets. It is getting easier to find fresh tuna: previously the best found its way to Japan for exorbitant sums of money and the rest went to be canned. It's a marvellous meaty fish and in its raw state has the appearance of red meat. You should eat tuna raw or rare as an overcooked tuna steak will have much the same texture as the canned and often ends up very dry and cardboardy. In this dish, I roll tuna loin in finely ground black pepper and star anise. The steak is then seared dry in a white-hot frying pan, just lightly charring the pepper. It is allowed to cool, then is thinly sliced and served with a lentil salad flavoured with chillies, limes and coriander, and a mayonnaise flavoured with Japanese green horseradish or *wasabi*.

The duck breast is pre-cooked skin-side down for 15 minutes over a slow heat to extract most of its fats, then allowed to cool and marinated in a mix of carrot, ginger, garlic and lemon. When ready to eat the duck breast is quickly chargrilled, retaining a pink centre. This is served with chargrilled marinated *bok choy* and a spiced aubergine compote. When buying duck breasts, try to buy the French (female) *canettes* which are leaner than their French male counterparts. English duck breasts are acceptable, but they tend to be a bit flabby.

Crème brûlée is a terrific classic pud. Originally called Cambridge burnt cream, I assume it was renamed when it became fashionable to write menus in French. Now that the Brits are producing food they can be proud of and English menus are in vogue, I wonder whether we'll revert to its original name. In the meantime natural *crème brûlée* is wonderful - or it makes a great vehicle for carrying different flavours. In this recipe, in keeping with the Oriental influences, I have infused the cream with star anise.

Serves 4

SEARED PEPPERED TUNA SASHIMI
WITH SPICY LENTIL SALAD

1lb (450g) trimmed tuna loin, in the piece

2oz (50g) finely ground black pepper, mixed with ½ teaspoon powdered star anise

2 dessertspoons wasabi powder (Japanese green horseradish)

6 tablespoons Mayonnaise (see below)

Dipping Sauce (see below)

Spicy Lentil Salad (see below)

2 teaspoons chopped coriander leaves

Place the black pepper mix in a shallow tray and roll the tuna in it, pressing the pepper into the flesh. Heat a thick-based frying pan without fat over a high flame until extremely hot. Place the tuna in the pan and sear each side until the heat has penetrated ⅙in (4mm) all round. The pepper will be nicely charred and aromatic. Set aside and, when cool, refrigerate until ready to serve.

Mix the *wasabi* powder to a smooth paste by gradually adding warm water. Allow to rest for at least 10 minutes. If it becomes too dry, add a little more water. Mix the *wasabi* paste little by little into the mayonnaise until the desired fieriness is achieved. (You can use Hellman's mayonnaise but I prefer to make my own.)

FINAL PREPARATION AND PRESENTATION

Have ready the mayonnaise, lentil salad and dipping sauce.

Remove the tuna from the fridge and cut it into ⅜in (9mm) slices using a simple, single draw from top to bottom with a sharp long knife. The flesh of the tuna will cut like butter so do not be tempted to use a sawing motion.

Stir the lentils incorporating all the juices. Place a heap of lentils on each of four plates. Lean 3 slices of tuna in a fan against the lentils. Garnish with coriander leaves and if you're feeling particularly inspirational, pipe the *wasabi* mayonnaise through the thinnest plain nozzle of a piping bag or through a paper piping bag in zig-zag lines over the tuna slices. Failing that, serve the mayonnaise and the dipping sauce in two separate dishes on the table.

MAYONNAISE

There's nothing to fear about making a mayo; just make sure all the ingredients are at room temperature and it should be plain sailing. If by any chance the mayo breaks and separates, simply add a couple of spoons of warm water to a clean bowl and whisk the broken mayo slowly into the warm water; the mayonnaise will immediately rediscover its thick personality.

Whisk 2 large egg yolks with ½ teaspoon Colman's English mustard, 1 dessertspoon lemon juice, a pinch of salt and a smaller pinch of freshly ground white pepper. Measure out 7fl oz (200ml) corn or vegetable oil and gradually add it to the mix drop by drop, increasing to a steady stream, until it has all been accepted. Remember, add the oil slowly to start, increasing the speed as it emulsifies. If very thick, whisk in 1 dessert-spoon white wine vinegar and 1 dessertspoon warm water. Check seasoning. Many chefs make the mistake of using extra virgin olive oil. This is fine for aïoli and other powerful flavour needs, but for a simple mayonnaise we usually want a much blander taste, hence the vegetable oil.

Spicy Lentil Salad

8oz (225g) lentilles du Puy, washed
Vegetable Stock (see page 148) or water
3 cloves garlic, peeled
1½ red onions, peeled and finely diced
grated zest and juice of 2 limes
3 fl oz (85ml) extra virgin olive oil
4 large red chillies, chargrilled or roasted, peeled, seeded and mashed
salt and freshly ground black pepper

Cover the lentils in stock or water by about 1in (2.5cm) and cook with the whole garlic cloves over a medium heat. Bring to the boil and simmer for 20-25 minutes or until cooked but still firmish and intact.

Drain the lentils and fold in the remaining ingredients while the lentils are still warm. Season to taste, and cool.

Dipping Sauce

1 teaspoon juices from grated fresh ginger
5fl oz (150ml) light Japanese soy sauce
½ teaspoon wasabi paste (see above)

Mix all the ingredients together and allow to stand for half an hour. Whisk again just before serving.

MARINATED DUCK BREAST WITH CHARGRILLED CHINESE GREENS AND AUBERGINE COMPOTE

4 duck breasts, 6-8 oz (175-225g) each
Garlic and Ginger Marinade (see page 76)
Aubergine Compote (see page 76)
4 heads Chinese greens or bok choy, split lengthwise
olive oil
salt and freshly ground black pepper
Dipping sauce
8fl oz (250ml) strained marinade
4 spring onions, finely sliced
1 red pepper, roasted or grilled, peeled, seeded and diced
2 tablespoons each of chopped coriander, basil and mint

THE DAY BEFORE

Heat a non-stick pan over a medium flame. Place the duck breasts in the pan, skin-side down, and cook gently to remove the excess fats. Drain the pan from time to time. Cook for about 15 minutes. Allow the duck breasts to cool. Place in the marinade overnight in the refrigerator.

FINAL PREPARATION AND PRESENTATION

Remove the duck breasts from the marinade. Strain the marinade and use some in the dipping sauce: simply combine all the ingredients and pour into a bowl.

Have ready the aubergine compote.

Bring a pan of salted water to the boil and

blanch the Chinese greens for 2 minutes. Drain well, drizzle with olive oil, and season to taste. Chargrill them at the last minute.

Grill or pan-fry the duck breasts for approximately 4 minutes on each side, depending on how rare you like your meat. Slice each breast across at an angle and arrange with the Chinese greens on four plates. Serve the aubergine compote and the sauce separately, allowing guests to serve themselves.

Garlic and Ginger Marinade
5fl oz (150ml) good olive oil
4 cloves garlic, peeled and finely chopped
1 tablespoon grated fresh ginger
½ onion, peeled and finely diced
grated zest of 1 lemon and 1 orange
3oz (75g) carrots, grated
1 red chilli, seeded and diced
1 teaspoon freshly ground black pepper
6fl oz (175ml) dry white wine
3fl oz (85ml) water
4fl oz (120ml) katchup manis or soy sauce
4 fl oz (120ml) Chinese oyster sauce
1 bay leaf
3 tablespoons clear honey

Heat the olive oil in a saucepan over a medium heat. Add the garlic, ginger, onion, citrus zest, carrots and chilli and cook gently for 5 minutes without allowing to colour. Add the remaining ingredients and bring to the boil. Simmer gently for 30 minutes, removing any scum that floats to the surface. Allow to cool.

Aubergine Compote
3 large aubergines
2 tablespoons sesame oil
4 tablespoons olive oil
½ red onion, peeled and finely diced
2 cloves garlic, peeled and finely diced
1 teaspoon finely grated fresh ginger
1 red chilli, seeded and finely diced
1 red pepper, roasted or grilled, peeled, seeded and diced
4 spring onions, finely sliced
2 tablespoons finely chopped coriander

Preheat the oven to 375°F/190°C/Gas 5. Prick the aubergines all over with a fork, rub the skin with sesame oil and bake on a tray in the oven for approximately 30 minutes or until they feel very soft. Keep warm.

Meanwhile heat the olive oil in a large pan and sweat the red onion, garlic, ginger and chilli until soft but not brown. Cut the aubergines in half lengthways and scoop out the flesh into a food processor with the sweated onion mix and the oil. Blend until smooth and pass through a fine sieve. This last measure is optional but occasionally the ginger can be a bit woody and these little bits can get stuck in your teeth, not a pleasant experience. Fold in the other ingredients and season to taste. Serve at room temperature.

STAR ANISE CREME BRULEE

1 pint (600ml) double cream

3 whole pieces of star anise

6 large egg yolks

caster sugar

Place the cream and star anise in a saucepan and heat to a high temperature without boiling. Remove from the heat and leave to stand for 30 minutes to allow the flavouring to permeate. Beat the egg yolks with 2oz (50g) of the sugar, and strain the cream on to the egg mixture. Whisk thoroughly and return to the heat. Cook over a medium heat and stir constantly with a wooden spoon. Do not use a whisk as you don't want to incorporate air into the custard. Cook until the custard coats the back of a spoon. A good test is to cover the back of a spoon with the custard, then run your finger down the middle of the spoon; if the custard does not join up again, it is ready. On no account allow the custard to boil otherwise it will split and separate, producing rather expensive scrambled eggs.

Strain the custard into four largish ramekins - at least 3-4in (7.5-10cm) in diameter - and allow to cool. Refrigerate overnight.

A couple of hours before serving sprinkle each custard with a thin layer of caster sugar. Preheat the grill. Place the ramekins in an ice filled tray and glaze the sugar under the grill until caramelised with delicious dark patches. Alternatively if you are a decorator use a blow-torch to caramelise the sugar. Once the sugar has been caramelised do not refrigerate. Place the ramekins on four side plates and present to your guests. Crack open the caramel and indulge in what is probably the greatest of British puds, albeit with a hint of the Orient.

WINE NOTES

Sashimi and saki belong together. Eating raw fish has an element of risk which is much reduced by a jar of hot rice wine. Over the years I've acquired the habit of rinsing the saki with Suntory beer, so a bottle of ice-cold lager between the first and second courses is to be recommended. It prepares you for duck and a stunning bottle of Châteauneuf-du-Pape, the kind produced by Domaine du Vieux Télégraphe or Château de Beaucastel. I have a great fondness for Châteauneuf, the one wine that really reminds one of the summer's heat, rich, spicy, great depth and packing a punch.

With the burnt cream, a neighbouring wine, Muscat de Beaumes de Venise, rich muscat flavour with overtones of orange, to be served chilled and in small glasses.

Altogether an alcoholic meal, so best taken at home, in bed. No belly-dancing please.

AN ITALIAN LUNCH

A Salad of Cos Lettuce, Lemon and Parmesan with Anchovy Grilled Bread

Shellfish Risotto with Saffron and Ginger

Balsamic Strawberries with Mascarpone Cream

A menu suitable for a light spring lunch. A salad starter with hints of Caesar, but I wasn't going to call it Caesar salad, as you get into such trouble with the 'foodies' when you give dishes labels. Caesar salad is one of the most popular starters of the 'ladies who lunch', good for the waistline and a great salad if made properly. There are so many food writers and chefs who consider theirs to be the definitive version, that I will stick to my description of this variation - all the traditional constituents are there, but it's more of a do-it-yourself version with a lemony dressing. The Cos lettuce is dressed and placed on a slice of toasted country bread which has been spread with anchoïade. The salad is garnished with fresh Parmesan shavings and a liberal sprinkling of black pepper.

I follow with a shellfish risotto to which I've added a few Oriental touches ... ginger, chilli, coriander and basil. It works well, but turns the head of a few purists. I've staked my reputation on being different and I'm not going to change now, although as I grow older, I find myself becoming a more mellow person - disturbing really.

Risotto is a wonderful vehicle for flavour making an extremely popular starter or main course. Very fashionable at the moment although, obviously, risotto has been a feature of Italian cooking for many centuries. Risotto, like soufflés, for some reason seems to frighten people. It's easy cooking if you follow the rules. I was demonstrating risotto at a catering college recently and had produced a particularly good one, when some young upstart told me that I had made it incorrectly. The student told me that the grains of rice should be separate and dryish and that I should have cooked it in the oven. Oh my God, I thought ... what hope is there for the future of restaurants, or risotto, for that matter, if students are being fed such information. His version of risotto was, I presume, a pilaff. Risotto, as we all know, is cooked on top of the stove by adding a hot liquid, usually stock, little by little to Arborio, Vialone Nano or Carnaroli rice. The starches which envelop the rice are dissolved creating a creamy emulsion. Butter and Parmesan are often added in the last minute of cooking to create a rich silkiness. Its texture should be fully cooked, but still firm towards the centre of each grain. The finished dish should be moist but not runny so that when you put a dollop on the plate it should hold its shape with only the slightest hint of movement.

My shellfish risotto uses the cooking juices from mussels and clams as the liquid, a touch of white wine and a little hot water. A fish stock would be too overpowering and sticky as it cooks and reduces, damaging the delicate flavours of the shellfish. I finish the risotto with a mixture of pan-roasted squid, the clams and the mussels - delicious. A salad of tomatoes is all that is needed.

A refreshing finish is made with ripe but not mushy strawberries macerated in balsamic vinegar and sugar. Yuk, you say - delicious, I say. The balsamic vinegar highlights the natural sweetness of the strawberries. Serve with a cream made with Mascarpone, a sweet soft Italian cheese. Weird but wonderful.

Serves 6

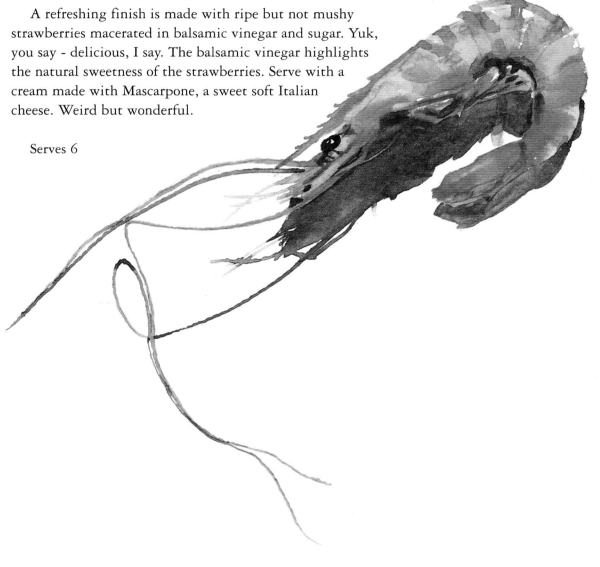

A SALAD OF COS LETTUCE, LEMON AND PARMESAN WITH ANCHOVY GRILLED BREAD

6 slices country bread
extra virgin olive oil
2 cloves garlic, peeled
6 tablespoons Anchoïade Rémoulade Sauce (see page 51)
2 Cos lettuces, washed and ripped in 1½in (3.5cm) pieces
5fl oz (150ml) Lemon Dressing (see below)
12 tinned anchovy fillets, rinsed and cut in half lengthways
6oz (175g) fresh Parmesan cheese
salt and freshly ground black pepper

Dribble the slices of bread with extra virgin olive oil and grill or chargrill. Rub with garlic and set aside. Spread each slice with 1 tablespoon anchoïade. Place a slice in the middle of each plate. Toss the salad leaves with some of the lemon dressing and place a handful of leaves on each slice of grilled bread. Garnish each salad with 4 halves of anchovy fillet. Shave the Parmesan into thin strips either with a sharp knife or a potato peeler. Lay some shavings carefully over each salad, and season with plenty of black pepper and a little salt.

Lemon Dressing
makes about 6fl oz (180ml)
1 teaspoon grated lemon zest
2 tablespoons fresh lemon juice
2 cloves garlic, peeled and finely chopped
1 dessertspoon finely snipped chives
1 teaspoon aged sherry vinegar
5fl oz (150ml) extra virgin olive oil
1 teaspoon freshly ground black pepper
½ teaspoon salt
½ tablespoon grated Parmesan cheese

Combine all the ingredients and leave to rest overnight. Shake before use.

SHELLFISH RISOTTO WITH SAFFRON AND GINGER

Mussels and clams	Risotto
1 shallot, peeled and finely diced	1 large onion, peeled and finely chopped
1in (2.5cm) fresh ginger, peeled and finely diced	3 cloves garlic, peeled and finely chopped
1 clove garlic, peeled and finely chopped	1in (2.5cm) fresh ginger, peeled and finely grated
3 tablespoons olive oil	1 red chilli, seeded and finely diced
1 bottle dry white wine	3oz (75g) unsalted butter
2lb (900g) small clams (Venus), cleaned	1fl oz (25ml) extra virgin olive oil
2lb (900g) mussels, cleaned	1lb (450g) Arborio rice or other rice suitable for risotto
	1 pinch saffron stamens, soaked in 1 tablespoon warm water

To finish
1lb (450g) squid, cleaned and cut into small pieces
2 tablespoons extra virgin olive oil
4 plum tomatoes, seeded and diced
2 tablespoons each of chopped coriander, basil and flat parsley
salt and freshly ground black pepper
2oz (50g) unsalted butter, chilled and cut into small cubes

THE MUSSELS AND CLAMS

Over a medium heat, sweat the shallot, ginger and garlic in the olive oil until soft but not brown. Add the white wine, bring to the boil and add the clams. Cover with a lid and cook at a fierce pace for 5 minutes. Add the mussels, cover and cook, shaking from time to time, until they have opened. Discard any that remain closed. Remove the shellfish and set aside. Add 2 pints (1.1 litres) water to the shellfish juices and simmer for 20 minutes. Strain the juices and return to the heat. Remove the meat from the shells and cut the clam meat into dice. Set aside.

THE RISOTTO

Sweat the onion, garlic, ginger and chilli in the butter and oil over a medium heat until soft but not brown. Add the rice and mix well with the onion. Allow the rice to become nutty and slightly perfumed, and then add a large ladleful of the shellfish cooking juices. The stock should bubble vigorously. Stir constantly with a wooden spoon. Add another ladle of the broth and stir again. As the liquor is absorbed, keep adding a further ladle of broth. Give the risotto your undivided attention, stirring most of the time. The risotto will take 20-25 minutes to cook. Halfway through cooking the rice, after about 10 minutes, add the saffron and its liquor and stir thoroughly.

FINAL PREPARATION AND PRESENTATION

While the risotto is cooking, pan-fry the squid in hot oil for approximately 2 minutes. Add the tomatoes, coriander, basil and parsley and toss together. Fold in the mussel and clam meat. Season with salt and pepper.

About 2 minutes before the risotto is fully cooked, add the squid mixture and mix thoroughly. Fold in the butter pieces and stir until emulsified. Check the seasoning and serve immediately from the pot with a salad of plum tomatoes.

PLUM TOMATO SALAD

Cut 1lb (450g) plum tomatoes into rough dice and toss with a finely diced shallot and 1 tablespoon snipped chives. Dribble over plenty of extra virgin olive oil and a splash of sherry vinegar. Season to taste with Maldon sea salt and plenty of freshly ground black pepper.

BALSAMIC STRAWBERRIES WITH MASCARPONE CREAM

2lb (900g) ripe, undamaged strawberries, stalks and hulls removed
4 tablespoons aged balsamic vinegar
4 tablespoons caster sugar
Mascarpone cream
2 tablespoons caster sugar
3 egg yolks
4 teaspoons Kirsch
8oz (225g) Mascarpone cheese
5fl oz (150ml) double cream

Macerate the strawberries in the vinegar and sugar for at least half an hour stirring from time to time.

Meanwhile prepare the Mascarpone cream. Beat the caster sugar with the egg yolks until ribboning and very pale. Fold in the Kirsch and then the Mascarpone. Whisk the cream to soft peaks and fold into the Mascarpone mixture.

Serve in a sauceboat or bowl with another bowl full of the strawberries - a delicious combination.

WINE NOTES

Not only an Italian lunch, but a ladies' Italian lunch, which in non-Mediterranean countries precludes red wine. Fortunately Italy produces a number of delicious white luncheon wines that will happily cope with Parmesan and shellfish risotto: Pinot Grigio from the region of Grave del Friuli, Lugana from Lombardy (my favourite being Santa Cristina), and Vernaccia di San Gimignano from Tuscany.

And then, with the coffee, an old-fashioned glass of Sambuca with its obligatory roast coffee bean - but preferably without the flames they love to light in London's Italian restaurants, so that you run the risk of burning your lips.

A SUMMER BRUNCH

Apple and Cinnamon Muffins

Mushrooms and Kidneys on Tapenade Toast

Salmon Hash with Smoked Salmon
Soured Cream and Crispy Bacon

Pain Perdu with Strawberries and Crème Fraîche

This brunch menu is very simple, delicious, late breakfast fare. I love any sort of muffins, but apple and cinnamon or Cheddar and chilli are my favourites. Despite public opinion, America has some excellent recipes to offer, with foods unique to their continent. Some of the best foods I've eaten in recent years have either come from Australia or America, in particular New York, Chicago, Los Angeles or San Francisco. Nothing inspires me quite so much as individuals not tied by any of the cookery cultures you might find in France or Italy. There are exciting times ahead for cookery in these countries.

Pan-fried kidneys and mushrooms are served on warm olive bread grilled or toasted and spread with a light coating of tapénade. Lamb's kidneys are cheap and delicious, but make sure you buy fresh ones still wrapped in their suet rather than the frozen variety available. It would be a truly fabulous dish if you used *cèpes* or porcini, but it works very well with large black field mushrooms.

As an alternative to the American hash using corned beef, try this dish with salmon. Potatoes are pan-fried from raw with garlic, onion, chilli and red peppers and allowed to cool, then mixed with beaten egg and cooked salmon. Tip the mixture into a frying pan and cook until brown, ending up with a wonderful crunchy mix of crispy eggy bits.

Unless you have demon knife skills it's probably best to buy smoked salmon ready sliced from your fishmonger or supermarket. As a rule of thumb, the more you pay the better the salmon, but if you find one you like and it's cheap then go for it. I prefer one which is much lighter, less oaky-smoked, moister and rawer in texture than the traditional, often over-salted variety. With the salmon, I serve soured cream mixed with spring onions and some crispy bacon. Everything including the hash itself can be prepared the night before. The end result gives you hot and cold, smoked and spicy, soft and crunchy taste and texture sensations.

Pain perdu is a favourite of mine, bringing back memories of childhood and more recently America where they call it French toast. As a child I remember it as 'eggy bread'. It can be made with slices of brioche, croissant or good ordinary slices of hand-cut white bread. The bread should be a couple of days old - if it is too fresh it will absorb too much of the 'custard' mix. The bread is dipped in a rinse of eggs beaten with milk and flavoured with cinnamon, orange zest and a dash of Cointreau. It's pan-fried in clarified butter then dusted with cinnamon sugar and served with strawberries, maple syrup, and a bowl of crème fraîche or Greek yogurt.

Serves 6

APPLE AND CINNAMON MUFFINS

makes 16 muffins
2 apples, peeled, cored and diced
7oz (200g) soft brown sugar
4oz (100g) unsalted butter
1 teaspoon lemon juice
4oz (100g) plain flour
a pinch of salt
3 teaspoons baking powder
1 teaspoon baking soda (bicarbonate of soda)
1 teaspoon ground cinnamon
2 eggs, lightly beaten
5fl oz (150ml) milk
5fl oz (150ml) golden syrup

In a small saucepan, cook together the apples, 2 oz (50g) of the soft brown sugar, 1oz (25g) of the butter and the lemon juice until the apples are soft but not mushy and the liquid has evaporated. Allow to cool.

Preheat the oven to 350°F/180°C/Gas 4. Sift together the flour, salt, baking powder, baking soda, the cinnamon and the rest of the soft brown sugar.

In another bowl combine the rest of the butter, melted, the eggs, the milk, the golden syrup and the apple.

Pour the wet mix over the flour mix and stir only enough to bind. The batter should not be smooth. Spoon into buttered muffin tins, filling each one two-thirds full. Bake for about 20 minutes or until a knife pushed into the centre comes out clean.

MUSHROOMS AND KIDNEYS ON TAPENADE TOAST

12 fresh lamb's kidneys in suet, trimmed of all but a thin coating of fat
6 large field mushrooms, stalks removed
salt and freshly ground black pepper
6 slices country bread
extra virgin olive oil
6 tablespoons Tapénade (see page 49)

Preheat the oven to 350°F/180°C/Gas 4. Pop the kidneys in a large metal ovenproof frying pan. Cook over a high heat for 2 minutes on each side; remove the kidneys and set aside.

Place the mushrooms in the same pan, gill-side down. Season with salt and black pepper. Cook for 2 minutes each side. Return the kidneys to the pan and place in the oven for a further 5 minutes if you want the kidneys pink, longer if not. Remove from the oven and keep warm.

Dribble the bread with a little olive oil and grill until golden brown on both sides. Spread the bread with tapénade. Place a mushroom on each slice. Cut each kidney in 4 and position 8 slices on top of each mushroom. Check the seasoning and serve immediately.

SALMON HASH WITH SMOKED SALMON, SOURED CREAM AND CRISPY BACON

1 red chilli, seeded and diced
1 clove garlic, peeled and crushed
1 red onion, peeled and finely diced
2 red peppers, finely diced
olive oil
4 medium waxy potatoes, peeled and diced
12oz (350g) cooked salmon, drained
2 tablespoons finely chopped dill
5 eggs, beaten
salt and freshly ground black pepper
To serve
8oz (225g) Scottish smoked salmon
10fl oz (300ml) Soured Cream Dressing (see below)
18 slices Crispy Bacon Pieces (see below)

Pan-fry the chilli, garlic, onion and red pepper in 1 tablespoon olive oil until soft but not brown. Transfer to a stainless-steel mixing bowl.

In a non-stick pan, heat 2 tablespoons olive oil and pan-fry the potatoes until tender. They should be lightly browned. Drain and add the potatoes to the onion mix. Allow to cool, and stir in the salmon and dill. Add the eggs to the bowl and mix well. Season with salt and black pepper.

Heat yet another tablespoon of olive oil in another non-stick pan. Pour in the mix and allow to cook for approximately 8 minutes. Invert the hash on to a plate and slide back into the pan to brown the other side.

PRESENTATION

Serve the hash from the pan, cutting it in wedges. Place a plate of smoked salmon, a bowl of soured cream dressing and a bowl of crispy bacon pieces on the table.

CRISPY BACON PIECES

Preheat the oven to 325°F/160°C/Gas 3. Place 18 slices of streaky bacon on a rack above a roasting tray and place in the oven. Cook until the bacon is golden and crispy, having released most of its natural fats. Remove from the oven, drain the fat (retain for other uses) and allow the bacon to cool. When at room temperature, break the bacon into small pieces.

Soured Cream Dressing
10fl oz (300ml) soured cream
1 clove garlic, peeled and crushed
a pinch of salt
a pinch of ground cumin
2 spring onions, finely chopped
1 tablespoon finely chopped coriander
1 tablespoon finely snipped chives

Combine all ingredients in a bowl.

PAIN PERDU WITH STRAWBERRIES AND CREME FRAICHE

4 eggs, beaten
10fl oz (300ml) single cream
10fl oz (300ml) milk
½ teaspoon ground cinnamon
½ teaspoon each of grated lemon and orange zests
2 teaspoons Cointreau
6 slices stale country bread, crusts removed (or brioche)
4oz (100g) Clarified Butter (see below)
2 tablespoons caster sugar mixed with ½ teaspoon ground cinnamon
To serve
10fl oz (300ml) maple syrup
8oz (225g) ripe strawberries
10fl oz (300ml) crème fraîche or Greek yogurt

Beat the eggs with the cream and milk. Fold in the cinnamon, citrus zests and Cointreau. Dip the bread in this mix and allow to sit for 30 seconds. Heat a tablespoon of clarified butter in a non-stick pan and fry 2 slices of 'eggy' bread at a time. Dust with the cinnamon sugar and keep warm. Repeat for the other slices of bread.

Serve with a jug of warm maple syrup, a bowl of strawberries and a bowl of crème fraîche or Greek yogurt.

CLARIFIED BUTTER

Melt 8oz (225g) unsalted butter in a saucepan over a low heat. Remove the pan from the heat and allow to rest for 10 minutes. Using a tea-strainer or spoon, carefully remove any scum that has risen to the surface. Pour the clear fats into a bowl: this is the clarified butter. Discard any solids or watery fluids that are at the bottom of the pan. Refrigerate. Clarified butter can be kept for several weeks and can be heated without burning to a much higher temperature than conventional butter.

WINE NOTES

Brunch is one of the many opportunities to restore the fortunes of those poor Champagne houses, forced to donate their best to over-excited racing drivers who haven't learned yet that the stuff is for drinking and not for showering gorilla armpits.

For brunch, a delicate Champagne. The most delicate (if you can afford it) is of course Roederer Cristal, but there are others, especially the Blanc de Blancs once known as Crémants (a description now forbidden by bureaucrats). Blanc de Blancs contain only Chardonnay and are bottled with a slightly lower pressure, which gives them the 'creamy' flavour. Ideal breakfast fizz.

If you don't like Champagne, and happen to take your brunch somewhere from mid-October to Christmas, then I thoroughly recommend some 'vin nouveau', ideally Beaujolais Nouveau. The fruitiness of the freshly made wine beats any fruit juice, passion or otherwise. People have been known to return to bed after a brunch with Beaujolais Nouveau, which can't be a bad thing.

ENTERTAINING WITH EASE

Herbed Leaf Salad
Crispy Duck Confit with Lentils
Baked Peaches with Zabaglione Sauce

The simpler the better is a phrase that sums up the direction in which food is going. This definitely applies to restaurant philosophies, but it should also apply to the British at home. There is a problem in that the British, and especially the English, are a nation of occasional diners. By that I don't mean the Brits only eat on occasions, but that they only entertain for that special occasion. Of course, this statement is a huge generalisation, but for the majority of our population it is definitely true.

It is the reason why, especially out of London, restaurants are so busy at weekends because that is when the populace will celebrate birthdays, weddings, anniversaries, bar mitzvahs, passing exams, etc. The policy I have for my restaurants is that customers should have fun, eat reasonable food (not necessarily *haute cuisine*), and drink enjoyable wines, all at incredibly reasonable prices. My strategy is not necessarily geared towards 'occasion' eating, but for meals on a day-to-day basis for people who don't necessarily want to eat at home.

My aim is to help to create a café society in London, similar to Paris, Milan, Barcelona and New York, where people use restaurants, *bistrots* and cafés as meeting places. It shouldn't be too difficult in England to produce establishments to satisfy these wants. At the moment we have the pub, not an attractive proposition when most of them are directed at the male citizen; not places in which one can relax. Britain, and especially our brewers, need to realise that it is not just the male who needs to be entertained: the females of the species are becoming more and more important, as are their offspring. It is no longer acceptable for the female to be left at home to be mum, but the pub isn't the right environment for family entertainment. Now maybe the *bistrot*, well that's another story. We are in the 1990s, life in general should be of better quality and there should be better integration of the family unit.

Similarly, home entertainment needn't be just for the special occasion; not just for the Christmas Day relatives' visit or the occasional Sunday lunch. Throw open your doors and have fun and relaxed times with your friends. Don't stand on ceremony. Too often entertainment at home means digging out the best china, polishing the crystal, ironing the linen tablecloth, cleaning the silver. Forget it. Get on the phone and say to a mate: Fancy coming over for supper? I've got a great moussaka, Irish stew or cassoulet in the oven. No need for that fancy little roulade from the Cordon Bleu school of thought, or the smoked salmon mousse, encapsulated in cucumber served on Granny's Spode or Meissen. Plonk a big bowl of something on the table, maybe a herby leaf salad and some fruit or cheese. Your guests want your company, they don't want to go away at the end of the evening thinking they can't return the invitation as they couldn't compete with your standards. Forget going 'OTT', there's a time for that but not on a regular basis; on a regular basis you want to relax and chill out, but enjoy doing it with friends.

A good leaf salad is an easy healthy starter. Any combination of leaves works but try to make it colourful. In France you can purchase *mesclun* which has all manner of leaves mixed together with a good selection of herbs. In this country, while the supermarkets undoubtedly are getting better, the customer who wants to make a good salad does get taken to the cleaners with their pricing policies. Poky little bags of designer salad leaves cost a fortune compared to the prices restaurants pay. Supermarkets have cornered the market as opposed to what happens in France and Italy where there is a market on every corner, and the British customer ends up paying through the nose. Profit margins in supermarkets have doubled from approximately 4.5 to nearly 9 per cent, far ahead of margins made in other parts of the world. They are ruthless, blowing away the little shopkeeper, and then exploiting you, their customers, by raising prices - that's my soapbox for the day; back to the menu.

Gardens are invaluable for excellent salads - nasturtiums, hedgerow buds, wild sorrel, garlic flowers, all types of soft herbs. A good dressing is essential - nothing creamy, it should just kiss the leaves, making them shine and stand out. Another prime rule is make sure your leaves are dry. A salad spinner is one of my favourite kitchen gadgets; failing that shake the leaves and pop them into an old pillow-case - a marvellous trick my grandmother showed me. The leaves crisp up every time.

Duck confit with lentils is a popular *bistrot* dish in France. On page 117 I explain how to make the confit. It is a useful stand-by, but it is also perfectly acceptable to buy a bottled or canned product. Simply remove it from its fat and roast in a hot oven for approximately 20 minutes. Dried lentils, especially *lentilles du Puy*, are always a useful larder stand-by. I could bash on about how healthy and good these are for you, but my reason for cooking and eating is to have fun. If we listened to every scare about food that reached the column inches we would be hard put to eat anything. My life-style policy is 'Excess on occasions, but as a general rule, everything in moderation.'

My simple pud is baked peaches with zabaglione sauce. On the surface it might appear daunting, but the mystery surrounding zabaglione produced in Italian restaurants is unveiled, it's simplicity itself. Hot peaches doused in honey and spices are an easy treat. If you really won't try the zabaglione, then just place some Ricotta in the centre of the peach and bake as per the recipe.

Serves 4

HERBED LEAF SALAD

1 clove garlic, peeled

4 tablespoons mixed fresh soft herbs, washed and dried (chervil, tarragon, dill, basil, marjoram, flat leaf parsley, mint, chives or sorrel)

10oz (300g) mixed salad leaves, washed, dried and ripped (curly endive, baby spinach, rocket, radicchio, chicory, watercress, trevise, oakleaf, dandelion, geranium and nasturtium)

salt and freshly ground black pepper

4 tablespoons Salad Dressing (see below)

Rub a wooden salad bowl with the raw garlic. Combine the herbs and the salad leaves and mix thoroughly. When seasoning salad, you can either put the salt and pepper in the dressing or alternatively season the salad direct. This is the dangerous method. Why? Because if you season directly on to the leaves and the leaves are damp, you're likely to end up with a mouthful of salt. As a precaution, before dressing the salad, season around the edge of the bowl and toss the leaves over and over and they will pick up an even amount; that's the principle anyway - try telling that to my chefs. Dress the leaves, but don't drown them. Serve immediately, don't allow the salad to sit for any length of time ready dressed. Croûtons or flakes of Parmesan or Pecorino make good accompaniments.

SALAD DRESSING

A good dressing for a simple salad doesn't muck about with nut oils or fancy flavoured vinegars, they had their day in the 1980s. We're in the 1990s now, and we're talking about 'back to basics', with good home cooking.

Too often dressings tend to be too acid with the proportion of vinegar to oil too high; this is hopeless for drinking wine which is one of the main constituents of home entertaining and one of the reasons I love my profession. Good wine, good food, good fun and goodness knows what else, in any order or combination, what better reason for being alive. I digress ...

Mix together 5fl oz (150ml) extra virgin olive oil with 2 tablespoons aged red wine or sherry vinegar; season with Maldon salt and freshly ground black pepper if you haven't seasoned the salad bowl. And for that extra special treat, add a tablespoon of the meat jelly that sets under the chicken or beef fat from the roasting tray, melted. I always keep the dripping from the roasting tray, whether of chicken, beef or lamb, for spreading on toast - only in moderation, of course!

CRISPY DUCK CONFIT WITH LENTILS

4 legs Duck Confit (see page 117) with some of their fat

Lentils

12oz (350g) lentilles du Puy, washed but not soaked

1 onion, stuck with 1 bay leaf and 1 clove

1 carrot, peeled

4oz (100g) salt belly of pork, soaked overnight

1 sprig thyme

2 whole garlic cloves, peeled

1 pint (600ml) Chicken Stock (see below)

1 pint (600ml) cold water

1 teaspoon caster sugar

1 dessertspoon duck fat

1 shallot, peeled and finely diced

3oz (75g) unsalted butter, cut in small pieces

salt and freshly ground black pepper

Prepare the lentils first. Place the lentils in a saucepan and cover with water; bring to the boil; drain and rinse under cold water. Return the lentils to the saucepan and add the onion, carrot, belly of pork, thyme, garlic, chicken stock, water and sugar. Bring to the boil over a high heat, then reduce the heat, cover the pan, and simmer until the lentils are tender but not mushy, about 35-40 minutes. Drain the lentils, retaining the liquor, but discard the onion, carrot, thyme and garlic.

Cut the belly of pork into small dice and return to the saucepan with the duck fat and the shallot. Pan-fry over a low heat until the pork is crispy and add half the cooked lentils. Keep warm. Place the remaining lentils in a liquidiser or food processor and blend with 5fl oz (150ml) of the cooking liquor. With the machine still running and the purée now smooth add the butter in small pieces one at a time. Pour this sauce on to the whole lentils, mix and season to taste with salt and black pepper. Return to the

heat and bring back gently to a hot temperature.

Meanwhile, preheat the oven to 375°F/190°C/Gas 5. Place the duck in a dish, skin-side down with a little fat, and cook in the oven for 10 minutes. Turn the duck skin-side up, and cook for a further 10 minutes or until the duck skin is crisp.

Pour the hot lentils on to a hot serving platter and top with the duck legs.

Chicken Stock

Makes about 2½ pints/1.5 litres

2¼lb (1kg) chicken carcasses and giblets (except liver), chopped

1 pig's trotter or calf's foot, chopped

2 whole onions, spiked with 2 cloves each

1 carrot, thinly sliced

2 garlic cloves, peeled and crushed

1 celery stalk, sliced

whites of 2 leeks, sliced

1 bouquet garni

½ bottle dry white wine

1 teaspoon white peppercorns, crushed

Put the carcasses, giblets and trotter in a large saucepan, and add water to cover. Bring to the boil, then skim well and strain, discarding the water. Return the carcasses, etc. to the pan and add all the remaining ingredients, along with 3½ pints (2 litres) water. Bring to the boil, then reduce the heat and simmer very slowly for 3-4 hours, skimming regularly. Add more water to top up if needed.

Strain through a fine sieve and leave to settle. Remove the fat, skimming off the last traces with kitchen paper. Return to the heat and reduce to the strength or volume required. Store in the fridge for a day, or freeze.

BAKED PEACHES WITH ZABAGLIONE SAUCE

4 peaches (yellow or white), halved and stone removed

juice of 2 limes

a pinch of grated nutmeg

4 tablespoons soft brown sugar

2oz (50g) unsalted butter

10fl oz (300ml) Zabaglione Sauce (see below)

Place the peach halves in a bowl and cover them with boiling water for 20 seconds. Drain and peel off their skins. Mix together in a food processor or mixing bowl the lime juice, nutmeg, brown sugar and butter to make a paste.

The oven is already hot from the duck confit. Place the peaches, cut side up, on a baking dish and divide the sugar paste between the peach halves. Bake until the syrup is bubbling and the peaches are wearing golden brown bits. Baste the peaches every 5 minutes with the syrupy juices that will find their way to the bottom of the dish. Serve hot with the zabaglione sauce.

ZABAGLIONE SAUCE

In a glass or stainless-steel bowl, beat 4 egg yolks with 2 tablespoons caster sugar until thick and pale. Place the bowl over a pan of very hot but not boiling water and continue to beat, adding 2 tablespoons dry sherry and 2 tablespoons dry white wine. Continue to beat until the mixture is very light and can hold its shape. Pour into a bowl and serve with the peaches.

For a variation, fold in 2 stiffly beaten egg whites at the end of cooking.

WINE NOTES

Wine vinegar distorts the flavour of wine, so ignore those who say you can't drink wine with salad, because they fail to appreciate this sublime opportunity to get rid of unwanted bottles, especially acid wines. Any sour wine, well chilled, will taste perfectly acceptable. If not, just increase the amount of vinegar in the salad ...

Confit de canard is a much more serious matter. Italian, I should say, like Barolo made by Ceretto, Pio Cesare or Aldo Conterno. More original even would be a Barbera from Argentina, or my personal preference, Malbec from Mendoza in Argentina. Malbec is the grape grown in Cahors where it makes rather hard and tannic wines; Argentine Malbec is streets ahead, *rich, round, quite powerful.*

At one stage or another you'll say 'Where do I find all these wines?' I have a friend who buys Christmas presents all the year round. He starts with the sales in January, but stays at home in December. I, on the other hand, decide every year that Christmas presents will be abolished. Only on 24 December panic gets the better of me, and out I rush, paying way over the odds for things no one really wants. Buying wine is a bit like that. If you really wish to pair food and wine, you'll need a cellar, by which I do not mean the place under your house, but any odd cupboard or space without central heating capable of holding 12,000 bottles ...

Raw Artichoke and Parmesan Salad

Roast Lamb, Garlic and Rosemary
Baby Carrots and Sugar Snap Peas
Gratin Dauphinoise

Snow Eggs with Raspberries in Armagnac

A menu of powerful flavours, starting with a dish I didn't imagine possible until I ate it at Il Tre Merli on West Broadway, SoHo, New York. A lovely Italian combination of finely shredded or grated artichokes, mixed at the last minute with lemon juice, extra virgin olive oil, grated Parmesan and plenty of black pepper.

To follow, a simple leg of lamb infused with rosemary and garlic, roasted pink on a bed of root vegetables and served with tiny new carrots and sugar snap peas. These are so much tastier than the now overplayed mangetouts. A leg of lamb well-roasted is one of my all-time favourite Sunday lunches. Use new season baby lamb when available - it's worth the extra expense and is one food which remains seasonal and to which we can look forward now that most things are available year-round. With the lamb, there's the chef's bonus. By roasting the joint on slices of carrot, potato and onion, you keep the meat from burning on the bottom of the pan, and during the cooking process they absorb all the wonderful juices and become nice and grungy with delicious crunchy bits - not at all attractive to serve, but heavenly to taste. That wonderful concoction of potatoes, cream and cheese, *Gratin dauphinoise*, is a perfect accompaniment.

Snow eggs or *oeufs à la neige* make a light finish. A dreamy concoction of poached beaten egg whites served with raspberries which have been macerated in Armagnac; a recipe inspired by Paula Wolfert's *Cooking of South-West France*. Half the raspberries are puréed to make a colourful and vibrant sauce for the snow eggs.

Serves 6

RAW ARTICHOKE AND PARMESAN SALAD

6 large or 12 baby artichokes

extra virgin olive oil

2 tablespoons freshly squeezed lemon juice

2 egg yolks

6 tablespoons freshly grated Parmesan cheese

grated zest of 1 lemon

salt and freshly ground black pepper

6 slices country bread, chargrilled or grilled

1 garlic clove, peeled

18 oil-marinated black olives, stoned and finely chopped

6 basil leaves, ripped

Remove all the coarse outer leaves (especially on large artichokes) from the artichokes, cut off the tips and remove the hairy choke. Coarsely grate or very thinly slice the artichokes into a non-reactive bowl. Toss the gratings with 3fl oz (85ml) of the olive oil and the lemon juice and fold in the egg yolks, Parmesan and lemon zest. Season to taste with a little salt and plenty of ground black pepper.

Rub the grilled bread with the raw garlic clove and dribble with extra virgin olive oil. Place one slice of bread on each of six plates. Place some of the artichoke mix on each slice. Scatter with the black olives and ripped basil leaves. Do not be tempted to prepare this dish too far in advance; always mix the grated artichoke with the dressing ingredients immediately otherwise the artichoke will become discoloured.

ROAST LAMB, GARLIC AND ROSEMARY, WITH BABY CARROTS AND SUGAR SNAP PEAS, GRATIN DAUPHINOISE

1 x 6lb (2.75kg) leg of British lamb
1 head garlic, split into cloves, 6 cloves peeled and thinly sliced
2 sprigs rosemary, broken into little spriglets of 4 or 5 leaves
salt and freshly ground black pepper
dripping, lard, butter, or duck fat
1 potato, peeled and sliced
1 onion, peeled and sliced
1 carrot, peeled and sliced
Gravy
6fl oz (175ml) light red wine
1 sprig rosemary
10fl oz (300ml) stock or cooking water from the vegetables
1 dessertspoon redcurrant jelly
To serve
Baby Carrots and Sugar Snap Peas (see below)
Gratin Dauphinoise (see below)

THE LAMB

Make deep incisions with the point of a sharp knife about 1in (2.5cm) apart all over the lamb. Into each hole place a sliver of garlic and a tuft of rosemary. Allow the lamb to rest in the fridge overnight or for at least 4 hours.

Season the lamb all over with salt and black pepper and smear it with a fat of your choice. Preheat the oven to 400°F/200°C/Gas 6. Place the sliced vegetables in the bottom of a roasting tray with the remaining peeled garlic cloves and some more fat. Place the lamb on top and place it in the middle of the oven. Cook for 20 minutes at this temperature and then turn the oven down to 350°F/180°C/Gas 4. Baste the lamb with the melted fat every 20 minutes. Cook for a further 1-1½ hours depending on how rare you enjoy your meat. Remove the lamb and vegetables from the oven to rest for at least 15 minutes (this helps the juices to settle) while you make the gravy.

THE GRAVY

Drain the fat from the roasting tray, leaving behind any juices that have exuded from the meat. Place the tray over a medium heat and pour in the red wine. Bring to the boil, scraping all the grungy bits that have caramelised in the bottom of the pan. Boil for 3-4 minutes then add the rosemary, stock and redcurrant jelly. Boil for a further 8 minutes. Season to taste with salt and freshly ground black pepper and strain into a gravy boat. The gravy can be thickened with a little flour mixed into a paste with an equal quantity of butter if you so desire. I don't.

FINAL PREPARATION AND PRESENTATION

Have ready the baby carrots and sugar snap peas and the potatoes. Place them on the table, reminding your guests not to touch the gratin dish - youch! Carve the lamb vertically and not horizontally and offer your guests some of the immensely tasty but not immensely attractive roasted vegetables that were under the lamb. Serve the gravy separately. At all costs avoid

95

guest requests for mint sauce and redcurrant jelly. Tell them to trust your judgement that it doesn't need the normal English trimmings.

Baby Carrots and Sugar Snap Peas
2 bunches baby carrots, scrubbed but not peeled (leave 1in/2.5cm green tops)
salt and freshly ground black pepper
1 teaspoon caster sugar
2oz (50g) unsalted butter
1lb (450g) sugar snap peas, topped and tailed
1 dessertspoon chopped mint

Place the carrots in a saucepan and just cover them with water. Add ½ teaspoon salt, the caster sugar and the butter, and cook over a moderate heat until the water has all but evaporated. The butter, sugar and the remaining juices will produce an emulsified, moreish sauce.

In a separate pan, boil a decent amount of salted water and add the sugar snap peas. Boil for approximately 5 minutes depending on how crunchy you like your vegetables. Drain (use the water in the gravy if you like) and add them to the carrots with the chopped mint. Toss together and season to taste with black pepper. Pour into a vegetable dish ready for the table.

Gratin Dauphinoise
1½lb (675g) waxy potatoes, peeled, thinly sliced and dried
15fl oz (450ml) milk
15fl oz (450ml) double cream
salt and freshly ground black pepper
a pinch of grated nutmeg
6oz (175g) Gruyère cheese, grated
2 cloves garlic, peeled and crushed to a fine paste with a little salt
2 eggs, beaten
3oz (75g) unsalted butter
3 tablespoons fresh breadcrumbs

Boil the milk and cream together and allow to cool. Place the potatoes in a bowl and season with salt, pepper and nutmeg. Mix in three-quarters of the Gruyère cheese and the garlic. Fold the eggs into the milk, whisk together, then pour this mix over the potatoes. It should just cover the potatoes.

Butter a glazed earthenware or Pyrex, shallow (3in/7.5cm) dish with half the butter and pour in the potatoes, pushing down well; arrange the top layer into overlapping slices. Mix the breadcrumbs with the remaining Gruyère and sprinkle this mix over the potatoes. Place the dish on the lower shelf of the oven underneath the lamb and bake for approximately 40 minutes. When the lamb is removed from the oven move the dish up one shelf and increase the oven temperature to 400°F/200°C/Gas 6. Bake for a further 15-20 minutes or until bubbling and golden.

SNOW EGGS WITH RASPBERRIES IN ARMAGNAC

8 egg whites, at room temperature
a pinch of salt
a dash of lemon juice
4oz (100g) caster sugar
Caramel (see below)
1½ pints (850ml) Raspberries in Armagnac (see below)

Bring a large shallow saucepan full of water to the boil. Place the egg whites in an immaculately clean bowl, stainless steel or copper preferably. If there is any dirt or grease on the surface of the bowl, the eggs will not fluff up properly. As a safeguard rub the surface of the bowl with extra lemon juice and wipe dry with kitchen paper. Add the salt and the lemon juice and whisk until the whites have reached the soft peak stage. At this point add the sugar, a little at a time, continuing to whisk until you can turn the bowl upside down without the whites dropping out (alternatively use an electric mixer). This is a confidence test - it can be messy if you haven't whisked the eggs sufficiently.

With a large tablespoon, scoop out the egg whites and form into large ovals. Place a spoonful of the beaten whites on the surface of the water, repeat. Cook about 4 at a time. Turn them after a couple of minutes to make sure all sides are fully cooked. Remove the egg whites and set aside on kitchen paper. When the whites have cooled dribble them with the caramel by dipping a spoon in the caramel and waving it backwards and forwards over the whites with the caramel dribbling off the end of the spoon.

Float the eggs on the surface of a bowl of the raspberries in Armagnac. Serve each of your guests 2 snow eggs and a spoonful of raspberries. Accompany with an iced shot of raspberry *eau de vie*. A great contrast in tastes, sweet and dry.

CARAMEL

Place 8oz (225g) caster sugar in a pan (copper if possible) with 3fl oz (85ml) water over a medium heat and bring to the boil, stirring from time to time. As the mixture boils, brush the sugar crystals (that form on the pan walls just above the surface of the syrup) with a brush dipped in water. Increase the heat and cook until the syrup is golden brown.

Raspberries in Armagnac
3lb (1.4kg) raspberries
1lb (450g) caster sugar
Armagnac to cover (approx. 1½ bottles - wow!)

Make sure the raspberries are perfect, with no mould or damage. Toss them gently in a bowl with the caster sugar. Carefully place the raspberries in Kilner jars and top up with Armagnac. Seal and store in a dark place for at least 30 days. Invert the jars every other day.

Before serving, take half the raspberries and liquidise with all the juices. Pour the remaining raspberries into a glass bowl and pour on the raspberry and Armagnac purée.

WINE NOTES

Magnum time. No need to waste energy on bubbly or white, straight into the red, French and Italian, Portuguese and Greek fashion. Europe.

Roast leg of lamb and Sunday suggests a great bottle of wine. A magnum of red Bordeaux, something with age, say a 1982 or 1985 St-Emilion or Pomerol, or one of the better-known names from the Médoc. 'Good' and not too wildly expensive St-Emilions include Châteaux Grand Mayne, Rolland-Maillet and Beauséjour; good Pomerols, Château Clinet, Petit-Village and La Croix du Casse. In the Médoc go for old faithfuls like Château Montrose, Cos d'Estournel, Lynch-Bages, Léoville-Barton, Gruaud-Larose, Lascombes or Brane-Cantenac - the list is long ...

For the pudding, a light and fruity sweet wine from Monbazillac, Cérons or Loupiac, all lesser cousins to Sauternes and Barsac which might be a bit too much of a good thing with fluffy egg white.

A VEGGIE ANTIPASTO LUNCH

Baby Artichokes in Olive Oil

Panzanella

Caponata

A Mediterranean Sandwich

Spanish Tortilla with Cavolo Nero

Aubergine Caviar

Chargrilled Vegetable Salad

Hummous

Tomato and Basil Salad

Tabbouleh

Tapenade Crostini

A Fruit Salad of Mango, Blueberries and Strawberries with Fresh Lime

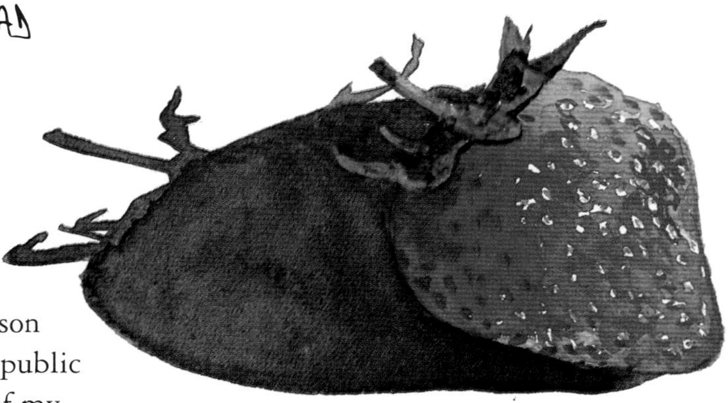

Before we start, let's get one thing clear. I have nothing against vegetarians. While I don't necessarily agree with the principles upon which they base their eating habits, I see no reason for alienating a section of the eating-out public by ignoring their wishes. I create many of my dishes or menus in the various restaurants using vegetarian ingredients, because at present there is a strong Mediterranean influence in fashionable restaurant food, making it hard to ignore so many wonderful vegetable-based dishes.

Many of my best friends are vegetarians, but only a few years ago, it was hard to find any vegetarian food for your partner on restaurant menus without stooping to the nut cutlet. Now you can go into many restaurants and find something suitable for them to eat without phoning 24 hours ahead to arrange a menu with the chef. I do not believe vegetarians should be labelled, nor do I believe that they go around in open-toed sandals wearing predominantly brown or green clothes, or have very pallid complexions. Neither do I label vegetarian dishes on my menus with a big V, customers simply have to discover the dishes that suit them. If I did mark them thus, I'm sure it would dissuade meat-eaters from choosing some quite delicious dishes.

What I don't understand is why a certain sector of vegetarian society needs to use veggie products, such as Quorn or soya, to reproduce the shape and texture of a meat product. It's nonsensical to produce vegetarian shepherd's pie or moussaka when there are so many wonderful vegetable-based dishes. Enough said about vegetarians - they're very welcome in my restaurants.

I have based this menu loosely on the Mediterranean style that is fashionable today, and it consists of dishes such as chargrilled vegetable salad, hummous, aubergine caviar, a Spanish tortilla with cavolo nero, tabbouleh, a Mediterranean sandwich, caponata, panzanella, tapenade crostini, tomato and basil salad and baby artichokes with olive oil - all served with big chunks of grilled country bread.

To present the menu, scatter the surface of a large kitchen table (preferably aged pine) with various leaves from the trees in your garden. Arrange the various salads on brightly coloured pottery plates and bowls. I think you'll agree that all these classic Mediterranean dishes deserve to be enjoyed not just by vegetarians; go for it and invite a few meat-eaters as well.

For pudding I offer a simple fruit salad of mango, blueberries and strawberries, macerated in caster sugar and fresh lime.

Serves 6

BABY ARTICHOKES IN OLIVE OIL

1 bunch basil
4 tablespoons finely chopped parsley
6 cloves garlic, peeled, ½ left whole, ½ finely diced
2 onions, peeled and sliced
2 carrots, peeled and sliced
7fl oz (200ml) extra virgin olive oil
juice of 2 lemons
18 baby artichokes, trimmed, choke removed
4 sprigs thyme
2 bay leaves
15fl oz (450ml) dry white wine
salt and freshly ground black pepper

Rip the basil and mix it with the parsley and finely diced garlic. Leave to one side. Sweat the onions and carrots in the extra virgin olive oil for 5 minutes. Add the lemon juice, artichokes, thyme, bay leaves and whole garlic cloves. Pour in the wine and sufficient water to just cover. Cook slowly for 15 minutes and then over a high heat for a further 15 until cooked. Remove the artichokes and set aside.

Liquidise the vegetable ingredients, then add the chopped parsley mixture. Season to taste with salt and plenty of black pepper. Return the artichokes to the emulsified sauce and serve warm or at room temperature.

PANZANELLA

This is an Italian bread salad. Toast 4oz (100g) of thick-cut country bread with the crusts removed. Cut the slices into ½in (1cm) cubes and set aside in a bowl. Toss with a tomato passed through a food mill and a little salt. Allow to stand for 15 minutes.

Mash 1 tablespoon rinsed capers with 1 peeled clove garlic. Mix with ½ red pepper, roasted, peeled, seeded and cut into dice, 5 tablespoons extra virgin olive oil, 1 tablespoon aged red wine vinegar, salt and freshly ground black pepper.

Skin, seed and dice another 3 tomatoes and combine with ½ cucumber, peeled, seeded and diced, ½ finely sliced red onion, 12 ripped basil leaves, 6 diced black olives and the caper mix. Pour this mixture on the bread and season with plenty of black pepper. Toss to combine.

CAPONATA

1lb (450g) aubergines, peeled and sliced lengthways, each strip cut in 2
8 tablespoons extra virgin olive oil
salt and freshly ground black pepper
½ onion, peeled and finely chopped
2 celery stalks, diced
4 ripe tomatoes, peeled, seeded and chopped
2oz (50g) stoned black olives
2 tablespoons small capers, rinsed and drained
2fl oz (60ml) red wine vinegar
1 tablespoon caster sugar, dissolved in 4fl oz (120ml) water
2 tablespoons chopped almonds, toasted
1 tablespoon chopped parsley

Salt the aubergines generously, then transfer to a colander and leave to drain for 30 minutes. Wash and dry. In a frying pan, cook the aubergines in 3 tablespoons oil for 10 minutes.

In the remaining oil, cook the onion and celery for 5 minutes. Add the tomatoes, olives and capers and cook for 10 minutes. Raise the heat and let the mixture reduce for 5 minutes. Remove from the heat and add the remaining ingredients, plus the aubergines, combining well. Season to taste with salt and black pepper. Allow to cool to room temperature.

MEDITERRANEAN SANDWICH

1 pugliese *loaf (round Italian country bread)*
1 clove garlic, peeled and halved
4 fl oz (120ml) olive oil
4 tablespoons Tapenade (see page 49)
5oz (150g) aubergine, sliced lengthways and chargrilled
5oz (150g) courgette, sliced lengthways and chargrilled
1 red and 1 yellow pepper, chargrilled, seeded and skinned
30 large basil leaves
5oz (150g) sun-dried tomatoes
4 tablespoons Pesto (see page 69)
14oz (400g) buffalo Mozzarella, thinly sliced
4oz (100g) stoned black olives
2oz (50g) red onion, peeled and thinly sliced
2oz (50g) rocket leaves
1 tablespoon balsamic vinegar
2oz (50g) spinach leaves
salt and freshly ground black pepper

Cut a lid off the top of the loaf and hollow out the bread, leaving a crust of about ½ in (1.5cm) all the way round. Rub the cut surface of the bread and lid with the garlic, then drizzle with the olive oil. Spread the tapenade on the bottom of the loaf then layer up all the ingredients in an interesting and colourful order, using about two layers of everything, and seasoning generously with salt and black pepper between each layer. Pour on the vinegar between the rocket leaves and spinach leaves. Replace the lid and wrap the loaf in cling film. Place in the refrigerator and leave pressed under a heavy weight overnight.

Cut the sandwich into wedges with a sharp knife.

SPANISH TORTILLA WITH CAVOLO NERO

16fl oz (475ml) olive oil
6 medium potatoes, peeled and cut into ⅙in (4mm) slices
2 large onions, peeled, 1 thinly sliced, 1 chopped
2lb (900g) cavolo nero, washed, thick stems removed (or spinach or spring greens)
3 tablespoons extra virgin olive oil
2 cloves garlic, peeled and crushed
2 tablespoons finely chopped parsley and thyme
coarse salt and freshly ground black pepper
a pinch of paprika
6 eggs, beaten with 4 tablespoons double cream

Heat the olive oil in a deep frying pan. Add the potatoes alternating in layers with the thinly sliced onion. Cook gently, covered, until the potatoes are just tender (they should remain separate, but not brown).

Meanwhile, place the greens in salted boiling water for 15 minutes with 1 tablespoon of the extra virgin olive oil. Drain and chop coarsely.

In a frying pan, heat the remaining extra virgin olive oil. Fry the chopped onion until wilted, then add the greens and continue cooking for a further 8 minutes. Add the garlic, parsley and thyme, salt, pepper and paprika.

When the potatoes are cooked, drain them of excess oil, and mix with the greens. Transfer this mixture to a shallow non-stick frying pan

that will go in the oven. The dish may be made in advance to this point.

Preheat the oven to 375°F/190°C/Gas 5. Pour the eggs and cream over the pan, shake and place in the oven for 15 minutes or until the eggs have set. Allow to cool; turn out on to a plate and dribble with extra virgin olive oil.

AUBERGINE CAVIAR

Preheat the oven to 350°F/180°C/Gas 4. Prick 4 aubergines in several places with a fork. Brush with olive oil and bake in the oven for approximately 45 minutes or until the aubergines are soft to the touch. Cut in half lengthways and scoop out the flesh. Pound the flesh in a pestle and mortar or blend in a food processor with 3 cloves finely chopped garlic, 1 teaspoon salt and several turns of the black pepper grinder. Add 6 tablespoons extra virgin olive oil, drop by drop, until you obtain a smooth emulsion. Add lemon juice to taste and pour into a pottery bowl. Serve with Crostini (see page 166).

CHARGRILLED VEGETABLE SALAD

1 aubergine, sliced lengthways
2 courgettes, sliced lengthways
6 spring onions, blanched for 2 minutes
1 red pepper, roasted, skinned, seeded and cut into 4
1 yellow pepper, roasted, skinned, seeded and cut into 4
12 asparagus stalks, peeled if necessary
olive oil
salt and freshly ground black pepper
Grilled Vegetable Marinade (see below)

Heat the chargrill or grill. Dip the vegetables in oil, season with salt and pepper and grill on both sides until cooked to your liking.

Marinate overnight in the marinade and serve at room temperature.

Grilled Vegetable Marinade
1 shallot, peeled and diced
1 red chilli, seeded and finely diced
1 clove garlic, peeled and diced
6 basil leaves, ripped
8 tablespoons olive oil
1 tablespoon sherry vinegar
salt and freshly ground black pepper

Simply combine all the ingredients in a bowl or dish.

HUMMOUS

Drain a 15oz (425g) tin of chick peas and place in a food processor with 4 tablespoons tahini (sesame paste) and 2 cloves garlic, crushed with a little salt. Blend until smooth; then add 6 tablespoons extra virgin olive oil, drop by drop, until emulsified. Add 4 tablespoons lemon juice and season with paprika. Garnish with black olives and serve with Crostini (see page 166).

TOMATO AND BASIL SALAD

Slice 6 plum tomatoes and arrange them on a large plate. Scatter with 1 tablespoon finely diced red onion and 8 ripped basil leaves. Season with Maldon salt and plenty of black pepper. Mix together 2 tablespoons extra virgin olive oil and 1 dessertspoon balsamic vinegar and pour over the tomatoes.

TABBOULEH

This is a cracked wheat salad with parsley and mint. Soak 3oz (75g) burghul (cracked wheat) in cold water for 10 minutes, drain and squeeze dry. Put the burghul in a glass bowl and season with salt and black pepper, add the juice of 2 lemons and 3fl oz (85ml) extra virgin olive oil. Allow to rest for 30 minutes before adding 8 tablespoons chopped flat-leaf parsley, 3 tablespoons chopped mint and 1 bunch of spring onions, washed and finely sliced. Check the seasoning and serve in a ceramic bowl lined with vine leaves, fresh if possible. Top the salad with 3 plum tomatoes which have been seeded and diced. Dribble with a little more olive oil.

TAPENADE CROSTINI

(See page 49)

A Fruit Salad of Mango, Blueberries and Strawberries with Fresh Lime

2 ripe mangoes, peeled, sliced and cut into ½in (1cm) dice
6oz (175g) blueberries, washed
6oz (175g) strawberries, hulled and cut in ½ lengthways
2oz (50g) caster sugar
juice and grated zest of 3 limes

Place the fruits in a large bowl and sprinkle with the sugar, lime juice and zest. Allow to macerate for 1 hour, tossing the fruit gently from time to time.

Wine Notes

This is not the ideal luncheon for hungry deckmen, but a déjeuner dégustation, neither to quell hunger nor to still thirst but to linger, sampling. In the Middle East they drink raki or ouzo on such occasions, but absinthe is not to the Englishman's taste, so let inspiration come from Spain and tapas: dry sherry. Remember sherry? An almost forgotten drink served in 'orrible thimbles in pubs, sherry deserves to make a come-back, if just for this dainty lunch. Dry sherry or Fino comes as Tio Pepe or Garvey's San Patricio. Manzanilla, another Fino, might even be better for the occasion, because it is fresher and crisper, and if you worry about the alcohol content, there is dry Montilla, similar in flavour but unfortified. Sherry and Montilla should be served well chilled in normal wine glasses, just as you would any white wine.

Grape variety and a very special vinification give these wines a unique nutty flavour. Although made from different grapes, you can find a hint of this deliberately oxidised flavour in Hungarian Tokay. Dry Tokay is labelled 'Tokaji Szamorodni' (as against the sweet and more famous Tokaji Aszú). If the first sip seems a bit odd, persist. Like sherry, it is an easily acquired taste.

SUNDAY BLOODY MARY

Jug of Bloody Mary

Crab 'Blinis' with Poached Eggs and Hollandaise

Marinated Beef Carpaccio with Fennel Shavings and Truffle Oil

Poached Red Wine Pears with Creamy Gorgonzola

A light 'brunchy' lunch. Simple power-packed flavours are the obvious pattern behind this menu. I start with crab blinis which are not so much blinis but more like American pancakes. I use a base of cornmeal or polenta with plain flour and various spices and hints of fire through chilli, cumin, coriander, olive oil, lime juice and mint. The base mix can be made a day ahead; beaten egg whites, crab and fresh herbs should be added just before cooking. These are served with poached eggs which are also easy to prepare ahead. In fact a little known fact about poached eggs is that they should be cooked ahead in water and vinegar (no salt) and then removed with a slotted spoon and plunged into ice-cold water. At the time of service just slip them into hot salted water. Why cook them ahead? Several factors really: (a) no salt should be put in the initial poaching water as this can cause the breakdown of the white; (b) cooking ahead gives you a chance to reheat them in salt water and redress the flavour balance as well as removing traces of any excess vinegar; (c) cooking ahead will reveal how old the egg is - if they are old, the whites spread out on contact with the water, creating a flat 'fried-egg' shape instead of the perfect spherical shape; (d) it enables you to trim any wayward threads of cooked egg white, thereby impressing your guest with the egg's perfect shape and beauty; (e) it lets you relax before the brunch, enabling you to savour the wonders of a Bloody Mary. Hollandaise sauce accompanies these eggs. Another sauce which causes panic - follow the rules and it's simple; panic and you'll lose it. Trust me with the recipe and you'll have a wonderful brunch dish.

This is followed with a *carpaccio* of beef with fennel, a combination of two Italian ideas. I first ate beef and fennel together at Andrea Riva's restaurant in Barnes. I receive a lot of inspiration from the food at Riva, simple homely tastes but perfect application of flavours. From the regular raw beef fillet I tried a variation based on Franco Taruschio's Bresaola at the Walnut Tree in Wales. Instead of totally raw beef, I marinated topside in a brine of red and white wines, salt, herbs, juniper, cloves, garlic, chillies, orange peel and star anise. The meat needs to marinate for approximately 7 days and instead of air-drying it as for bresaola, I freeze it and slice it on a meat slicer. Now I can appreciate that most households do not have slicers readily to hand, so instead you can chill the meat and then slice snippets as thinly as possible which are then beaten between sheets of cling film. The beef is served on a pile of rocket leaves and shavings of fennel which have been marinated in extra virgin olive oil, lemon and lots of black pepper. To finish I use a dribble of truffle oil which sends the dish into another dimension.

A sweet and savoury pud with pears poached in red wine flavoured with pepper, nutmeg, cinnamon, coriander, cloves, bay, lemon, orange, ginger and redcurrant jelly served with a wedge of creamy Gorgonzola or Dolcelatte, superb Italian blue cheeses. The flavours are powerful but work well together.

Serves 6

JUG OF BLOODY MARY

makes enough for 10 glasses
2fl oz (60ml) Worcestershire sauce
1 tablespoon Heinz tomato ketchup
1 teaspoon Tabasco sauce
1 teaspoon celery salt
5 tablespoons freshly squeezed lemon juice
1 tablespoon orange juice
1 teaspoon grated horseradish
1 teaspoon finely chopped shallot
½ teaspoon ground black pepper
3 pints (1.75 litres) V8 juice or tomato juice
2 tablespoons dry sherry

To serve
10fl oz (300ml) vodka (pepper vodka if you like more bite)
ice cubes
celery stalks, washed thoroughly

Blend the first 11 ingredients in a liquidiser. Transfer to a jug and refrigerate overnight to allow the flavours to develop. Strain the mixture through a fine sieve then stir in the vodka. Serve in an ice-filled highball glass and garnish with a stick of celery. A perfect way to start the day.

CRAB 'BLINIS' WITH POACHED EGGS AND HOLLANDAISE

Blinis
4oz (100g) cornmeal or polenta
2oz (50g) plain flour
1½ teaspoon baking powder
1 teaspoon salt
½ teaspoon freshly ground black pepper
½ teaspoon each of ground cumin and coriander
1 tablespoon extra virgin olive oil
½ teaspoon each of chilli oil and sesame oil
2 eggs, separated
2 tablespoons freshly squeezed lime juice
2 tablespoons each of finely chopped coriander, mint and basil leaves
1 red chilli, seeded and finely diced
1 teaspoon pickled ginger (not stem ginger)
up to 10fl oz (300ml) milk
8oz (225g) white crabmeat, preferably fresh
2 tablespoons finely chopped spring onion

Clarified Butter (see page 86) for frying
To serve
12 Poached Eggs (see below)
Hollandaise Sauce (see below)
8oz (225g) white crabmeat
coriander leaves

THE BLINIS

In a food processor combine the cornmeal, flour, baking powder, salt, black pepper, cumin and coriander and pulse quickly. With the machine running add the three oils, the egg yolks and the lime juice. Add the chopped herbs, chilli and pickled ginger. Turn off the machine, remove lid and scrape down with a rubber spatula to make sure all is combined. Replace the lid, activate the machine and add three-quarters of the milk to make a fairly thick batter. Transfer the mixture to a non-reactive bowl and leave for at least an hour (or overnight) in a cool place. This allows time for the dry ingredients to swell. If the mixture is too thick add some more milk. Mix well and fold in the crab and the spring onion.

Just before cooking the blinis, whisk the egg whites until stiff and fold into the batter. Heat some clarified butter in a large non-stick frying pan over a medium heat and spoon in 1 tablespoon of the mixture for each blini. Cook in batches of 4. Use a metal pastry cutter for the perfect round shape if you wish. Cook the mixture until it's starting to set and then carefully turn each blini. Cook until golden brown on each side. Repeat until all the mixture has been used. Keep warm.

FINAL PREPARATION AND PRESENTATION

Poach - or warm through - the eggs, and make the hollandaise.

Place a plate of hot blinis on the table with a plate of soft poached eggs, a bowl of hollandaise, a bowl of crabmeat and some fresh coriander leaves. Allow your guests to help themselves.

POACHED EGGS

Use a large, wide-mouthed saucepan filled two-thirds full of water and add 1 tablespoon of mild vinegar for each 2 pints (1.1 litres) of water. Bring to the boil. Break the egg into where the water is bubbling. Cook up to 6 eggs at a time. Move the pan to the edge of the heat source so the water continues to simmer gently.

After approximately 3 minutes' cooking, remove the eggs carefully with a slotted spoon and slide them into iced water to arrest the cooking. When cold, trim any ragged ends from the cooked egg white. When ready to serve heat a pan of salted water and warm the eggs; do not allow the water to boil.

HOLLANDAISE SAUCE

In a small saucepan combine 1 tablespoon white wine vinegar, 1 tablespoon water and a pinch of crushed white peppercorns. Reduce this mixture over a medium heat until only 1 teaspoon remains. Cool the mixture then add 3 egg yolks and a further 2 tablespoons of water. Combine the ingredients well, making sure to scrape up all the vinegar mixture from the bottom. Place the saucepan in a double boiler over hot but not boiling water. Whisk the egg yolks until they are thick and creamy; do not cook too fast or they will become grainy. When the egg yolks reach the correct stage start to incorporate 8oz (225g) butter, either melted or in small pieces. When cooking hollandaise think mayonnaise, so add the butter little by little, emulsifying it with the egg yolks before making each addition. Add a little salt. If the hollandaise becomes too thick add a few drops of warm water. The sauce should be light but quite thick. Keep warm over a low heat. Too hot and the eggs will separate from the butter. If this happens heat 1 tablespoon water in another pan and add small amounts of the separated sauce, whisking vigorously until a smooth emulsion is re-established.

MARINATED BEEF CARPACCIO WITH FENNEL SHAVINGS AND TRUFFLE OIL

1½lb (675g) Marinated Beef (see below)

2 large fennel bulbs, tough outside layer removed

4fl oz (120ml) extra virgin olive oil

juice of 1 lemon

salt and freshly ground black pepper

4oz (100g) rocket leaves, washed and dried

1fl oz (25ml) white truffle oil

On a mandoline, a meat slicer or with a very sharp knife, thinly slice the fennel; it should be almost transparent. Marinate the fennel shavings with 3fl oz (85ml) of the extra virgin olive oil, 2 tablespoons of the lemon juice, some black pepper and a pinch of salt for an hour.

Half freeze the beef to ease the process of cutting it extra thinly. If you are unable to cut it that thin, never fear. Place the slices between 2 sheets of cling film and flatten with a meat mallet or cutlet bat. Failing that, you'll have to eat the meat a little thicker, it's not the end of the world.

Just before serving dress the rocket leaves with the remaining olive oil, salt and black pepper and a dash of lemon juice. Make a pile of rocket leaves in the centre of six cold plates. Arrange the fennel shavings around the rocket leaves. Top the leaves and half the fennel with slices of beef. Dribble the beef with a little truffle oil and give it a couple of turns of the black pepper grinder.

MARINATED BEEF

Make this dish in larger quantities than you need for this recipe. It keeps well or you could air-dry it or freeze it. Trim a 5lb (2.25kg) roll of topside, removing any fat that your butcher might have wrapped around it.

Make the marinade by combining 1 bottle of gutsy red wine, 1 bottle of Chardonnay white wine, 1½lb (675g) of Maldon rock salt (it is a form of brine after all), ½ bunch of rosemary, ½ bunch of thyme (both washed thoroughly), 8 juniper berries, roasted and slightly crushed, 2 tablespoons caster sugar, 24 cloves, 12 bay leaves, 20 black peppercorns, 4 garlic cloves, slightly smashed, 12 hot dry red chillies, 4 strips dried orange peel, and 1 piece of star anise. Immerse the beef in this mix for 7 days. Remove and dry. Use as for the recipe.

If you want to make a form of air-dried beef (bresaola) then wrap the meat in muslin and hang in a cool cellar for up to 14 days. A drier, more sophisticated taste.

POACHED RED WINE PEARS WITH CREAMY GORGONZOLA

6 pears, peeled but not cored

1 pint (600ml) red wine

8oz (225g) caster sugar

12 black peppercorns

a pinch of grated nutmeg

a pinch of ground cinnamon

1 teaspoon coriander seeds, toasted

1 clove

2 bay leaves

juice of 1 lemon

juice of 1 orange

2 tablespoons redcurrant jelly

2 pieces of dried orange peel

1in (2.5cm) piece of fresh ginger

12oz (350g) Gorgonzola cheese, in the wedge

In a saucepan large enough to hold the 6 pears standing up, combine all the other ingredients except for the Gorgonzola, bring to the boil and simmer for 30 minutes. Place the pears in the liquid, making sure they are submerged. Top up with water if necessary. Cook for 20 minutes over a medium heat or until the pears are cooked but still firm. Strain the pears and place them in a glass bowl. Continue to cook the liquor until it becomes syrupy. Pour over the pears and allow to cool.

Place a large wedge of Gorgonzola on the table with the bowl of pears and allow your guests to serve themselves, making sure they taste the cheese with the pear. A fine experience.

WINE NOTES

Poached eggs and hollandaise are rich, so a leanish French Chardonnay from the Côte Chalonnaise of a recent vintage ('89, '90, '91) to balance the richness: Montagny, Rully Blanc or Mercurey Blanc.

You could happily take the white through the carpaccio, but this is Sunday, so let's add a glass of fresh and fruity red from the Loire, Saumur-Champigny rather than Chinon, or the latest vintage of a Gamay from the Ardèche, less expensive but as good as decent Beaujolais.

AUBERGINE, GOAT'S CHEESE AND RED PEPPER 'SANDWICH'
ROAST MULLET ON A STEW OF WHITE BEANS AND DUCK CONFIT
CRUNCHY GRANOLA AND RASPBERRY PUDDING

Memories of the Mediterranean found in Sydney, Australia. The aubergine, goat's cheese and red pepper sandwich was a dish created by Chris Manfield at the Paragon Café, Sydney. An exciting marriage of flavours. I wasn't given a recipe, but I think I've come up with a satisfactory result based purely on my investigatory taste buds. The components of the dish can be prepared ahead, but last-minute construction is essential to prevent the textures and tastes from combining before they hit the back of your throat. For each participating diner you require slices of aubergine, a wodge of creamy soft goat's cheese and roasted peppers. I use a soft goat's cheese made just outside London called Gedi.

Australia has some great cooks, young, enthusiastic and really keen to learn. So when they walk through my doors looking for jobs, I snap them up, especially the feminine variety. Not that I've got anything against the male cook, but in my modest experience, as a general rule, the girls tend to have a natural feel for food, a better understanding of what I'm trying to achieve and, of prime importance, a better taste ability.

Red mullet is one of those fish that remained out of favour for many years in this country. Perhaps it had something to do with the amount of bones, perhaps it was that dated British attitude to being unadventurous with their fish. As a generalisation the Brits can be adventurous with chicken and shellfish - with our colonial roots we've always enjoyed a Chinese or an Indian - but rarely a fish dish or a fish curry. Thank goodness times are changing.

These beautiful looking, beautiful tasting red mullet now have a place at our tables with or without the bones. If bones bother you, ask your fishmonger to scale, fillet and pin-bone (that's removing the little bones) the fish, but reduce the cooking time accordingly. In this recipe the fish are dusted in flour and cayenne and the cavity is spread with some tapenade, seared in hot olive oil on both sides and roasted with some confit of garlic. The confit caramelises wonderfully and can be eaten whole (the confit process removes the harsh flavours) or spread on crostini.

The beans are white haricots cooked with other delicious goodies, cassoulet-style, finished with duck fat and shredded duck confit (which can be bought in the 'better' food shop or prepared ahead from the recipe below). It is a combination of powerful flavours that red mullet, being a bit meaty itself, can take. The dish is finished with a scattering of black olives and torn basil, and is accompanied by a rocket salad dressed only in olive oil, salt and pepper.

The pudding is healthy without being boring. Lots of nuts, oats, brown sugar, honey, spices and citrus are baked, allowed to cool and then broken into crunchy bits, mixed with some dried apricots, dates and sultanas. This can be made well in advance and stored. At the time of service mix with Greek yogurt and top with raspberries. For the ultimate experience top with Raspberries in Armagnac (see page 97).

Serves 4

AUBERGINE, GOAT'S CHEESE AND RED PEPPER 'SANDWICH'

1 large aubergine, cut widthwise into 8 slices

salt and freshly ground black pepper

extra virgin olive oil

plain flour for dredging

12oz (350g) soft goat's cheese (preferably Gedi), cut into 4 discs

2 red peppers, roasted or grilled, peeled and seeded, cut in thin strips (julienne)

4fl oz (120ml) Anchovy and Oregano Dressing (see below)

some fresh oregano leaves

Sprinkle a little salt over the aubergine slices. Allow half an hour for the salt to extract any bitter juices from the aubergine. Rinse the aubergine and pat dry on kitchen paper. In my experience this salting step is unnecessary if the aubergine you buy has beautiful shiny, taut skin but it does seem to be common practice among the aubergine 'purists'.

Take a frying pan, heat to a high temperature and add a dash of good olive oil. Dip the aubergine slices in seasoned flour and dust off any excess. Pan-fry the aubergine in

two batches; the slices should not overlap. When the aubergine has developed a golden crust, turn over and repeat with the other side. Remove the slices and place on kitchen paper; keep warm. Repeat with the second batch.

Meanwhile pop the goat's cheese and the pepper julienne into a warm oven - 300°F/150°C/Gas 2 - and heat through without letting the cheese melt. Season with salt and pepper.

FINAL PREPARATION AND PRESENTATION

Place a slice of aubergine on each of four warmed plates. Top each slice with a dribble of the anchovy and oregano dressing, a slice of goat's cheese, some julienne of red pepper, another dribble of dressing and top with the remaining aubergine slices. Garnish the top of the sandwich with a few strands of the red pepper, a dribble of dressing, a couple of fresh oregano leaves and a couple of turns from the black pepper grinder. Arrange a swirl of dressing on the plate and serve immediately.

Anchovy and Oregano Dressing

6oz (175g) tinned anchovy fillets, soaked in milk for 15 minutes, drained and dried

3 tablespoons finely chopped fresh oregano or marjoram

1 clove garlic, peeled and finely chopped

juice of 2 lemons

6fl oz (175ml) extra virgin olive oil

freshly ground black pepper

2 teaspoons finely chopped sun-dried tomatoes in olive oil

Mash the anchovies and place them in a mortar and pestle with the herb and garlic. Pound to a smooth paste, slowly adding the lemon juice. Beat in the olive oil as you would for mayonnaise until the oil has been absorbed. Season with black pepper and fold in the sun-dried tomato flecks.

(This dressing would also be suitable for any leaf salad, a tomato salad, or for flavouring char-grilled squid or cold fillets of Mediterranean fish.)

ROAST MULLET ON A STEW OF WHITE BEANS AND DUCK CONFIT

1lb (450g) Stew of White Beans (see below)

12 cloves Garlic Confit (see below)

4 x 12oz (350g) red mullet, cleaned but retaining their livers

2 teaspoons Tapenade (see page 49)

plain flour seasoned with cayenne pepper and salt

extra virgin olive oil

To serve and garnish

Rocket and Parmesan Salad (see below)

8 basil leaves, torn

8 black olives, marinated in olive oil and herbs, stoned and finely diced

freshly ground black pepper

Prepare the beans and the confit in advance.

Preheat the oven to 375°F/190°C/Gas 5. Make two diagonal slashes on each side of each of the red mullet. Spread a little tapenade in the cavity of each fish and dust each fish in seasoned flour, removing any excess. Heat a large frying pan to a high temperature. Pour in 2 teaspoons olive oil and pan-fry the mullet with the garlic confit for 1 minute on each side. This high-speed cooking seals in the fish's valuable juices. Pop the mullet in the oven and roast for about 10 minutes. Remove the fish and garlic from the oven and keep warm.

FINAL PREPARATION AND PRESENTATION

Pour the warm beans into a china serving dish. Arrange the roast fish and the garlic on top and scatter with torn basil leaves and chopped olives. Dribble the fish with a little extra virgin olive oil and ground pepper. Place on the table with the rocket salad and allow guests to serve themselves.

Stew of White Beans

8oz (225g) white haricot beans
1 carrot, peeled
1 onion, spiked with a bay leaf and a clove
8oz (225g) pork rinds, cut into small squares of ¼in (5mm)
8oz (225g) belly of pork, blanched for 10 minutes and cut into lardons
1 sprig thyme
2 pints (1.1 litres) Chicken Stock (see page 91) or water
2 tablespoons duck fat
2 onions, peeled and finely diced
6 cloves Garlic Confit (see below)
1 dessertspoon tomato purée
12oz (350g) firm, ripe plum tomatoes, skinned, seeded and diced

6 fl oz (175ml) Dry Martini
8oz (225g) belly of salt pork, blanched in 2 changes of water, 20 minutes each
2 legs Duck Confit (see below), skin and bone removed, broken into small pieces
salt and freshly ground white pepper

Cover the beans with cold water in a saucepan, bring to the boil and simmer for 15 minutes. Remove from the heat and allow to stand in the water for a further 30 minutes. Drain and set aside.

Place the beans in another saucepan with the carrot, onion, pork rind, belly of pork and thyme. Cover with chicken stock or water, bring to the boil and simmer for an hour.

Remove the carrot, onion and thyme.

In the duck fat, fry the chopped onion and the garlic confit until golden brown. Mash the garlic cloves with the back of a fork. Add the tomato purée, the tomatoes and the Martini. Cook for 10 minutes over a high heat, then add to the beans. Purée the salt pork and fold this into the beans. Simmer gently for a further hour. During the last 10 minutes of cooking add the duck confit. Check the seasoning and adjust as necessary.

Duck Confit
2lb (900g) Maldon rock salt
4 tablespoons mixed dried herbs (thyme, marjoram and crumbled bay leaf)
1 tablespoon white peppercorns, lightly crushed
4 cloves
½ tablespoon roasted juniper berries, lightly crushed
1 teaspoon saltpetre (optional)
1lb (450g) caster sugar
6 legs of fattened duck
4 pints (2.3 litres) equal parts duck fat and pork dripping (both can be bought)
lard for sealing the confit

Combine the salt, herbs, peppercorns, cloves, juniper, saltpetre and caster sugar. Put a layer of this aromatic salt in a large crock or glazed bowl. Place the duck legs on top and cover with the rest of the spiced salt. Cover with muslin and leave in a cool place for at least 24 hours.

Remove the duck pieces (retain salt for further batches) and shake legs free of salt. Wipe clean with a soft cloth. Heat the two fats and insert the duck legs so they are completely covered Slowly bring to the boil and then reduce the heat so that the fat occasionally 'burps'. The duck must cook extremely slowly. It will take 2 hours approximately before a needle will easily penetrate the meat. By this time the fat should be clear. Carefully remove the legs, remembering that the meat is very fragile and could easily fall off the bone.

Take a large earthenware crock and place a layer of the fat on the bottom. Allow to harden. Place a single layer of legs on top, making sure the legs don't touch the side. Cover with another layer of fat and so on until all the duck is covered. Allow the fat to set hard in the fridge. The next day cover the surface of the fat with a layer of melted lard which will form a totally airtight seal. The longer you leave the confit in the fat the better the flavour. When removing the duck, be very careful not to damage the complete leg.

GARLIC CONFIT

Peel the cloves on 2 heads of garlic or more. Simmer for 5 minutes each time in three changes of water; this removes the harshness of the flavour and has the effect of sweetening the taste. Drain and dry on kitchen paper. Pop the garlic cloves into melted duck or pork fat and bring to the boil. Reduce the heat as in the previous recipe and gently cook for approximately 45 minutes. Follow the duck confit recipe for storage method.

A useful standby for a great selection of dishes including roast chicken, garlic potatoes and, of course, the red mullet dish.

ROCKET AND PARMESAN SALAD

Wash and dry 6oz (175g) rocket leaves. Rub a salad bowl with raw garlic and season the bowl with a little salt and freshly ground black pepper. Toss the leaves in the bowl to take up the seasoning. Pour on 1½fl oz (45ml) extra virgin olive oil and toss again. Top with 1oz (25g) of Parmesan shavings (not grated) and serve with 4 wedges of lemon.

CRUNCHY GRANOLA AND RASPBERRY PUDDING

8oz (225g) Granola (see below), broken into small pieces
1oz (25g) dried apricots, finely diced
1oz (25g) dates, finely diced
1oz (25g) sun-dried cherries
1oz (25g) sultanas
1½lb (675g) Greek yogurt
8oz (225g) raspberries

Fold the granola and dried fruits into the yogurt. Pour the mixture into a glass bowl and top with fresh raspberries.

Granola
8oz (225g) rolled oats
4 tablespoons flaked almonds
2 tablespoons chopped Macadamia nuts, unsalted
2 tablespoons hazelnuts, skins removed, roughly chopped
2 tablespoons Brazil nuts, roughly chopped
6 tablespoons soft brown sugar
1 dessertspoon grated orange zest
a pinch of grated nutmeg
a pinch of ground cloves
a pinch of ground cinnamon

6oz (175g) unsalted butter, cut into cubes
3 tablespoons golden syrup

Preheat the oven to 325°F/160°C/Gas 3. Combine the rolled oats, all the nuts, the soft brown sugar, orange zest and spices. Melt the butter and golden syrup in a large saucepan. Add the oat mixture and combine until well mixed. Pour into a lightly buttered shallow tray. Pat the mix down and bake in the preheated oven for 25 minutes. Place another buttered tray over the hot tray and invert. Pat the granola down firmly again and return to the oven for a further 25-30 minutes or until golden brown. Remove from the oven and cool completely - it will become brittle - then break into small chunks. This will make more than you need, but it's an excellent sweet or it could be strewn over your breakfast yogurt.

WINE NOTES

There is no doubt, Antony's taste is Mediterranean, and as I'm sitting here, looking out over my sunny village and a sea dotted with white sails, I know that wines will also have to come from chez nous to compete with the strong flavours of goat, olive and rouget.

A fruity Syrah Rosé to start with, sold under the description of vin de pays (Roussillon, Languedoc, etc.) or even as plain vin de table. Then a spicy red, because red mullet is a red wine fish hereabouts: something that can better the fruity rosé, like a Bandol (Tempier, Pibarnon) or a slightly lighter red from the Coteaux d'Aix-en-Provence, or better still, the Coteaux de Baux-en-Provence and one of my all-time favourites - Domaine de Trévallon. Although Trévallon is made with Cabernet Sauvignon, its flavour is surprisingly 'Provence', similar to but a bit classier than Bandol.

A GARLIC DINNER

Mini Aïoli

Garlic Terrine

White Garlic Gazpacho

Chargrilled Squid with Chilli and Garlic Oil

Roast Chicken with 40 Garlic Cloves
Asparagus with Paprika
Pan-fried Potatoes with Garlic, Walnuts and Parsley

Fried Custard with Banana Ice Cream

From time to time, we have special theme menus in our restaurants and undoubtedly the most popular has proved to be the garlic menu. To many readers that might seem strange, but garlic lovers are a bit like vegetarians, there are a lot of them around. You either love it, or hate it, and I definitely love it. The only problem is the next morning, you have to have an understanding partner, or alternatively chew a big bunch of parsley before you go to bed. Not a pleasant thought? But think of the benefits: not only is garlic excellent for the circulation, but parsley is full of vitamin C, what more could you want. There is of course an alternative - Dr Sakar Garlic, which has been processed to remove most of its lingering potency - but you will pay the best part of double the price, and anyway why spoil the fun of munching through that bunch of parsley!

I start this mega-dinner off with a mini or petit aïoli. I say mini because there is a famous French dish, a monster aïoli which fills a whole table - great bowls of fish, vegetables and meats eaten with a pungent garlic mayonnaise. The ingredients look wild and wonderful: squid, octopus, mussels, snails, lobster, salt cod, chicken, beef and a vast array of different vegetables and hard-boiled eggs. Forget all that, nobody will have room for the rest of the menu, so I'm going to serve a baby version with the aïoli.

Aïoli can be made in a food processor but ideally it should be made in a mortar and pestle which brings out the real flavour of Provence.

To follow, an explosion of garlic, a revelation, a garlic terrine created for Bistrot 190. As I mentioned in the introduction, I have seen only one similar dish and that was in the now defunct Jacques Maximin's restaurant in Nice. In the early days, I created a monster, raising many eyebrows and causing near divorce situations. A story follows ... In my infancy as a garlic terrine maker I failed to understand the principles of cooking the garlic slowly in several different waters to reduce the pungency. A friend of mine, Janet, editor of a well-known magazine, chose to eat the terrine whilst out on the 'loose' with another friend Lorna, also an editor. Suffice to say that the evening was not going to be that 'loose'... What was worse, when Janet returned home, even her husband wouldn't sleep with her, in fact she was exiled to the garden shed for the entire weekend. Sorry Janet, sorry 'hubbie', but believe me, it is one of the great dishes of my *bistrot* world, sweet garlic layered with olives, tomatoes, peppers and basil set in vegetable jelly.

Fast on the tail of the terrine comes a classic Spanish cold soup often called white gazpacho. As you know, the 'norm' is a pungent tomato-based soup bound with bread and served with cucumber, peppers, and flavoured with garlic and vinegar. The white gazpacho is also bread based but is mixed with garlic, powdered almonds, oil and white grapes. Serve a small refreshing portion.

And next, another favourite, grilled squid with chilli and garlic oil. Forever popular in all of the restaurants, really fresh squid is heaven. Too often the public perception of squid is a rubbery band or a little ring of some Dunlopillo substance surrounded by batter, but that needn't be. Fresh squid can be prepared by your fishmonger, cut into 5 oz (150g) steaks, slashed with a criss-cross pattern and chargrilled for about 30 seconds each side. You end up with a perfect, flavoursome, tender offering.

For the main course a superior roast chicken highly flavoured with garlic, what else? I push a mixture of garlic confit and butter under the skin, a similar principle to the butterball turkey except nicer, the self-basting leaving behind a garlicky residue. This dish is popular in Provence in various forms, occasionally roasted, more often pan-fried. We add further garlic cloves to the roasting tray with some new potatoes, which form a wonderful crust yet retain their waxiness in the centre. I serve this with asparagus cut into 1in (2.5cm) lengths and pan-fried with garlic and paprika. It's a simple dish without being too heavy to follow the previous course.

For pudding I'm going to spare you the garlic. As much as I've played around with various dishes that included garlic, in my heart of hearts I couldn't subject you to this punishment. Don't get me wrong, it has been done. A restaurant opposite dell'Ugo called Garlic 'n' Shots has almost everything with garlic, including puddings and drinks. I really can't entertain this idea.

Serves 12

MINI AIOLI

2lb (900g) baby carrots, scrubbed and blanched for 5 minutes in salted water, served warm

2lb (900g) Jersey new potatoes, scrubbed and cooked, served warm

2lb (900g) broad beans, outside and inside skins removed, served raw and cold

12 hard-boiled eggs, shelled and served whole

12 baby artichokes, tough outer leaves removed, cut in quarters, rubbed with lemon, served cold and raw

Aïoli (see below)

Arrange all the vegetables and eggs on two large platters. Serve with three bowls of aïoli. Allow guests to help themselves with fingers, or to fill up their plates and eat as a salad.

AIOLI

2 heads garlic, cloves peeled and finely chopped
2 teaspoons salt
1 pint (600ml) extra virgin olive oil
4 egg yolks
2 teaspoons Dijon mustard
juice of 3 lemons
1 pinch saffron soaked in 1 tablespoon warm water
½ teaspoon freshly ground white pepper

Place the garlic cloves in a mortar and pestle, and crush with the salt and 1 tablespoon of olive oil until a smooth paste. Add the egg yolks and the mustard and combine thoroughly. Add the oil drop by drop to start with, and then in a slow continuous flow, until the consistency is thick. Add the lemon juice and the saffron water. Season with the pepper and extra salt if necessary. If the aïoli splits or separates for any reason, rectify as you would for mayonnaise (see page 73).

GARLIC TERRINE

10 bulbs garlic, cloves peeled, cut in half and green inner germ removed
salt
1 pint (600ml) clear Vegetable Stock (see page 148)
10 leaves gelatine, softened in cold water
2 red peppers, roasted, peeled and finely diced
6 tomatoes, peeled, seeded and diced
3 shallots, peeled and finely diced
18 black olives, stoned and chopped
2 tablespoons chopped parsley
2 tablespoons snipped chives
To serve
a few dressed rocket leaves
slices of toast
extra virgin olive oil

Cook the garlic cloves in boiling salted water for 5 minutes, remove from the heat then plunge into cold water, and drain. Meanwhile, heat another pan of salted water to boiling point and plunge the garlic into this water; cook for another 5 minutes. Repeat this process eight to ten times, treating the garlic more gently each time to retain the shape.

Whilst this process is being completed, bring the vegetable stock to the boil and melt the gelatine in this liquor. Set aside. Using a conventional terrine mould (12 x 3in/30 x 7.5cm), scatter some of the garlic cloves over the bottom in one layer, then sprinkle with a little of each of the other vegetable and herb constituents, repeating each layer until the terrine is full. When full, pour over the warm, well stirred vegetable stock. Tap lightly to remove any bubbles, and allow to cool at room temperature. Refrigerate for several hours.

To remove, dip the bottom and sides of the dish in hot water for a few seconds, then tip the terrine out on to a plate. Cut it into ¾in (2cm) slices and place a slice on each of twelve plates. Garnish with a few dressed rocket leaves and serve with toasted country bread dribbled with a little olive oil.

WHITE GARLIC GAZPACHO

10oz (300g) white country bread, crusts removed, broken into small pieces

10oz (300g) flaked almonds

6 cloves garlic, peeled and crushed to a paste with 3 teaspoons salt

12fl oz (350ml) extra virgin olive oil

5fl oz (150ml) sherry vinegar

4 pints (2.25 litres) iced water

1 bunch white grapes, cut in half and seeded

1 teaspoon paprika

Cover the bread in cold water for an hour. Squeeze the bread of excess water. In a food processor combine the bread, almonds and garlic. With the machine running add the oil in a thin stream until emulsified. Add the vinegar and 1 pint (600ml) water and blend until smooth. Pour into a bowl, cover with cling film and refrigerate.

When ready to serve, add further iced water to obtain the desired consistency, which should be similar to a thick gazpacho. Season with paprika and more salt and vinegar if required. Fold in the grapes and pour into a colourful pottery bowl. Dribble with extra virgin olive oil and serve ice cold.

CHARGRILLED SQUID WITH CHILLI AND GARLIC OIL

12 x 4 oz (100g) pieces of squid, cleaned

6 sets of squid legs, cut in half lengthways

Chilli and Garlic Oil (see below)

salt and freshly ground black pepper

3 red peppers, roasted, peeled, seeded and cut in 4 lengthways

12 lime wedges

Salsa Verde (see page 167)

Cut the outside of the squid pieces with a sharp knife in a criss-cross fashion half the depth of the flesh. Dip the squid legs in the oil and season with salt and black pepper. Place on the chargrill and cook for 1 minute each side, remove and keep warm. Likewise with the squid pieces, but only cook for 30 seconds each side. If the squid is very thick cook a little longer. It is important that the squid does not overcook, otherwise it will end up being tough. Chargrill the peeled peppers for 30 seconds on each side. Arrange one piece of squid and one set of legs on each plate, dribble with chilli and garlic oil and garnish with a piece of red pepper and a lime wedge. Serve the bowl of salsa separately.

Chilli and Garlic Oil
5fl oz (150ml) sesame oil
10fl oz (300ml) corn oil
2 tablespoons dried chilli flakes
2-6 garlic cloves, to taste, peeled and sliced

Place the oils in a small saucepan and heat through together for several minutes. To check that it's the right temperature, add a pinch of the dried chilli flakes - the oil should foam, but the flakes must not blacken. If all right, add the remaining chilli flakes and the garlic slices and remove from the heat. Cover and leave to infuse overnight.

The next day, strain the oil through a fine mesh strainer, and discard the flakes and garlic. Bottle and store in a cool dark place.

You could make a chilli oil alone, by omitting the garlic. And, instead of adding the garlic as above, you could pop a couple of peeled cloves into the strained oil when you bottle it. Leave for a week or so before using.

ROAST CHICKEN WITH 40 GARLIC CLOVES, ASPARAGUS WITH PAPRIKA, PAN-FRIED POTATOES WITH GARLIC, WALNUTS AND PARSLEY

3 x 3lb (1.4kg) roasting chickens
4 heads garlic, cloves separated but not peeled
olive oil
salt and freshly ground black pepper
Savoury butter
6oz (175g) unsalted butter, at room temperature
3 tablespoons finely chopped parsley
juice of 2 lemons
3 tablespoons water
6oz (175g) fromage blanc
4 tablespoons finely chopped shallots
2 tablespoons finely snipped chives
2 tablespoons finely cut tarragon
6oz (175g) clean button mushrooms, finely chopped
Sauce
1oz (25g) unsalted butter
3 tablespoons chopped shallot
5 tablespoons sherry vinegar
¾pint (450ml) dry white wine
¾ pint (450ml) Chicken Stock (see page 91)
5fl oz (150ml) double cream
4 tomatoes, skinned, seeded and diced

Preheat the oven to 400°F/200°C/Gas 6. Roast half the garlic cloves dribbled with a little olive oil in the hot oven for 15 minutes. Remove from the oven and, when cool enough to handle, push the garlic out of its skin by using the back of a knife. Set the garlic pulp aside and make the stuffing.

Place the unsalted butter in the bowl of a food processor with the parsley, lemon juice, 2 teaspoons salt, water and 1 teaspoon black pepper. Blend until smooth. Add the garlic pulp and the fromage blanc and pulse until just amalgamated. Remove the mix to a non-reactive mixing bowl and fold in the shallot, chives, tarragon and chopped mushroom.

Lift the skin of the chickens on the breast and around the legs by carefully inserting your fingers between flesh and skin, be careful not to rip the skin. The skin can be lifted from both ends of the chicken. Divide the stuffing in three and push a third under the skin of each chicken, spreading an even layer all over the breasts and thighs.

Rub the outside skin of the chicken with a little olive oil, season with salt and pepper and place in a roasting tray, breast side up, with the remaining garlic. Cook for 1 hour, basting regularly with the fats that exude from the chicken. After 1 hour turn off the oven. Transfer the chickens to a serving dish and pop back in the lower part of the oven until ready to serve. Leave the garlic cloves in the roasting tray.

To make the sauce pour the fats from the roasting tray into a bowl and replace with the unsalted butter. Cook the shallot in the butter over a medium heat until soft but not brown. Deglaze the pan with the sherry vinegar, scraping up all the encrusted bits from the bottom. Add the white wine and chicken stock, increase the heat, and reduce by half. Add the double cream and then pass everything through a food mill or fine sieve, pushing through as much flavour as possible, especially from the garlic cloves. Return the sauce to a saucepan and add the diced tomato. Season to taste with salt and ground black pepper. Keep warm.

FINAL PREPARATION AND PRESENTATION

Prepare and cook the asparagus and potatoes.

Place a bowl of potatoes and a platter of asparagus on the table and present the chickens. Carve the chickens, giving each guest some breast and leg. Serve the sauce separately.

ASPARAGUS WITH PAPRIKA

Remove the woody ends and peel the stems of 3lb (1.4kg) asparagus. Heat 4fl oz (120ml) virgin olive oil in a large frying pan and fry 3 slices of bread cut into cubes until golden with 3 cloves peeled garlic. Remove the bread and garlic to a food processor and blend until fine breadcrumbs. Meanwhile, in a little more oil, cook the asparagus with 1 tablespoon paprika for 5 minutes. Add 1¼ pints (750ml) boiling salted water to the pan and cook for about 12 minutes over a high heat or until the asparagus is tender. Returning to the food processor add 3 tablespoons Chicken Stock (see page 91) to the breadcrumbs. Tip the breadcrumbs into a mixing bowl and add 1 teaspoon salt, 1 teaspoon paprika, 3 hard-boiled eggs (peeled and finely chopped), and 3 tablespoons finely chopped parsley. Drain the asparagus and toss with the breadcrumb mix. Set aside and keep warm.

PAN-FRIED POTATOES WITH GARLIC, WALNUTS AND PARSLEY

Heat 5fl oz (150ml) good olive oil, add 3 finely sliced onions, 5 finely chopped cloves garlic and 1 teaspoon soft thyme leaves. Over a medium heat cook until soft but not brown, then add 8 potatoes, peeled and cubed, with 6oz (175g) broken walnuts. Add water to cover, and increase the heat. Cook until the water has evaporated and the potatoes are tender and golden. Drain off the oil, and toss the potato with 2 teaspoons salt, 1 teaspoon freshly ground black pepper and 2 tablespoons chopped parsley. Keep warm.

FRIED CUSTARD WITH BANANA ICE CREAM

2 pints (1.1 litres) milk
peel of 1 lemon and 1 orange
1 cinnamon stick
2 bay leaves
7 egg yolks
2 tablespoons banana liqueur
4oz (100g) caster sugar
2oz (50g) cornflour
2 eggs, beaten
breadcrumbs
oil for frying
6 tablespoons caster sugar mixed with 1 tablespoon ground cinnamon for dusting
To serve
Banana Ice Cream (see below)

In a medium saucepan bring to the boil the milk with the citrus rind, the cinnamon and the bay leaves. Allow the flavours to meld for half an hour off the heat. In a metal bowl beat the egg yolks with the banana liqueur, caster sugar and cornflour until smooth; add a little milk and continue whisking until smooth again. Add the remaining milk and return to the heat. Stir continuously with a wooden spoon until the custard is quite thick. Pour through a fine strainer into a greased tray at least 1in (2.5cm) deep. Allow to cool and refrigerate overnight.

The next day cut the custard into 3in (7.5cm) squares, dip them in beaten egg and coat them with breadcrumbs. Fry them in shallow oil in small batches, turning once. The squares of custard can be kept warm for at least half an hour. Before serving dust the squares in the cinnamon sugar.

To serve, place the custard squares on a platter, and the ice cream in a bowl. Allow your guests to help themselves.

Banana Ice Cream
1 pint (600ml) double cream
1 vanilla pod, split and scraped
1 sprig thyme
2 very ripe bananas
5 egg yolks
4 tablespoons caster sugar
5fl oz (150ml) soured cream
1 tablespoon lavender honey
2 tablespoons banana liqueur

Bring the cream, vanilla and thyme to the boil together in a non-reactive saucepan. Remove from the heat, cover, and allow the flavours to infuse for 30 minutes. Meanwhile, mash or purée the bananas and set aside.

In a large stainless-steel bowl beat together the egg yolks and sugar until the mixture is thick and pale yellow. Bring the cream back to the boil. Pour a quarter of the cream on to the egg yolks, whisking continuously. Return this mixture to the saucepan and whisk with the remaining cream. Cook over a low heat, stirring constantly until the mixture coats the back of a spoon.

Return the mixture to the stainless-steel bowl and whisk for a couple of minutes to cool. Stir in the mashed banana, soured cream, honey and liqueur. Pour the mix through a fine strainer and chill. Freeze in an ice-cream machine according to manufacturer's instructions.

WINE NOTES

AWT may have found a way to make garlic socially acceptable, but I loathe garlic, especially when other people breathe it over me. Of course, I've been known to secretly enjoy escargot à la bourguignonne *and frogs' legs* fines herbes, *but publicly I'm garlic's enemy No. 1. I shall therefore condemn this meal to unsubtle powerful red. Listed in order of decreasing brutality:*

1. *Primitivo from southern Italy, a deep dark red, with a flavour to match its name;*
2. *Black Bobal from Jumilla, Spain;*
3. *Mascara from Algeria;*
4. *14.7° Zinfandel from California.*
In fact, a decent red Burgundy would do wonders for this meal.

SUPPER BY THE MEDITERRANEAN

Purple Figs with Parma Ham and Minted Yogurt

Braised Squid with Clams, Potatoes and Peas

Pecorino with Rocket, Chilli and Extra Virgin Olive Oil

Perfect for a lunch or dinner as well, and very easily prepared. The main course can be cooked the day before and reheated.

Figs make a pleasant alternative to the usual melon in the first course. Choose figs that are ripe yet have a firm tight skin. Treat them with respect as they are very delicate and bruise easily. I prefer purple figs but green varieties are perfectly acceptable. Parma ham must be sliced very thinly from a whole ham; beware the pre-sliced packets. Ask the shop assistant to cut off the rind before slicing. To most this is common practice, but there are many who don't. As an alternative try the more expensive San Daniele ham or a Serrano from Spain, but best of all, and you have to taste it at least once in your lifetime, is the ham from a rare species of Spanish pig, *cerdo ibérico*, a black-haired species, commonly known as the *pata negra* (black foot); to obtain this necessitates a trip to Spain and when you get there you're talking big bucks to purchase ham of this quality. This breed of pig has a high fat content and is fed almost exclusively on acorns.

I have added one of my little quirks, a minted yogurt sauce which goes very well with the figs. I can't make up my mind why I introduced it to this dish; there was probably some in my fridge at the time, or maybe it's because I love yogurt and mint, but for me the dish works.

For the main course, I have chosen a squid stew inspired by a Spanish dish. Other meaty fish such as turbot, monkfish, octopus or cuttlefish could easily be substituted. Potatoes, onions and peas are cooked separately in fish stock and added to the squid later. The squid is fried with onions, garlic and chilli in good olive oil, ignited with brandy and cooked with tomatoes and white wine. Towards tenderness, clams are added and then the potatoes, onions and peas.

To finish, a simple platter of mature Pecorino or Parmesan slices, scattered with rocket leaves, rock salt, diced chilli and dark green, first-pressing extra virgin olive oil.

Serves 4

PURPLE FIGS WITH PARMA HAM AND MINTED YOGURT

8 figs

8oz (225g) thinly sliced Parma ham

Minted yogurt

2 tablespoons finely diced cucumber

salt and freshly ground black pepper

10fl oz (300ml) Greek yogurt

1 tablespoon chopped mint

lemon juice, to taste

For the minted yogurt, salt the cucumber and leave for half an hour, then rinse and drain. Pat dry. Combine all the ingredients and season to taste with freshly squeezed lemon juice and black pepper. The recipe should not need extra salt.

Allow 2 figs per person. Slice them vertically into 4 and arrange to the side of the plate. Serve each person with 2oz (50g) of the thinly sliced ham and offer the yogurt separately.

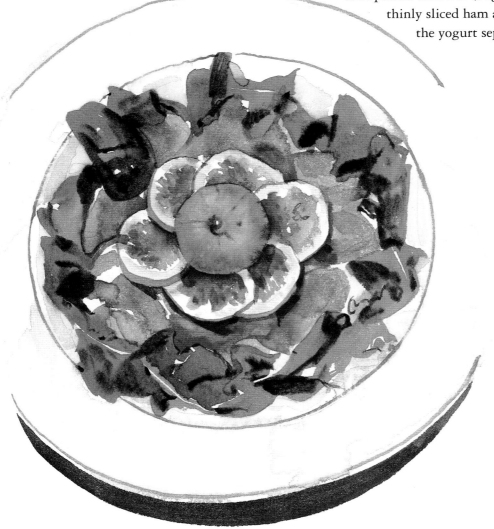

BRAISED SQUID WITH CLAMS, POTATOES AND PEAS

2lb (900g) cleaned medium sized squid (ask your fishmonger to clean it for you), cut into 3in (7.5cm) chunks

4fl oz (120 ml) good olive oil

4 cloves garlic, peeled and finely chopped

2 green chillies, seeded and finely chopped

1 onion, peeled and finely chopped

3fl oz (85ml) brandy

10fl oz (300ml) white wine

1lb (450g) tomatoes, peeled and cored, crushed with a fork

1lb (450g) floury potatoes, peeled and cut into chunks

24 baby white onions, peeled

8oz (225g) shelled fresh peas

1 bay leaf

1 sprig thyme

1½ pints (900ml) Fish Stock (see below)

24 clams (Venus or Cherrystone), scrubbed

1 teaspoon paprika

salt and freshly ground black pepper

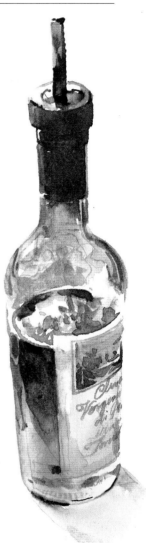

Fry the squid pieces in hot olive oil for 2 minutes, turning regularly. Add the garlic, chilli and onion and cook over a medium heat until they start to brown.

Warm the brandy in a separate small pan and ignite; pour it carefully over the squid. Add the white wine and the tomatoes and simmer gently for 30 minutes, or until the squid is tender.

Meanwhile, in a separate pan, cook the potatoes, onions and peas with the bay leaf and thyme in half the fish stock until tender, about 10-15 minutes.

Add the clams and the remaining fish stock to the squid pan and bring to the boil; simmer until all the clams have opened, a few minutes only (discard any that remain closed). Add the vegetables with their reduced juices, first removing the thyme and bay leaf. Stir in the paprika and check the seasoning, adding salt and black pepper as necessary.

Simmer for a further 5 minutes. If preparing the previous day, allow to cool completely then refrigerate. Reheat gently when required.

Serve in hot flat soup bowls with chunks of crusty country bread.

130

Fish Stock
makes about 2½ pints (1.5 litres)
3¼lb (1.5kg) bones and heads of white fish, skin and gills removed
salt
14fl oz (400ml) dry white wine
1 celery stalk
white of 2 leeks
2 tablespoons mushroom trimmings
1 onion, peeled and stuck with 2 cloves
1 bouquet garni
a few parsley stalks
juice of 1 lemon
1 teaspoon white peppercorns, crushed

Soak the fish bones and heads in iced salted water for 30 minutes. Break up the bones, then put them in a saucepan with the remaining ingredients. Cover with 3½ pints (2 litres) water, and bring to the boil. Simmer for 20 minutes (no longer), skimming regularly.

Strain through a fine sieve lined with kitchen paper or wet cheesecloth. Return to the heat and boil until reduced to the strength or volume required (1 pint/600ml for the strongest flavour).

PECORINO WITH ROCKET, CHILLI AND EXTRA VIRGIN OLIVE OIL

12oz (350g) Pecorino (or Parmesan) cheese, shaved into thin slices
2oz (50g) rocket leaves, torn (leave a few whole)
1 green chilli pepper, seeded and finely diced
rock salt
extra virgin olive oil
freshly ground black pepper

Arrange the thin slices of cheese on four plates or one platter, scatter with the rocket and chilli. Sprinkle with rock salt and drizzle with a decent amount of olive oil. Add a few turns of black pepper.

WINE NOTES

Purple figs, grown in my garden, and wrapped with a mint leaf in Parma ham are one of my wife's favourite appetizers. They inevitably ruin my wine, although I have not as yet tried the combination with Lambrusco. A possibility, I wonder?

Braised squid Spanish style offers at least an opportunity to open a bottle from your Iberian collection, nothing too fine and white or too heavy, mature, oaky and red, but middle of the spectrum: a buttery white Rioja from the Marqués de Murrieta or CVNE (Compañia Vinicola del Norte de España), or a light red from Marqués de Cáceres. Better still, if you can find it, a Rioja Tinto from Martinez Rujanada or the Rioja Crianza from the Bodegas Benito Urbina.

ANOTHER COUNTRY: ANOTHER BARBIE

Twice-Cooked Leeks and Mushrooms on Tapenade Toast

Chargrilled Saddle of Hare with Tolosa Beans

Pears, Prunes, Oranges and Walnuts in Spiced Red Wine

A real country menu with lots of exciting flavour sensations, perfect for a barbecue. I remember as a boy picking big beautiful mushrooms from a nearby field. These mushrooms had a touch of magic, something I haven't tasted for many years; if you can't pick them, buy field mushrooms for this dish and where possible, try to buy ones with pinkish gills which signify freshness. Cook them over open coals - a wonderful taste experience. Accompany the mushrooms with leeks which are lightly steamed over bay leaves and then chargrilled producing an enticing marriage. The pairing is served on tapénade-spread charcoal grilled country bread. If you don't possess a chargrill or barbie, use an ordinary domestic grill or better still, buy a Le Creuset griddle which fits over gas or electric rings and recreates the grill markings on the bread. Porcini mushrooms or *cèpes* are good substitutes, but I'm bound to say that in this case, I prefer the common field mushroom. Tapénade is easy to make at home using a food processor (see page 49). I find the plump black olives marinated in olive oil and herbs are best for this recipe. Make a decent sized batch as it keeps well and is perfect for a pre-dinner nibble spread on crostini with a little tomato and basil.

The main course dish of hare has a Mediterranean influence as it's served with an old Spanish recipe for Tolosa beans. When buying hare, make sure the animal is no older than a year. Its fur should be shiny, the feet small and the toenails undeveloped. Of course you could buy just saddles for this dish, but on their own they tend to be expensive.

The saddle of the hare is wonderfully tender and after an overnight marination needs only a short period of cooking. This is another sophisticated barbecue dish following on from the grilled starter. The Tolosa beans originate from the Basque country and are a heady mixture of red kidney beans, bacon, garlic, chorizo, cabbage and *morcilla* or other blood sausage or black pudding which can be cooked ahead and reheated in a pan on the barbecue.

For the pudding, I have chosen a compote of stewed fruits with the addition of oranges and walnuts. I use a light red Beaujolais spiced with cinnamon, vanilla, ginger, bay leaves and cloves. The walnuts add extra flavour and extra texture and in fact, a compote made with walnut wine acquires an extra dimension. This can be eaten as is, or served with a dollop of Cinnamon Ice Cream.

Serves 4

TWICE-COOKED LEEKS AND MUSHROOMS ON TAPENADE TOAST

8 large field mushrooms
extra virgin olive oil
1 teaspoon sesame oil
2 cloves garlic, peeled and halved
salt and freshly ground black pepper
20 bay leaves
10 slices dried orange rind
4 leeks (or 16 baby leeks), washed thoroughly
4 x ½in (1cm) slices country bread
about 2oz (50g) Tapénade (see page 49)
Garnish
finely chopped coriander
olive oil dressed rocket leaves

Make sure the mushrooms are clean, then remove and discard their stalks. You need beautiful fresh field mushrooms - don't buy mushrooms with dehydrated, wrinkled skins. If you wish to peel them, feel free to do so, but it's not necessary.

Heat 3fl oz (85ml) of the olive oil and the sesame oil in a large frying pan. When hot, add the garlic, cook until golden and then remove and discard. Add the mushrooms, gill-side down, and cook over a medium heat for 5 minutes. Turn them over and cook for a further 5 minutes. Season and remove the mushrooms, setting them aside until ready to serve.

Prepare a pan for steaming the leeks. Salt the water and arrange the bay leaves and the orange rind in the top half of the steamer, cover with a lid and bring to the boil. Place the leeks in the steamer and cook for between 6-12 minutes, depending on their size. If the leeks are large, cut them in half lengthways. Remove the leeks and allow to cool. Everything to this point can be prepared the day before.

FINAL PREPARATION AND PRESENTATION

Drizzle both sides of the country bread with extra virgin olive oil and chargrill or grill. Spread the toast with a fine layer of tapénade. Set aside to keep warm.

Grill the leeks and mushrooms until lightly charred; season with salt and black pepper. Share them evenly between the 4 slices of tapénade toast.

Place the loaded toasts on four plates, sprinkle with chopped coriander and garnish with a few dressed rocket leaves.

CHARGRILLED SADDLE OF HARE WITH TOLOSA BEANS

2 saddles of hare, each cut horizontally in 2

8oz (225g) blood sausage or good black pudding, cut into 8 slices

salt and freshly ground black pepper

Hare marinade

1 teaspoon thyme leaves

¼ teaspoon powdered bay leaf

1 onion, peeled and finely sliced

1 clove garlic, peeled and finely diced

2 tablespoons Armagnac

Tolosa beans

12oz (350g) red kidney beans, soaked overnight

4oz (100g) belly of salt pork (or unsalted bacon), diced

4fl oz (120 ml) extra virgin olive oil

1 onion, peeled and finely chopped

3 pints (1.75 litres) Chicken Stock (see page 91) or water

2 cloves garlic, peeled and finely chopped

cayenne pepper

8oz (225g) Spanish chorizo sausage, sliced in 1in (2.5cm) chunks

1½lb (675g) Savoy cabbage, shredded

Gremolata

2 teaspoons chopped parsley

1 teaspoon chopped garlic

½ teaspoon chopped red chilli

½ teaspoon grated lemon rind

THE DAY BEFORE

Place the hare in a non-reactive bowl and mix with the marinade ingredients, salt and pepper to taste. Marinate for at least 8 hours, turning from time to time.

2 HOURS BEFORE SIT-DOWN

Drain the beans and place them in a medium saucepan with the salt pork or bacon, 3 tablespoons olive oil, half the onion and the chicken stock. Bring to the boil and cover with a lid. Simmer over a low heat for approximately an hour, adding more stock or water as necessary to keep the beans covered. Stir from time to time.

Pan-fry the remaining onion and the garlic in the remaining olive oil with a pinch of cayenne pepper until soft but not brown. Add the onions, oil and chorizo sausage to the beans and cook for a further hour.

Meanwhile, cook the cabbage in plenty of boiling water for approximately 12 minutes or until tender. Drain and add to the beans. Everything up to this point can be prepared the day before.

FINAL PREPARATION AND PRESENTATION

When you are ready to serve, remove the hare from its marinade and place on a preheated chargrill. Cook for approximately 8 minutes on each side, basting with the marinade juices.

Reheat the beans in a saucepan placed to the side of the chargrill. Dip the black pudding slices in seasoned olive oil and grill for 2 minutes on each side.

Mix together the gremolata ingredients and fold into the beans. Tip the beans onto a large platter and arrange the meats on top. Serve immediately.

PEARS, PRUNES, ORANGES AND WALNUTS IN SPICED RED WINE

4 pears, peeled, but not cored
2 oranges
8 Agen prunes
16 walnut halves
fresh bay leaves
Spiced wine
1 pint (600ml) red Beaujolais
7oz (200g) caster sugar
6 black peppercorns
a pinch of grated nutmeg
a pinch of ground cinnamon
½ teaspoon roasted coriander seeds
1 clove
2 bay leaves
½ vanilla pod
juice of 1 lemon
juice of 1 orange
2 tablespoons redcurrant jelly
2 tablespoons grated orange rind
2 thin slices fresh ginger

Combine all the ingredients for the spiced wine and simmer for approximately 30 minutes. Strain and return the liquor to a pan just large enough to hold the pears. Top up with water as necessary to cover the pears. Simmer for approximately 30 minutes or until the pears are cooked through. Remove the pears and return the liquor to the heat. Reduce the liquor by boiling vigorously until 15fl oz (450 ml) remains. Return the pears to the liquor and allow to cool in a glass bowl.

Meanwhile, peel and de-pith the oranges and slice each into 6 horizontally. Add to the pears along with the prunes and walnut halves.

Chill overnight in the refrigerator.

Serve 'natch' or with Cinnamon Ice Cream (see below). In the latter case, place both bowls on the table, garnish the compote with fresh bay leaves and allow your guests to tuck in.

CINNAMON ICE CREAM

Combine 10fl oz (300ml) milk with 10fl oz (300ml) double cream and 1½ cinnamon sticks and heat until nearly boiling over a medium heat. Remove from the heat and allow the flavours to develop for 1 hour. Cream 4 egg yolks with 3oz (75g) caster sugar. Strain the cream mix on to the egg yolks and cook over a medium heat until the custard thickens enough to coat the back of a spoon. Do not allow the mixture to boil. If you are nervous, the custard can be cooked over hot water or in a bainmarie, but it takes longer, so requires more patience. When thickened, cool the mixture over ice cubes. When cold, strain into the ice-cream machine and freeze according to manufacturer's instructions. When the ice cream has set, turn into a bowl and store in the freezer until ready for use.

WINE NOTES

Reading on, I'm relieved to learn that 'Barbie' has nothing in common with my daughter's doll. Far too skinny to be grilled or roasted.

This is a truly Mediterranean menu, more Languedocian than Provençal, and not one for white wine, although that shouldn't stop you from

drinking a glass of fresh Austrian Grüner Veltliner or a Muscadet for apéritif.

Languedoc food with Languedoc wines: an abundance of choice, shelves piled high in all the supermarkets, from plain vin de pays *(Pyrénées-Orientales, Aude, Hérault, Gard) to really excellent reds like Faugères from the Hérault. My own choice is usually a good plain Côtes de Roussillon-Villages, like Caramany, or a Fitou of which Madame Parmentier (from the Co-op) is the most popular in the UK. Minervois and Corbières (Domaine de Villemajou) are part of that region, as are the lesser known Côtes de Malpère.*

It is always difficult to pair fruit in red wine with another wine, but I was recently served a Clairette de Die 'Tradition', a slightly fizzy, Muscat-flavoured wine, and the combination was rather enjoyable. 'Optional.'

GRILLED GOAT'S CHEESE IN GRAPE LEAVES WITH WALNUT PICKLE

BRAISED STUFFED BREAST OF VEAL

Stewed Peas in Extra Virgin Olive Oil

Buttered Noodles

TARTE TATIN

A definitely Frenchie menu ... nothing wrong with the French apart from their arrogant belief that the rest of the world can't cook. On yer bike, Frenchie, the Brits are coming. Even now, London has to be one of the best restaurant capitals in the world, with a startling choice of restaurant nationalities - far greater than any other city. And within these nationalities, some of the best cooks perform their magical art. But back to the French. They *can* cook and they apparently invented the *bistrot*, so they are worthy of a little support, but, as far as I'm concerned, there will always be an intense rivalry between the UK and France as to who achieves the highest culinary standards.

I start with a satisfying cheese dish grilled in grape leaves (which are of course vine leaves, but somehow grape has a nicer ring to it). For the goat's cheese I use a Crottin de Chavignol which is firmer than some and keeps its texture better. The cheese is seasoned, dribbled with olive oil and wrapped in blanched grape leaves which can be bought ready-prepared in Greek shops or supermarkets. Should you have a vine

growing in your garden, the satisfaction is that much greater.

I serve the cheese with a few salad leaves and some delicious walnut pickle, a legacy from my Great-Aunt Nancy who picked up the recipe and many other things during her lengthy army penance in India. Lots of exciting recipes were developed by the colonials and their cooks including, I understand, Worcestershire sauce ... a bit of a winner that one!

The main course uses the only inexpensive cut of veal. The breast is boned and stuffed horizontally with a mixture of pork, spinach, Parmesan cheese, pancetta and onion. This is braised slowly in white wine, aromatics and stock. Best done the day before so that the cooking juices can be de-fatted when cold. An excellent easy dish for reheating. I serve it with a slow braise of fresh peas and spring onions which stew with some pancetta, garlic, sugar and extra virgin olive oil. Buttered noodles or new season Mids from Jersey or the waxy Egyptian potatoes accompany this dish.

The pudding is the classic upside-down apple pie, tarte tatin, which everybody loves, but most cooks are scared of making. Easy-peasy really, just take your new-found cookery confidence and follow the recipe. It'll work, it'll be good and what's more, you will have made it yourself. Some chefs caramelise the apple, butter and sugar with the pastry cover on already. I prefer to cover the apples after they have been caramelised: (a) you can see what's happening in the caramelisation process and (b) I think the pastry stays a little crisper. If you don't want to make it, you can buy a very acceptable version at Marks and Spencer, but to eat the finest in the world, you must find Roger Pizey, who is a superb pastry chef, introduced to the world by Marco Pierre White at his old restaurant Harvey's and now at the new restaurant, Marco's New Number, at the Hyde Park Hotel. His tarte tatin is to die for, unbelievably dreamy. Serve it with clotted cream.

Serves 6

GRILLED GOAT'S CHEESE IN GRAPE LEAVES WITH WALNUT PICKLE

6 hard, individual goat's cheeses (preferably Crottin de Chavignol)
6 large vine leaves, if fresh, blanched for 2 minutes in boiling water; otherwise bought (available in Greek shops)
1 tablespoon oregano leaves
salt and freshly ground black pepper
extra virgin olive oil
3 slices country bread, cut into ½in (1cm) croûtons
6oz (175g) or 1 small head curly endive or frisée, washed and dried
1 teaspoon balsamic vinegar
a little Walnut Pickle (see below)

Lay the vine leaves on a flat surface and place a goat's cheese in the centre of each. Sprinkle with oregano leaves, salt and pepper and dribble with some olive oil. Fold the leaves over, brush with olive oil and refrigerate the packages on a tray, folded side down. Allow to marinate for an hour.

Sprinkle the croûtons with olive oil and season with salt and black pepper. Place on a baking tray in a low oven (300°F/150°C/Gas 2) until golden and crisp. (These can be pre-prepared and stored in an airtight container. Reheat in the oven or under the grill when required.)

Place the cheeses under the grill - preferably on a chargrill - and cook under (or over) a medium heat for approximately 5 minutes on each side.

While the cheeses are cooking, dress the leaves with 2 tablespoons extra virgin olive oil, the balsamic vinegar, salt and pepper. Toss the leaves with the warm croûtons and divide the salad leaves between six plates or arrange on a large platter. When the cheeses are soft, place them on the salad leaves and serve immediately. Serve the walnut pickle separately.

Walnut Pickle
makes 2lb (900g)
1 onion, peeled and finely chopped
4 tablespoons walnut oil
1lb (450g) walnut halves, lightly toasted, roughly chopped
1 teaspoon grated nutmeg
1 teaspoon paprika
5oz (150g) soft brown sugar
4 garlic cloves, peeled and crushed with 2 teaspoons salt
1in (2.5cm) fresh ginger, peeled and grated
1 chilli, seeded and finely chopped
1 Bramley cooking apple, peeled, cored and diced
2 cloves
1 hard green pear, peeled, cored and diced
10fl oz (300ml) cider vinegar

Sweat the onion in the oil in a non-reactive saucepan until soft but not brown. Add the walnuts and cook for a further 5 minutes, stirring from time to time. Add all the remaining ingredients and bring to the boil. Cover the pan and cook for 20 minutes, stirring regularly. Spoon into hot sterilised Kilner jars and seal. Allow flavours to develop for 2 weeks if you can resist from picking. Also great with cold roast pork.

BRAISED STUFFED BREAST OF VEAL, STEWED PEAS IN EXTRA VIRGIN OLIVE OIL AND BUTTERED NOODLES

1 breast of veal (approx. 6lb/2.7kg), ask your butcher to remove the bones
16 sage leaves
salt and freshly ground black pepper
Stuffing
1 onion, peeled and finely chopped
4 cloves garlic, peeled and finely chopped
3oz (75g) unsalted butter
1 tablespoon olive oil
4oz (100g) pancetta, coarsely chopped, or ham
4oz (100g) pork fat, finely diced
2lb (900g) chard or spinach, tough stems discarded, cooked and chopped
1 dessertspoon finely chopped sage
4 tablespoons grated Parmesan cheese
4 tablespoons moistened breadcrumbs, squeezed dry
4oz (100g) hazelnuts, roasted, skinned and roughly chopped
4 tablespoons chopped flat parsley
a pinch of grated nutmeg
2 eggs, beaten
Cooking the veal
5oz (150g) unsalted butter
1 tablespoon olive oil
1 carrot, cut into rings
3 cloves garlic, peeled
1 celery stalk, sliced
1 onion, peeled and sliced
8oz (225g) pork rind, diced
1 bay leaf
1 sprig sage
1 sprig thyme
1 dessertspoon caster sugar
½ bottle dry white wine

1 pint (600ml) Chicken Stock (see page 91) or water
To serve
Stewed Peas in Extra Virgin Olive Oil (see below)
Buttered Noodles (see below)

THE STUFFING

Sweat the onion and garlic in the butter and olive oil until soft but not brown. Add the pancetta and pork fat and cook for a further 5 minutes. Transfer to a bowl and add the cooked chard or spinach, sage, Parmesan, moistened breadcrumbs, hazelnuts and parsley. Allow to cool and knead or squeeze between your fingers until all the ingredients are bound together. Fry a nugget of the stuffing in the same pan to test seasoning; taste and season with ground black pepper, salt and nutmeg. Add the eggs, combine and the stuffing is now ready.

STUFFING AND COOKING THE VEAL

Slit the veal horizontally through the centre without cutting the ends and without cutting completely through the third side. The veal will have two closed ends and one long side also closed. With the tip of a sharp knife criss-cross the top of the veal as if playing noughts and crosses. Again on the top of the veal make 16 small gashes and insert a sage leaf into each cut. Season inside and out, fill the cavity with the stuffing and sew the opening with butchers' string.

In a casserole large enough to hold the veal,

pan-fry it in 2oz (50g) of the butter and the olive oil for approximately 10 minutes until all sides are brown. Remove the veal and set aside. To the same pan add the carrot, garlic, celery, onion, pork rind, bay leaf, sage and thyme. Fry over a high heat until the vegetables are brown. Add the caster sugar and lightly caramelise.

Deglaze the pan with the wine, scraping all the naughty bits from the bottom. Return the veal to the pan and add the water or stock. The liquid should barely cover the meat. Bring to the boil and cover the pan. Place in a moderate oven (325°F/160°C/Gas 3) and cook for approximately 2½ hours.

When the meat is cooked, remove it from the pan and keep warm on a platter. Place the casserole on top of the stove and boil the cooking juices until only 15fl oz (450ml) remains. Fold in the remaining butter, cut into small cubes, and boil to emulsify. Pour the contents of the pan through a fine sieve into a smaller pan and keep warm.

FINAL PREPARATION AND PRESENTATION

Have ready the buttered noodles and the peas. Remove the string from the veal. Place the noodles and peas in two separate casserole dishes on the table with a separate boat of sauce. If the sauce has separated, bring it to the boil and whisk to bring the components back together. Check the seasoning. Carve 2 slices of veal per person and allow guests to help themselves to everything else.

The veal can be cooked the day before and reheated in a hot oven half an hour before you wish to serve. Make sure the veal comes up to temperature by using a meat thermometer - better to be safe than sorry. Serve a side dish of grated Parmesan to accompany the noodles.

Stewed Peas in Extra Virgin Olive Oil

1lb (450g) shelled or frozen peas (I concede to frozen peas being an excellent substitute)
4oz (100g) pancetta, or streaky bacon, cut in lardons
½ onion, peeled and finely diced
1 clove garlic, peeled and finely diced
1 dessertspoon caster sugar
6 spring onions, washed and cut in 1in (2.5cm) lengths
1 sprig thyme
1 sprig sage
5fl oz (150ml) extra virgin olive oil
10fl oz (300ml) water
salt and freshly ground black pepper

Place the pancetta in a saucepan and cook over a high heat until crisp and a fair amount of fats have been exuded; add the onion and garlic, reduce the heat and sweat until soft. Add the sugar, spring onions, thyme, sage and peas. Stir briefly and add the olive oil and water. Bring to the boil and cover. Reduce heat and simmer gently for 45 minutes. Remove lid and season to taste with salt and pepper.

Buttered Noodles

1lb (450g) noodles or fettucine, home made or otherwise
salt and freshly ground black pepper
1 teaspoon olive oil
2oz (50g) unsalted butter
1 tablespoon finely chopped flat parsley

To serve

freshly grated Parmesan cheese

Bring a pan of salted water to the boil 15 minutes before serving the veal. Add the olive oil and the noodles and return to the boil, stirring from time to time. Simmer until cooked (4-12 minutes depending on whether fresh or dried). Drain and toss in the butter and parsley. Season to taste. Serve with the Parmesan cheese.

TARTE TATIN

4lb (1.8kg) apples (Egremont Russet or Granny Smith) peeled, cored and cut into sixths
10oz (300g) unsalted butter
8oz (225g) caster sugar
1 teaspoon grated nutmeg
2 teaspoons grated orange rind
juice of 2 lemons
Pastry
2 eggs
3oz (75g) butter, softened
2 tablespoons caster sugar
1 tablespoon grated lemon rind
a pinch of salt
1lb (450g) plain flour, sifted
water as necessary

Make the pastry first. The quick way: place the eggs, butter, sugar, lemon rind and salt in a food processor and blend until it is reminiscent of scrambled eggs. Add the flour all at once and pulse until the dough comes together in a loose ball. If it's too dry add a little water. Knead the dough gently to form a soft ball and wrap in cling film. Refrigerate for an hour.

The not-so-quick way: place the flour in a mound on a floured marble slab preferably, if not, your favourite work surface. In the centre of the mound form a well and add the eggs, salt, sugar, butter and lemon rind in no particular order. Mix and rub all the ingredients together between the palms of your hands, adding water as necessary to form a smooth soft ball. Do not overwork the dough. Wrap dough in cling film and refrigerate as before. Now clear up the mess - practice makes perfect.

Using 8oz (225g) of the butter, generously grease two 9in (23cm) deep, round, tart tins. Sprinkle half the caster sugar over the butter. Arrange the apple slices tightly together in the bottom of the pans and sprinkle with the remaining sugar. Melt the remaining butter and dribble over the apples. Place the tart pans over a high heat for about 15 minutes, watching with a wary eye to ensure that the sugar and butter are melting and caramelising evenly. You want to achieve no more than a light golden brown. Sprinkle the apples with the nutmeg, orange rind and lemon juice.

Roll out the pastry to 2 circles slightly larger than the tins. Cover the apples with your pastry, pushing the edges down the side of the apples.

Bake the tarts in a moderate oven (375°F/190°C/Gas 5) for approximately 30 minutes, then invert onto two serving platters. Allow to cool for a few minutes so that the sugars set slightly. Serve with nothing more than the love it took to make this masterpiece of puddingship, unless like me you're a piglet - in which case, lashings of clotted cream.

WINE NOTES

I've been brought up on rustic food, most certainly not on rustic wines, although my first memorable bottle would probably qualify as such. It had a decisive impact on the further course of my life (she yielded ...) and was a Moulin-à-Vent 1947, drunk in Rotterdam in 1952. In those days, the wines of Beaujolais were certainly rustic, except that a great Beaujolais like Moulin-à-Vent of an outstanding vintage like 1947 must have been of the gentleman-farmer variety. Unlike Hilaire Belloc who on such an occasion couldn't remember the place, or the girl ('but the wine, by George, was Chambertin!'), I seem to have a much more precise recollection of the girl ...

Good old-fashioned Beaujolais then for the stuffed breast, and there is only one recent vintage that can lay claim to being 'old-fashioned': the 1991 vintage, ideally a Moulin-à-Vent from the Domaine des Rosiers, or a Juliénas 1991. Both are better value than the ever-popular Fleurie, although a bottle of Fleurie La Madonne 1991 would probably be just as good ...

With the Crottin de Chavignol goat's cheese a wine from the village where it is made: Sancerre. Avoid old Sancerre, Sancerre from the Co-op and bottles that say 'Prestige' and cost the earth. Instead select a grower's Sancerre from the village of Chavignol, Bué or Verdigny.

I've never yet enjoyed a sweet wine with tarte tatin - too much sugar, butter and apple-acidity. How about an aged Calvados?

Courgettes Frites with Anchoïade
Roast Yellow Pepper Soup with Chilli Cream
Roast Goose, Baked Apples with Prune and Parsley Stuffing
Braised Red Cabbage with Chestnuts
Roast Potatoes
Compote of Plums with Vacherin Mont d'Or

An autumn celebration menu. Goose is an underrated bird, occasionally used as an alternative for turkey at Christmas. Traditionally served at Easter and Michaelmas, it should be eaten more often. The French serve it on Christmas Eve but perhaps that's gilding the lily slightly as the average British family will enjoy a 'pig out' on Christmas Day. When buying goose, allow 1¼ lb (550g) per person as there is much bone and fat in proportion to the meat. As far as any major bird is concerned, the experience is often made more memorable because of all the trimmings and I've included small Cox's apples stuffed and baked with a prune and parsley stuffing, an original bread and bone marrow sauce inspired by the Italian *peira*, some delicious slow-cooked red cabbage with a compote of chestnuts and, of course, crunchy roast potatoes. I prefer cooking my stuffing separately; stuffed birds can have problems with undercooking as the temperature takes longer to reach the cavity.

Roast potatoes invoke a lot of passions in me and I'm sure in many other people. They must be crunchy on the outside and fluffy inside. To produce this effect you need a good floury potato, which must be par-boiled. Heat your roasting tray, fill with the potatoes and cook over a high heat in good meat dripping; pop the goose in the tray and cook in the oven until really crispy. The secret is in the blanching which allows the potato to absorb an unhealthy quantity of the fats. Who cares? Too often you see the deep-fried variety in restaurants where the potato immediately forms a protective seal ending up with what in essence is a rather large round chip. It's the crunchy edges that are important, who needs the perfect shape.

As pre-dinner drinks nibbles I'm offering the alternative chip: courgettes dusted in seasoned cornmeal and deep-fried, served with anchoïade. Despite the health risk, I've noticed a definite return to deep-frying in restaurants. It does produce good snacking food for that moment when you get an attack of the munchies.

As a starter, hints of the West Coast of America are apparent in my roast yellow pepper soup with chilli cream. A beautiful taste with vivid colour contrasts - the yellow of the peppers and the red tones of the chilli cream. If yellow peppers are a problem then you can substitute red, but I suggest you don't use green because (a) they don't have the same sweetness and (b) the colour can be a trifle yukky. Eye appeal still counts for a lot even in these days of *bistrot* cooking.

I finish with a simple country pud, a compote of plums with Vacherin Mont d'Or. My grandmother had great pleasure in forcing stewed fruits down my gullet on a regular basis as a child - something to do with regular bowel movements. I remember our garage shelved out with masses of autumn fruits and I was regularly fed stewed apples, pears and plums. I'm sure I was her little dustbin, enabling her to boast to her friends that she never wasted any of her precious fruits. Dear old Gran, her eyesight was a little to the left of Inspector Gadget, little did she know that most of her fruit was devoured by the local countryside rats. One year she had the bright idea of making her own cider so she invested large sums in a cider press, and yes, you guessed it, we had to suffer barrels of cider which was lethal and pretty nasty. Still, that's a country grandmother for you. It's funny how foods you hated as a kid often turn out to be favourites as an adult - liver, spinach, swede, steak and kidney pudding, stewed fruits - I still haven't learnt to enjoy rice pudding or tapioca, but I love my plums, especially with a creamy Vacherin Mont d'Or.

Serves 6

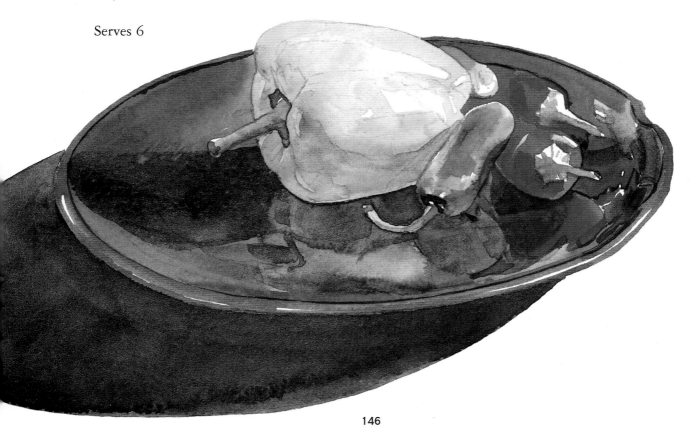

COURGETTES FRITES WITH ANCHOIADE

*4 courgettes, topped and tailed, cut into
'chips' 2 x ³⁄₈in (5cm x 9mm)*

*6 tablespoons cornmeal mixed with 1 teaspoon
cayenne pepper*

10fl oz (300ml) milk

salt

corn oil for deep-frying

*10fl oz (300ml) Anchoïade Rémoulade Sauce
(see page 51)*

Preheat the oil to 350°F/180°C. Where possible use a domestic deep-fryer. Allow a depth of 4in (10cm) of oil. Dip the 'chips' in milk and drop them into the cornmeal. Shake well to ensure the courgettes are evenly coated. Deep-fry the courgettes in batches until crispy and golden, about 3 minutes depending on your skill with a knife and how thick you've cut the 'chips'. Remove from the oil and drain on kitchen paper. Dust with salt and serve immediately with a bowl of anchoïade and plenty to drink.

ROAST YELLOW PEPPER SOUP WITH CHILLI CREAM

*8 yellow peppers, cored, seeded and cut in
4 lengthways*

olive oil

3oz (75g) unsalted butter

2 onions, peeled and finely chopped

2 cloves garlic, peeled and finely chopped

1 red chilli, seeded and finely chopped

*2 floury potatoes, peeled and cut into 1in
(2.5cm) cubes*

1½ teaspoons finely chopped oregano leaves

3 pints (1.7 litres) Vegetable Stock (see below) or water

salt and freshly ground black pepper

Parmesan Croûtons (see below)

Chilli Cream (see below)

Preheat the oven to 375°F/190°C/Gas 5. Place the pepper quarters on two baking sheets, skin-side up, and dribble with olive oil. Place the trays in the oven and roast until the pepper skins have black encrusted patches. Transfer the peppers to a paper or plastic bag. Seal the ends and allow the peppers to steam in their own heat for approximately 10 minutes. Remove from the bag and peel off the skins. The bag process makes the skinning of the peppers less daunting. Roughly chop the peppers and set aside, with any precious juices from the cooking.

In a saucepan over a medium heat, melt the butter and sweat the onion, garlic and chilli until soft but not brown (about 10 minutes). Add the potatoes, oregano, peppers and the stock or water. Bring to the boil and simmer for 40 minutes. Liquidise the soup, remembering not to fill the liquidiser goblet more than half full. Any fuller and the created vacuum can blow the lid off, creating a finely speckled yellow kitchen. Return to the pan, season to taste with salt and black pepper and serve piping hot with croûtons and the chilli cream served separately.

VEGETABLE STOCK

Fill a saucepan with 4 pints (2.3 litres) of water. Add all the following ingredients at the same time and bring to the boil: 2 onions, peeled and cut in wedges, 2 celery stalks, 3 peeled carrots, cut into 2in (5cm) chunks, 2 leeks, washed and cut in 2 lengthways, 1 turnip, peeled and quartered, 4 cloves garlic, 1 sprig tarragon, ½ bunch chervil, 3 bay leaves, ½ fennel bulb, 3 sprigs parsley, 1 large sprig fresh thyme, 12 black peppercorns, 12 coriander seeds, roasted, and 4oz (100g) clean button mushrooms, quartered. Simmer gently for 2 hours then pass through a fine sieve discarding the solids. Refrigerate for no longer than a couple of days, or freeze.

PARMESAN CROUTONS

Preheat the oven to 300°F/150°C/Gas 2. Cut 3 slices of country bread, crusts removed, into ½in (1cm) cubes. Dribble the cubes with olive oil, a little dried thyme and a dusting of salt and freshly ground black pepper. Place on a baking tray in the oven and cook for approximately 45 minutes, or until golden and very crisp. Halfway through the cooking time, dust the croûtons with freshly grated Parmesan.

The croûtons could be cooked in a frying pan but I prefer the oven method which makes them less greasy. The croûtons can be prepared ahead and stored in an air-tight container. Reheat in the oven before serving.

CHILLI CREAM

Preheat the oven to 350°F/180°C/Gas 4. Roast 6 large red chillies with 3 cloves garlic and a dribble of olive oil until the garlic is golden and the chillies have blistered and charred. Remove from the oven and peel, seed and core the chillies. In a food processor blend the chillies and garlic with 2 tablespoons balsamic vinegar, a pinch each of ground nutmeg, cumin and coriander, 1 teaspoon each of soft thyme leaves and oregano leaves, ½ teaspoon salt and a few turns of the black pepper grinder. This chilli paste will keep for a couple of weeks in the fridge.

Take 10fl oz (300ml) of crème fraîche or soured cream and fold in enough chilli paste to suit your fiery or not-so-fiery palate.

ROAST GOOSE, BAKED APPLES WITH PRUNE AND PARSLEY STUFFING, BRAISED RED CABBAGE WITH CHESTNUTS, ROAST POTATOES

1 goose, approx. 10lb (4.5kg), trussed for roasting
salt and freshly ground black pepper
a handful of celery leaves
2 tablespoons cider vinegar
Giblet stock
goose giblets, neck etc
2 tablespoons goose fat
1 onion, peeled and roughly chopped
1 celery stalk, roughly chopped
1 carrot, peeled and roughly chopped
2 pints (1.1 litres) water
Bread gravy
1 onion, peeled and finely diced
1 clove garlic, peeled and halved
1 sprig sage
10fl oz (300ml) red wine
4oz (100g) soft breadcrumbs
bone marrow from 3 x 2in (5cm) bones, diced
4 tablespoons grated Parmesan cheese
To serve
Braised Red Cabbage with Chestnuts (see below)
Roast Potatoes (see below)
Baked Apples with Prune and Parsley Stuffing (see below)

THE GOOSE

Remove excess fat and season the cavity of the goose with salt and black pepper. Keep the giblets for the stock. Place the celery leaves in the cavity. Prick the goose all over with a carving fork; this will release the fats during cooking. Rub the skin with cider vinegar and sprinkle with salt. Allow the goose to dry in the fridge for an hour. This helps to crisp the skin during the cooking process.

Preheat the oven to 350°F/180°C/Gas 4. Cook the goose in the same pan as the roast potatoes (see below), basting regularly during the cooking. As the fats are released remove them with a kitchen spoon. Cook for approximately 10-14 minutes per lb depending how rare you like your meat.

THE GIBLET STOCK

While the goose is cooking, make the giblet stock for the gravy. Brown the goose giblets, neck, etc. in the goose fat, with the roughly chopped vegetables, in a pan for 30 minutes. Add the water, cover and simmer gently for 1 hour. Strain the liquor and set aside.

THE BREAD GRAVY

When they are cooked, remove the goose and the potatoes from the oven, and keep warm while you make the gravy.

Remove most of the cooking fats from the goose roasting tray. Add the onion, garlic and sage to the tray and cook gently until soft and brown. During this cooking process, scrape all the coagulated bits from the bottom. Deglaze the tray with the red wine. Transfer this mix to a saucepan. Bring to the boil and add the strained giblet stock, the soft breadcrumbs and diced bone marrow. Bring to the boil, stirring all the time. Lower the heat to simmer, and season to taste with salt and plenty of black pepper. After 20 minutes' simmering you have a thickish brown bread sauce. Towards the end of cooking add the Parmesan cheese.

FINAL PREPARATION AND PRESENTATION

Place the roast potatoes, the red cabbage and the bread gravy in separate bowls. Present the goose surrounded by the apples to your guests, and then carve. Serve the meat with one apple on each plate with a little extra stuffing, and allow your guests to help themselves to the other accompaniments.

BRAISED RED CABBAGE WITH CHESTNUTS

Preheat the oven to 325°F/160°C/Gas 3. Take a medium red cabbage, cut it into quarters and remove the core. Shred the cabbage finely. Melt some duck or goose fat in a casserole, add 2 tablespoons caster sugar and stir until brown. Add 1 finely chopped onion and cook until golden. Add 3 tablespoons red wine vinegar and cook until the liquor has all but disappeared. Add 2 apples, peeled, cored and finely diced, 2 tablespoons redcurrant jelly, ½ teaspoon caraway seeds and the cabbage. Stir until all the ingredients are combined. Season with salt and freshly ground black pepper and add 10fl oz (300ml) dry red wine. Cover with a circle of buttered paper and then with a lid. Cook in the oven for 2 hours. This should be prepared the day before.

When you want to serve, mix with the cooked chestnuts. Prepare these ahead by making a small incision in each of 30 chestnuts and baking them in a hot oven (425°F/220°C/Gas 7) for 10 minutes. Remove from the oven and, when cool enough, peel the outside and inside skins (if this is too much effort, buy pre-prepared chestnuts in vacuum packs; *do not* buy sweet chestnuts). Finely dice 1 celery stalk, and add this to the chestnuts in a pan. Cover with a tin of beef consommé and add 2oz (50g) of unsalted butter. Cook over a medium heat, covered, for 25 minutes. Remove the lid and increase the heat to reduce the liquid to a thickish syrup. Set aside and mix with the red cabbage when you reheat. Adjust the seasoning.

ROAST POTATOES

Peel 6 medium floury potatoes. Cut the potatoes in half lengthways so you have two thinnish long sections of potato. Place the potatoes in cold salted water and bring to the boil. Cook for approximately 8 minutes and then drain; return the potatoes to the pan and allow them to dry out over a low heat. Scrape each potato with a fork to rough the surface up a little. This enables the potato to absorb more of the goose fat, giving the potato a crisper finish. Fry some of the goose fat from the cavity in a roasting tray until the released fats are hot. Add the potatoes and start the browning process. Make sure the potatoes are coated in the fats. Season with salt and pepper. Place the goose in the pan with the potatoes and cook in the normal way, basting the goose and the potatoes regularly; remember to pour off the excess fats that are released during cooking. If the potatoes become too brown remove them from the roasting tray and pop them in another dish in the bottom of the oven.

BAKED APPLES WITH PRUNE AND PARSLEY STUFFING

First prepare the stuffing by pouring 1 pint (600ml) hot orange pekoe tea (strained) over 8oz (225g) prunes and 2oz (50g) sultanas. Allow to stand for 15 minutes and then strain. Keep the liquor. Stone the prunes, and roughly chop them and the sultanas. Soak 4oz (100g) soft bread in the prune liquor, then squeeze out. Add this, along with 4oz (100g) butter melted, ½ teaspoon salt, a few turns of the black pepper grinder, 1 tablespoon finely chopped onion, and 4 tablespoons finely chopped parsley to the prunes. Mix well, combining all ingredients, and set aside.

Core 6 Cox's Orange Pippin apples and with the tip of a knife make a shallow incision around the circumference of each apple; this stops the apple bursting during the cooking. With a melon baller remove a little more from the apple cavity. Chop this apple and fold it into the stuffing. Fill the cavity with the stuffing and bake on a buttered tray in the oven for the last 30 minutes of the goose cooking time. Any stuffing remaining can be cooked separately.

COMPOTE OF PLUMS WITH VACHERIN MONT D'OR

The first of the season Vacherin cheeses from Switzerland adds a different dimension to the plums. Vacherin Mont d'Or is a wonderful cheese which is made from the milk of cows from herds that graze on the lower slopes of the mountains rather than the pastures. It has 45 per cent fat content and is shaped like a flat cylinder weighing 1½-6lb (675g-2.75kg). It should have a moist, smooth pink rind, and should feel soft and almost liquid. Don't buy one with a wrinkled rind or one so large that your guests won't be able to finish it, as once cut, the cheese can't be kept long. Never store it in the fridge.

Heat the sugar and water together in a saucepan and add the cinnamon stick and the remaining flavourings wrapped in muslin. Cook the syrup for 10 minutes then add the plums or greengages. Poach for 10 minutes, then remove and set aside in a bowl.

Remove the cinnamon stick and muslin bag and boil to reduce the syrup by half. Pour the syrup over the plums, cool then refrigerate overnight.

To serve, fold back the top rind of the Vacherin Mont d'Or and allow your guests to spoon the runny cheese on to their plates to eat with the cooked plums.

2lb (900g) dessert plums or greengages
1 small Vacherin Mont d'Or cheese
Spiced syrup
1lb (450g) caster sugar
1 pint (600ml) water
1 cinnamon stick
1in (2.5cm) piece fresh ginger
1 bay leaf
2 pieces dried lemon peel
4 allspice berries

WINE NOTES

An all white wine meal: a good rich Aussie Chardonnay to start off the courgettes, something like the widely popular Lindemans Bin 65 (whatever happened to Bin 64?) and then, with the goose, a really hefty Gewürztraminer

from a great year like 1989 or 1990. Not all Gewürztraminers hail from Alsace, indeed some of the finest come from Baden in Germany, from an area known as Kaiserstuhl. A rich Ruländer Auslese from the very same district would probably be my second choice, before looking for alternatives across the Rhine. Alsace Gewürz is not always up to scratch, certainly not the wines of the light 1991 and 1992 vintages, so select carefully and don't be mean: a 'Grand Cru' is well worth the extra money you'd pay for a non-vintage supermarket wine.

With the sweet, an Austrian Trockenbeerenauslese from the Neusiedler See, nowadays without the diethylene glycol which caused such a scandal years ago. Although no one came to harm, Austrian wines practically vanished from the shelves overnight. Italian wines, of course, continued enjoying their popularity despite 97 stiffs in southern Italy at precisely the same time: they had stretched their local brew with water and methyl-alcohol. I suppose they also collected a subsidy from Brussels ...

AUTUMN IN ITALY

Melted Taleggio over New Potatoes and Grilled Leeks with Prosciutto

Pumpkin Gnocchi, Mustard Fruits and Brown Sage Butter

Salad of Spinach and Chicory

Poached Figs with Blackberries in Red Wine

Definitely an Italian influence in the menu, although not necessarily inspired by my Italian travels. The first course is a mish-mash of wonderful Mediterranean flavours (with due deference to the Welsh in leeks). Taleggio is a smashing Italian creamy cheese which I make into a paste and spread over cooked new potatoes dressed warm, and serve with the leeks in an extra virgin vinaigrette. This combo is lightly grilled until the cheese starts to bubble and then served with paper-thin slices of prosciutto (Parma ham) and a scattering of rocket leaves. It's yummy.

The second course was inspired by a lunch I ate in Andrew Blake's restaurant in Melbourne with Rita Ehrlich, the famous restaurant critic from *The Age*. She was writing an article on my successes in a recession and my use of Australian staff in London restaurants. Chris Millar, my Australian Head Chef at One Ninety Queen's Gate, was with us and I remember fighting over who was to have the pumpkin tortellini with mustard fruits. I won - just as well, because here was a marvellous combination of flavours. Pumpkin is widely used in Australia and America, but sadly not so much over here. We seem to use it mainly for carving grotesque faces at Hallowe'en, such a waste. It makes fantastic sweet pies, great purées, excellent soups, and produces the best roast vegetable. Get with it Britain, use your pumpkin. Inspired by my friend Andrew's tortellini, I fashioned gnocchi from dry-roasted pumpkin, mixing it with hazelnuts, a little brown sugar, potato and flour. These are poached and dribbled with a burnt sage butter and a scattering of Mustard Fruits (see page 166 for the recipe, or they are now quite widely available at the better supermarket or deli).

As for the poached figs with blackberries in red wine, I first tried a similar dish from Paula Wolfert's *Cooking of South-West France* where she poaches figs in a purée of raspberries and red wine. Chefs tend to play around with food and I worked this dish with blackberries - a really dense explosion of taste, deep colours and moreish textures ... that's if you like figs in the first place, which many of you think you don't. Try them with this combination and you might change your mind. When buying the figs, make sure they are firm, but not hard, with shiny green or purple skins showing no signs of shrivelling. Treat them with respect in your shopping basket, as they bruise and are easily offended. Watch over them carefully during the cooking process as they must not overcook. Allow them to macerate in the reduced cooking juices for at least 24 hours. Serve plain or with vanilla ice cream.

Serves 8

MELTED TALEGGIO OVER NEW POTATOES AND GRILLED LEEKS WITH PROSCIUTTO

1½lb (675g) leeks, preferably baby, washed thoroughly
extra virgin olive oil
salt and freshly ground black pepper
New Potato Salad (see below)
2oz (50g) rocket leaves
fresh lemon juice
12oz (350g) thinly sliced prosciutto (Parma ham)
Taleggio cream
3oz (75g) unsalted butter
5fl oz (150ml) double cream
5oz (150g) Taleggio cheese, cut in small cubes

To make the Taleggio cream, melt the butter in a pan and add the cream and Taleggio. Simmer gently, stirring constantly, until all the components are blended together. Season to taste with salt and pepper. Allow to cool, and store until ready to use. May be prepared ahead to this point.

If the leeks are small, dip in olive oil, season with salt and black pepper and chargrill, pan-fry or grill for approximately 3 minutes each side. Set aside.

If using larger leeks, blanch for 3 minutes in boiling salted water, then drain, cool and dry. Split each leek in 2 vertically and chargrill as for small leeks. May be prepared ahead to this point.

Make the potato salad well in advance too.

FINAL PREPARATION AND PRESENTATION

If you wish to serve this starter on individual plates, mix the leeks and potato salad together and position in the centre of heatproof plates. Spread each salad combination with 1oz (25g) of the Taleggio cream and flash under your grill so that the salad warms through and the cheese begins to bubble and melt. Scatter the plates with the rocket leaves dressed in extra virgin olive oil, a squeeze of lemon, salt and ground black pepper. Arrange some slices of prosciutto on each plate just before serving.

Alternatively, serve the potato salad and leek mix, the rocket and the prosciutto in three separate bowls and allow your guests to serve themselves. Serve the Taleggio cream separately.

New Potato Salad
1lb (450g) new potatoes, preferably Jersey Mids, scraped but not peeled
salt and freshly ground black pepper
8oz (225g) streaky bacon, cut into lardons from a thick piece
2 shallots, peeled and finely diced

1 tablespoon aged red wine vinegar
4 tablespoons extra virgin olive oil
1 dessertspoon grain mustard
1 tablespoon finely chopped flat parsley

Boil the potatoes in salted water until tender. Drain and keep warm. Fry the bacon pieces in a dry non-stick pan until crisp,

then add the shallots and sweat until soft but not brown. Deglaze the pan with vinegar, add the olive oil and mustard, and toss the potatoes in this dressing. Sprinkle with parsley and season to taste with salt and black pepper. Always toss the potatoes in the dressing while they are still warm as they absorb the flavours more successfully. May be prepared ahead to this point.

PUMPKIN GNOCCHI, MUSTARD FRUITS AND BROWN SAGE BUTTER, SALAD OF SPINACH AND CHICORY

Gnocchi
2lb (900g) Roast Pumpkin (see below)
8oz (225g) dry mashed potato
3oz (75g) dry goat's cheese, mashed
2 eggs
9oz (250g) plain flour
2oz (50g) roasted hazelnuts, finely chopped
freshly grated nutmeg
salt and freshly ground black pepper
To serve
6oz (175g) unsalted butter
2 tablespoons finely chopped sage
juice of ½ lemon
6oz (175g) Mustard Fruits (bought or see page 166), finely chopped
24 sage leaves
oil for deep-frying
Parmesan cheese shavings

THE GNOCCHI

In a food processor, blend together the caramelised roast pumpkin and the mashed potato briefly until combined; do not overwork. Add the goat's cheese and combine with the eggs. With the processor

running, add the flour until you have produced a well mashed, smooth paste. Turn the mixture into a bowl and fold in the chopped hazelnuts, the nutmeg and salt and pepper to taste.

Put the paste into a piping bag with a wide smooth nozzle. Pipe the mix on to a floured tray and cut the lengths into ½in (2cm) pieces. Press the shortened lengths with the prongs of a fork. Alternatively, roll the paste into small balls between finger and thumb and, as before, indent each ball with the prongs of a fork.

Bring a large pan of salted water to the boil and cook the gnocchi in small quantities. The gnocchi will float to the surface after about 2-3 minutes. Continue to simmer for a further 5-6 minutes. Remove from the water and drain. Keep warm on a buttered tray covered with a damp cloth while cooking the remaining gnocchi.

FINAL PREPARATION AND PRESENTATION

Deep-fry the sage leaves in the hot oil until the sizzling stops, moments only. Drain well on absorbent paper. They will crisp up as they wait.

When all the gnocchi are cooked, heat a frying pan and drop in the butter with the chopped sage. Swirl the butter around until it has melted, then allow to cook until it froths, there are just hints of nutty aroma, and the butter turns pale brown. Add the lemon juice.

Arrange the gnocchi on a large serving dish or on eight plates. Scatter with the chopped mustard fruits and top with the nut brown butter which you pass through a fine sieve. Top with deep-fried sage leaves and Parmesan shavings.

If gnocchi is one of those dishes you panic about - don't. The trick is to balance the amount of flour you add - too little and the gnocchi will fall apart; too much and it will end up being too doughy. If in doubt, poach a piece on its own to test it. It should retain its shape and yet not be heavy in the mouth.

As a contrast to the sweetness of the dish, serve a bitter salad of baby spinach and chicory or Belgian endive, depending on where you originate from.

Roast Pumpkin
2¼lb (1kg) pumpkin with skin on, cut into 3in (5cm) cubes
olive oil
2 tablespoons soft brown sugar
salt and freshly ground black pepper

Roast the pumpkin pieces with a little olive oil in a hot oven (425°F/220°C/Gas 7) for approximately 45 minutes. Season with salt and black pepper. Allow to cool, remove any skin and cook in a saucepan with the brown sugar and seasoning until the pumpkin starts to caramelise and break down. Stir to prevent it from burning.

SALAD OF SPINACH AND CHICORY
Make a dressing with 1fl oz (30ml) balsamic vinegar, 4fl oz (120ml) extra virgin olive oil, and 1 peeled and mashed garlic clove, adding salt and freshly ground black pepper to taste. Allow to stand, preferably for a couple of hours. Wash and dry 4oz (100g) baby spinach leaves. Core and rip up the leaves of 3 heads of chicory. The general rule is not to use a knife when preparing salads as the cut ends of the leaves can go brown. However, if you feel more at home using a knife, do so but cut at the last moment. Toss the leaves in a little of the dressing, just before serving.

POACHED FIGS WITH BLACKBERRIES IN RED WINE

1½lb (675g) ripe, undamaged blackberries, washed	16 firm, fresh figs
juice of 2 lemons	3fl oz (85ml) Crème de Mûre (blackberry liqueur) or Crème de Cassis (blackcurrant liqueur)
juice of 1 orange	1 tablespoon finely chopped mint
6oz (175g) caster sugar	
1 bottle Zinfandel red wine	

In a food processor or liquidiser, blend the blackberries with the two citrus juices until smooth. Strain the resulting purée through a fine sieve into a non-reactive saucepan. Discard the pips. Add the sugar and the red wine and over a medium heat, bring to the boil. Reduce the heat and simmer. Skim off any scum that might rise to the surface.

When the sugar has dissolved, add the figs in batches of 4 and poach for 4-5 minutes depending on their ripeness. Remove the figs to a glass bowl.

When all the figs have been cooked, reduce the blackberry purée to approximately 15fl oz (450ml). Allow to cool and add the chosen liqueur and the chopped mint. Pour over the figs. If possible, prepare this dish 24 hours ahead. Turn the figs in the liquor from time to time. Delicious on their own as they are, you could also serve them with a rich vanilla ice cream.

WINE NOTES

A hairy menu. I mean, how can you serve any wine with mustard fruits? 'When in doubt,' my father used to say, 'drink Kalterersee.' He eventually drowned himself in it and the Italian speakers have renamed it Lago di Caldaro, although we German-speaking Tiroleans persist (with right) in calling it Kalterersee.

A South Tirolean wine or Alto Adige, if you belong to them, Merlot, because that is what we traditionally drink there. You'll find it under labels such as Lagreiner, Santa Maddalena or the cherished Kalterersee. Insist on a recent vintage, none of them is a wine that ages well. In their youth they are full of fruit, soft and ideal with almost any food, even Antony's.

Do as we Tiroleans do: drink it before, during, and after. A good time and headache will be had by one and all.

SUPPER FOR THE BOYS

Tomato and Basil Tart, Baby Spinach Salad

Chargrilled Double Lamb Chop, Kumquat and Chilli Marmalade

Corn Pudding and Green Beans

Banana Mango Fool

Most of the time the enthusiastic cook wants to cook simply but well. This menu starts with a simple tomato tart, best made in the summer when tomatoes are at their sweetest and full of flavour, and basil at its most aromatic. It makes a change from the usual tomato and basil salad and can be prepared well ahead to serve at room temperature or warm. Never serve Mediterranean-type food straight from the fridge - you need room temperature to develop flavours. The tart is made with a rich tomato sauce which is reduced down to a thick consistency, allowed to cool and folded into a quiche based custard with chopped spinach and Parmesan. The mixture is poured into a pastry case, topped with sliced tomatoes, baked in the oven and served with a baby spinach salad.

Lamb is the main course, using a Barnsley chop or cutlet, a double chop cut across the saddle of the lamb. It weighs about 12oz (350g) and has a marvellous flavour, perfect for chargrilling. The kumquat and chilli marmalade is an excellent substitute for the more common redcurrant or mint jelly, and has a punchy bite to it, well camouflaged by the initial hit of sweetness. Make it in large batches as it keeps well; a useful result for a fruit that apart from looking cute is really good for nothing.

The corn pudding is taken from a recipe from the southern states of America where corn appears to feature in just about everything. It's a nice dollop to have on your plate, hints of sweetness from the corn with a slightly smoky aftertaste caused by chargrilling the corn first before stripping it and combining it with the pudding ingredients. Maintaining the fiery undertones of the kumquat jelly, I serve some French beans tossed with onion, garlic and chilli.

To finish, I make a fool combining three of my favourite fruits: mango, banana and lime. It produces a wonderfully fresh zingy taste, so pure and concentrated that you might wonder why you bothered with any other flavours. Definitely one of the nicest fools I know.

Serves 6

TOMATO AND BASIL TART, BABY SPINACH SALAD

1 x 9in (23cm) blind-baked Pastry Crust
(see below)

Tomato base

½ celeriac, peeled and coarsely chopped

1 carrot, peeled and coarsely chopped

1 onion, peeled and coarsely chopped

2 cloves garlic, peeled and finely chopped

1 teaspoon soft thyme leaves

12oz (350g) firm, ripe plum tomatoes,
coarsely chopped

4oz (100g) tinned tomatoes, drained and
coarsely chopped

4oz (100g) sun-dried tomatoes, drained and
coarsely chopped

1 dessertspoon Pesto (see page 69)

10 basil leaves, ripped

4 tablespoons extra virgin olive oil

salt and freshly ground black pepper

Finishing ingredients

4 large eggs

2 tablespoons double cream

1½oz (40g) grated Parmesan cheese

4oz (100g) cooked spinach, roughly chopped

4 plum tomatoes, sliced

To serve

Baby Spinach Salad (see below)

Place all the tomato base ingredients in a non-reactive saucepan and cook over a medium heat for approximately an hour, stirring from time to time. Liquidise all the ingredients and pass through a fine strainer into another saucepan. Increase the heat and cook until the sauce has reduced to a thick consistency. Season with salt and black pepper. Allow to cool.

Preheat the oven to 375°F/190°C/Gas 5. Beat the eggs with the cream and fold in the Parmesan and spinach. Mix with the tomato sauce. Pour the mix into the blind-baked pastry case. Arrange the tomato slices on top of the filling. Bake in the centre of the oven for approximately 20-25 minutes or until the filling has set. Allow to cool for 15 minutes and then transfer it from the tart pan to a pie dish. Dribble with extra virgin olive oil. Serve with a simple baby spinach salad.

PASTRY CRUST

Place 8oz (225g) plain flour, 1 teaspoon salt and 2oz (50g) coarsely chopped walnuts in a food processor and blend until reasonably smooth. Add 3oz (75g) very cold butter, cut into small cubes, and process once again, leaving small lumps of butter still showing. Add 1 egg, and if the mix is too dry, a little cold water. When a ball has formed, remove from the processor, flatten into a small cake, wrap in cling film and refrigerate for at least 2 hours.

Butter a 9in (23cm) tart pan with a removable base. Knead the pastry briefly and roll out into a large circle about 1/8in (3mm) thick. Roll the pastry on to the rolling pin and lower it on to the buttered tart pan. Press down and cut off any excess pastry. Crimp the edges of the pastry. Prick the base in several places with a fork and line the inside of the pastry case with greaseproof paper.

Fill it with dried beans or specially made pastry beans. Bake in the oven preheated to 375°F/190°C/Gas 5 for approximately 30 minutes. Allow to cool slightly, and remove paper and beans before filling with the tomato mixture.

BABY SPINACH SALAD

Wash and dry 8oz (225g) baby spinach leaves and toss with 1fl oz (30ml) extra virgin olive oil and 1 tablespoon aged sherry vinegar. Season with salt and freshly ground black pepper. Serve in a salad bowl.

CHARGRILLED DOUBLE LAMB CHOP, KUMQUAT AND CHILLI MARMALADE, CORN PUDDING AND GREEN BEANS

6 x 12oz (350g) Barnsley chops, cut thickly across the saddle
salt and freshly ground black pepper
olive oil
soft thyme leaves
To serve
Kumquat and Chilli Marmalade (see below)
Corn Pudding (see below)
Green Beans (see below)

Season the chops with salt and black pepper, brush with olive oil and chargrill or grill for approximately 8 minutes on each side, depending on how rare you like your meat. Sprinkle with thyme leaves and serve with the kumquat and chilli marmalade, corn pudding and green beans.

KUMQUAT AND CHILLI MARMALADE

Slice 2lb (900g) kumquats and soak them overnight in 3 pints (1.75 litres) water mixed with 2lb (900g) caster sugar. Place this mix in a non-reactive pan and add 8oz (225g) seeded and thinly sliced mild green chillies (*jalapeño*) and stir well. Bring to the boil and simmer for about 30 minutes or until a sugar thermometer reads 225°F/110°C. Ladle into hot sterilised jars and seal. If possible, allow the marmalade to mature for 2 weeks.

CORN PUDDING

Chargrill 4 corn-on-the-cob until lightly charred all over. Allow to cool and cut off the corn niblets.

Preheat the oven to 325°F/160°C/Gas 3. Sweat 2 tablespoons finely diced shallot in 1oz (25g) of butter with 1 teaspoon thyme leaves

161

and 1 red chilli, seeded and finely diced, until soft but not brown. Mix with 12oz (350g) of the niblets, 2 beaten eggs, 1 teaspoon caster sugar, 1oz (25g) melted butter, 10fl oz (300ml) each of double cream and milk, 1 teaspoon salt and a few turns of the black pepper mill. Pour the mix into a buttered baking dish. Place the dish in a container of hot water (bain-marie) and bake in the preheated oven until firm, approximately 45 minutes. May be prepared ahead and reheated.

GREEN BEANS

Top and tail 1lb (450g) French beans. Cook in boiling salted water for 8 minutes. Drain and refresh in iced water. Drain again and set aside. Sweat 1 tablespoon finely diced shallot in 1oz (25g) of butter with ½ teaspoon finely chopped garlic, 1 teaspoon thyme leaves and 1 red chilli, seeded and finely diced, until soft but not brown. Just before you are ready to serve, toss the beans in this mixture and season with salt and freshly ground black pepper.

BANANA MANGO FOOL

1 ripe mango, peeled, stone removed, cut into chunks

4 ripe bananas, peeled and cut into chunks

3 tablespoons fresh lime juice

2 tablespoons soft light brown sugar

10fl oz (300ml) double cream

2 tablespoons caster sugar

½ teaspoon vanilla essence

grated lime zest

In a food processor, purée the mango flesh with the bananas, the lime juice and the soft brown sugar. Pour into a bowl and refrigerate until ready for use. Whip the cream with the caster sugar and the vanilla essence until just stiffer than soft peaks. Fold the cream into the fruit purée and ladle into six glasses. Sprinkle the top with grated lime zest.

WINE NOTES

Avignonesi Bianco from Tuscany, Orvieto Classico Secco by Antinori or the Spanish Viña Sol by Miguel Torres - any one of these three would be a perfect partner to tomato, basil and Parmesan.

When it comes to lamb I lack imagination: I've been brought up in the belief that any wine is good with lamb as long as it is red and comes from Bordeaux. The classic wine remains Pauillac (probably because baby lambs are known as pauillac?), so any decent Pauillac or St-Estèphe in your cellar should do, especially if it should be Château Latour. Many of these rather expensive names sport second labels, so if Latour sounds too steep, then Les Forts de Latour will do (almost) as well. Château Batailley is another good 'lamb' wine, as is Cos d'Estournel from St-Estèphe. Château Léoville-Las-Cases used to be my favourite, but ever since it has become an over-oaked 'super-second' at outrageous prices, I'd prefer Château Lynch-Bages.

For sheer originality, though, I should serve a wine to turn boys into men; Sassicaia from the Tenuta San Guido near Bolgheri in Tuscany, made with a blend of Cabernet Sauvignon and Sangiovese. Never will lamb have tasted better.

POT-AU-FEU ON A SUNDAY

Pot-au-feu
Prune, Rum and Raisin Semi-Freddo

Reputedly the French national dish, a symbol of family life and friendship. The Italians have a similar dish called *bollito misto*, again symbolising their strong family ties. The British have their own national dishes, of course, but there isn't quite the same ring to boiled beef and dumplings! On the surface, pot-au-feu could be conceived as a vulgar extravaganza or alternatively as a boring pile of boiled bones, but on both counts, you'd be very wrong. It can be a simple family dish using modest meats - brisket, chicken and marrow bones - or a wonderful showpiece. The choice is yours, the principle the same.

Food writers get very het up about what's right and what's wrong about pot-au-feu, but I believe nothing in cookery is engraved in stone. At the end of the day, this dish belongs to family and friends ... a different meat here, a different vegetable there, will not make the slightest bit of difference. What counts is your planning, your love, your confidence and your imagination. It's an excellent dish, deriving from peasant cookery; some cooks add lamb, some a duck neck sausage, some a partridge or old pigeon, perhaps some garlic sausage, country ham or bacon.

A dish designed to fight loneliness, it must be enjoyed with a group of friends or family, it can't be produced for one or two. Perfect one-pot dining with invitations issued without ceremony - no candles, no family silver, no wedding crockery, no rolled napkins - just chill out and have a party.

It's best prepared the day before; this allows fats to be removed from the cold stock, but more importantly it allows you to relax with your friends and enjoy your day. I suggest you serve it as a lunch dish with the broth served as a first course with two crostini; one topped with the delicious bone marrow cooked in the broth, and the other topped with melted Gruyère cheese. Then the meats are served with some of the reduced broth, the vegetables and a wonderful array of condiments - different mustards, rock salt, baby gherkins, pickled onions, sour cherries, mustard fruits, some salsas and a salad of grated celeriac with a mustard mayonnaise. You'll find a few suggestions following the pot-au-feu recipe.

You get a marvellous feeling of satisfaction watching your guests' reactions - some of startled surprise, some of amazement - and then see them launch into this dish with gay abandon. My version of this classic dish is an extravaganza, no holds barred, a lunch lasting from one until seven, easily simplified by reducing the types of meats and not attempting all the accompaniments. The choice is yours ...

The pot-au-feu will produce at least two or three lunches or dinners either reheated or minced and used for stuffing a cabbage.

There are times when you want to finish your lunch or dinner with a really 'moreish' pud, something that doesn't demand any form of intellectual thought patterns - a pud you just stick your spoon in, lift gently to the mouth, insert and allow its contents to disintegrate on your tormented tastebuds. Semi-freddo is one such pud, simply delicious, cold, creamy, grungy, not pretty, but heaven. Semi-freddo, as the name suggests, is a semi-frozen number, a combination of Italian meringue, a rum custard with prunes and raisins, and whipped cream. It can be prepared a couple of days in advance, stored in your freezer and revealed to dazzle your guests. A sort of frozen fool, but nicer.

Serves 12

POT-AU-FEU

4lb (1.8kg) beef short ribs

1lb (450g) knuckle of veal

2lb (900g) oxtail, cut into 2in (5cm) pieces

2lb (900g) brisket, tied with a long string so it can be easily removed

rock salt

black peppercorns

1 bouquet garni, made by tying bay leaf, sprigs of thyme, parsley stalks, chervil sprigs in the green leaves of the leek

1 garlic bulb, cut in half horizontally

1½lb (675g) leeks, washed, most of the green tops removed

8 juniper berries, pan-roasted for 5 minutes

3 medium onions, peeled and each studded with 4 cloves

1½lb (675g) carrots, peeled

2 heads of celery

1 fennel bulb

1 parsnip, peeled

½ stuffed breast of veal, about 5lb (2.25kg) in weight (see page 140)

½ chicken, about 3lb (1.4kg) in weight

½ leg of lamb, about 3½lb (1.6kg) in weight

3lb (1.4kg) rump steak, in one piece, fat removed, tied with a long string

6 marrow bones, cut into 2in (5cm) sections

12 small potatoes, peeled

12oz (350g) small turnips, peeled, but leave ½in (1cm) green top

24 baby onions, peeled

1 Savoy cabbage, cut into 6 wedges (cooked separately)

cooking liquor a rich colour. Place these in the bottom of the large pot; this stops the other meats coming into contact with the bottom of the pan. Add the oxtail and the brisket (tie the string to the pot handle). Cover with water and bring to the boil, leaving the pot uncovered. When the liquid boils, reduce the heat and draw the pot slightly to the side of the heat. This will produce a scum on one side of the pot which should be removed with a ladle. Simmer for 2½ hours. The liquid should just 'burp' from time to time. Skim off any impurities that rise to the surface. Top up the liquid as necessary.

Add rock salt (about 1oz/25g for every 8 pints/4.5 litres of liquid), some black peppercorns, the bouquet garni, the garlic, half the leeks (tied in a bundle), the juniper berries, the onions, half the carrots, the tops of the celery (retaining the hearts), the fennel, the parsnip and the breast of veal. Simmer for a further 40 minutes, skimming regularly.

Add the chicken and the lamb and simmer for a further 1½ hours. Remove the meats and set aside to cool in a suitable pan or dish, moistening with a few ladles of the liquor. Discard the beef bones (perfect lunch for the dog) and the vegetables. Strain the liquor through a fine sieve. Taste the liquor and if a little weak, reduce over a high flame. Adjust the seasoning. Allow to cool. Pour it over the meats and refrigerate or leave in a cold place.

THE DAY BEFORE

Preheat the oven to 425°F/220°C/Gas 7. Have ready a large 15 pint (8.5 litre) stockpot.

Brown the beef ribs and the knuckle of veal lightly in the hot oven; this will give your

1 HOUR BEFORE SIT-DOWN

Remove the solidified fats from the surface and return the liquor and meats to a suitable large pot, bring to a simmer and add the rump steak tied to the pot handle. Dab the end of each marrow bone with rock salt and tie a slice of carrot on each end with cotton or a thin thread to prevent the marrow escaping during its cooking.

30 MINUTES BEFORE SIT-DOWN

Add the remaining carrots, leeks, potatoes, celery hearts, the marrow bones and the potatoes. About 15 minutes later add the remaining vegetables except for the cabbage. Cook this separately until still crisp in a little water or pot-au-feu stock; I don't mind adding it to the same pot, but the flavour it imparts is not to everybody's liking. When the vegetables are cooked, after about 15-20 minutes, turn off the heat and summon everyone to the table.

FINAL PREPARATION AND PRESENTATION

Serve the broth with the bone marrow as a first course with some melted cheese crostini and some plain crostini. Tell your guests to scoop the bone marrow on to the plain crostini. When your guests have drunk half the broth offer to pour a slurp of red wine or port into their bowls to be drunk French style.

For the main course arrange the meats (having removed their strings) in the centre of a large platter and surround with the various vegetables. Moisten with a little broth and serve with a tray of sauces and accompaniments.

CROSTINI

Cut ¼in (5mm) slices on the diagonal from a French stick, dribble with olive oil and bake in a low oven - about 300°F/150°F/Gas 2 - until very crisp and golden. Allow to cool and rub with a raw clove of garlic. For the cheese crostini, sprinkle each slice with a mixture of grated Gruyère and Parmesan cheeses and melt in the oven or under the grill.

CELERIAC SALAD

Mix together 3 tablespoons lemon juice, 2 tablespoons grain Dijon mustard, 5fl oz (150ml) each of thick mayonnaise and soured cream or crème fraîche, salt and freshly ground white pepper. Cut a bulb of peeled celeriac into ⅛in (3mm) slices and then each slice into thin strips (*julienne*). Sprinkle lightly with salt and allow to stand for 30 minutes. Rinse the strips and pat dry. Mix immediately with the mustardy cream.

SOUR CHERRIES IN VINEGAR

Boil 2 pints (1.1 litres) white wine vinegar with a few pan-roasted juniper berries, 2 allspice berries, some black peppercorns, some coriander seeds, a few sprigs of tarragon and a little caster sugar. Strain and allow to cool. Pack black cherries (you'll want about 2lb/900g) into sterilised jars and top up with the flavoured vinegar, adding extra vinegar if necessary, to cover. Seal and store in a dark place for 1-12 months - the longer the better.

MUSTARD FRUITS

Mash 3lb (1.3kg) white seedless grapes in a mortar and pestle and place the resulting pulp in a bowl. Cover and refrigerate for 2 days. After 2 days, strain the pulp through a jelly bag into a non-reactive saucepan and bring to the boil with 3 tablespoons of mustard seeds. Reduce by half. Meanwhile, peel, core and dice 1lb (450g) hard pears and 1lb (450g) Granny Smith apples. Cook the fruit until tender with a bay leaf, sprig of thyme, a pinch each of ground cinnamon and nutmeg, 1 tablespoon caster sugar, a couple of cloves and a glass of dessert wine or Amontillado sherry (depending on how sweet you like the mix). When the fruit is softish and the liquor evaporated add the hot grape pulp. Add a good squeeze of lemon and allow to cool. Refrigerate. Mustard fruits and sour cherries can be bought in upmarket delis, but there's a certain satisfaction about making them yourself.

SWEET BROWN PICKLED ONIONS

Mix 5lb (2.25kg) peeled pickling onions with 4oz (100g) salt and leave overnight. In a non-reactive saucepan, combine 1lb (450g) soft brown sugar, 1lb (450g) golden syrup, 1 dessertspoon cloves, 2 tablespoons black pepper-corns, 3 quartered red chillies, seeded, a pinch of mustard seeds, ½ stick cinnamon, 2 bay leaves, 2 sprigs thyme, 6 slices ginger, 3 peeled garlic cloves and 2 pints (1.1 litres) of malt vinegar. Bring this mixture to the boil, remove from the heat and cool overnight.

The next day, drain and dry the onions and pack into sterilised storage jars. Boil the pickling liquor and pour it over the onions evenly distributing the herbs and spices. Seal the jars and store for 2 weeks.

SALSA VERDE

Mix together 6 finely chopped cloves garlic, 6 sliced spring onions, 3 thinly sliced lemongrass stalks, 1 bunch each of coriander and parsley leaves, stalks removed, 4 finely chopped green chillies, 6 finely chopped anchovy fillets and 6 tablespoons rinsed capers. Pound these ingredients in a mortar and pestle and add 3 tablespoons lemon juice and 3 tablespoons red wine. Slowly add up to 15fl oz (450ml) extra virgin olive oil and 3oz (75g) soft breadcrumbs. Check the seasoning.

RAW CHUNKY TOMATO SAUCE

Seed and dice 3lb (1.4kg) plum tomatoes and mix with 3 chopped shallots, 3 finely chopped garlic cloves, 6 tablespoons finely chopped coriander, 2 tablespoons balsamic vinegar, 4 red chillies (seeded and finely diced), 6 teaspoons lime juice and a teaspoon of caster sugar. Season to taste.

HORSERADISH SAUCE

Mix 3 tablespoons of grated horseradish with 5fl oz (150ml) double cream whipped to soft peaks, 1 teaspoon grain mustard, 5fl oz (150ml) soured cream and 2 tablespoons lemon juice. Season to taste.

AIOLI
(See page 122.)

PRUNE, RUM AND RAISIN SEMI-FREDDO

Fruit custard	Meringue
5oz (150g) raisins	8oz (225g) caster sugar
5oz (150g) Agen prunes, stoned and chopped	8fl oz (250ml) water
8fl oz (250ml) dark rum	9 large egg whites
12 large egg yolks	a large pinch of salt
8oz (225g) caster sugar	a few drops of lemon juice
5fl oz (150ml) dry sherry	
3fl oz (85ml) dry white wine	
1¾ pints (1 litre) double cream	

THE FRUIT CUSTARD
Soak the raisins and prunes in the rum for an

hour. Beat the egg yolks with 5oz (150g) of the caster sugar until pale and frothy. Add the fruits and their liquor, the sherry and the white wine. Place the bowl over a pan of boiling water and whisk until the mixture becomes thick. Be careful not to overcook or you will end up with scrambled eggs. Cool the mixture over ice, whisking continually.

THE MERINGUE

In a non-reactive saucepan melt 6½oz (190g) of the caster sugar with the water over a medium heat, and simmer until the syrup turns golden. While this caramel is forming, brush the inside of the saucepan just above the level of the syrup with cold water to prevent it from forming crystals. Keep warm.

Meanwhile in an immaculately clean bowl, whisk the egg whites (alternatively use a food mixer) with the salt and lemon juice. When the whites reach the soft peak stage add the remaining caster sugar little by little. Continue beating the eggs until they are stiff.

Pour the caramel syrup in a continuous stream on to the egg whites while you carry on beating.

FINAL PREPARATION AND PRESENTATION

Whip the double cream with the remaining caster sugar to soft peaks. Fold the cream into the fruit custard. Then fold in the meringue, a little at first, then the remainder, folding carefully so that you retain its airy lightness. Pour the mixture into a Pyrex bowl and freeze, at least overnight. (It can be prepared well in advance.) With its light texture it does not freeze hard, hence its name, semi-freddo, or half-frozen.

PRESENTATION

When ready to serve, place in your favourite bowl and spoon out into individual dishes. If you like, you can scatter a few alcohol-soaked Agen prunes on top.

WINE NOTES

I've never yet eaten pot-au-feu en famille in France, only poule-au-pot, and with that we invariably drink a youngish Côte de Beaune, ideally a Santenay or a Chassagne-Montrachet Rouge. On the other hand I've frequently enjoyed bollito misto, the very best of its kind in Ealing, prepared by a delicious Italian lady married to an almost proper Englishman, were he not Irish. He served Chilean Cabernet with the bollito misto, which I thought was OK, until I had the dish in Siena, where it was served with a Brunello di Montalcino made by Il Poggione. Another dimension. Brunello is just another name for the Sangiovese grape, so the wines made with the same grape variety in the region ought to do just as well: Chianti Classico, or Vino Nobile di Montepulciano.

Then prune, rum and raisin and a marvellous eau-de-vie to help digestion, ideally one of the white spirits of Alsace like Mirabelle, Prunelle, Fraise, Framboise, Myrtille, Quetsch. Quel Sunday afternoon!

Cassoulet
Chicory and Watercress Salad
Lemon Granita with Citrus Biscuits

One-pot dining at its best, France's version of sausages and baked beans, albeit a little more lavish. Different areas of western France have their own version with the only common ingredients being soisson beans or white haricots and confit of duck or goose. The package deal I use is a combination of salt pork, pork bladebone, duck confit, shank of lamb and garlic sausage in a rich stew of white beans made richer by the addition of diced pork rind and pig's trotter.

Make a large pot and invite a group of friends over for an alternative Sunday lunch. It takes organised pre-planning but once you've prepared the main pot, it's time to sit back and relax with your team, and enjoy a few bevvies, safe in the knowledge that this marvellous dish is bubbling away in the oven.

Fierce debates rage, usually fuelled by Jonathan Meades, restaurant critic for *The Times*, over whether a cassoulet includes tomatoes - he says not. I disagree, so if you like tomatoes, go ahead and put them in. It may not end up the classic cassoulet, but who cares, if you enjoy the finished result and flavours, go for it.

Serve the cassoulet with a simple salad of peppery watercress and bitter chicory or Belgian endive. I can assure you a starter is not required, merely finish your day with a lemon granita with citrus biscuits. Granita is the easy option to sorbet as it is made without an ice-cream machine. Simply make your lemon syrup and freeze in the coldest section of the freezer. As it freezes, break up the ice particles with a whisk or wooden spoon. Couldn't be simpler really, a refreshing end to a blow-out lunch. The citrus biscuits are adapted from a recipe in Julie Rosso and Sheila Lukin's *Silver Palate Cookbook*.

Serves 12

CASSOULET

Beans

3lb (1.4kg) soisson or white haricot beans,
soaked for 2 hours

2lb (900g) belly of salt pork, left in one piece

1 pig's trotter

2 onions, peeled and studded with 1 clove each

2 carrots, peeled

1 celery stalk, washed

4 sprigs fresh thyme

12 peppercorns tied in muslin

3 bay leaves

4 sprigs parsley

8 oz (225g) pork rinds, tied together

8 cloves garlic, peeled

4 pints (2.3 litres) Chicken Stock (see page 91) or water

1lb (450g) boiling garlic or Toulouse sausage
(large if possible)

Meats

4 lamb shanks

2lb (900g) pork bladebone

4 tablespoons duck fat

salt and freshly ground black pepper

4 onions, peeled and chopped

2 celery stalks, thinly sliced

8 cloves garlic, peeled and smashed

10 tomatoes, skinned, seeded and chopped

3 tablespoons tomato purée

3 sprigs thyme

2 bay leaves

1 pint (600ml) dry white wine

10fl oz (300ml) Chicken Stock (see page 91) or water

salt and freshly ground black pepper

Finishing the cassoulet

6 legs Duck Confit (see page 117) and some of their fat

1 tablespoon soft thyme leaves

fresh breadcrumbs

extra stock or bean cooking liquor

THE DAY BEFORE

Drain the beans then cover with fresh water and bring to the boil. Simmer for 5 minutes, remove from the heat and allow to stand for 30 minutes. Drain and discard the water.

Return the beans to a large saucepan with the other bean ingredients, except for the sausage. Place the pan on a medium heat and bring to the boil. Reduce the heat, cover the pan and simmer for 1¼ hours. Add the sausage for the last 30 minutes. The beans must be cooked through but retain their shape. Drain the beans, retaining the liquor. Discard all the other ingredients except the sausage, the pork rinds, the belly and the trotter. Cool and then refrigerate everything.

Meanwhile, preheat the oven to 250°F/120°C/Gas ½. In a large casserole, brown the lamb shanks and the pork bladebone all over in the duck fat. Remove the meats, season and set aside. Add the onion, celery and garlic to the fat in the pan, and cook until soft but not brown. Add the tomatoes, the tomato purée, the thyme, the bay leaves, the white wine and the stock. Return the meats to the pan. Bring the liquor to the boil, cover and place in the oven to braise for approximately 1¾ hours.

Remove the meats and set aside. Strain the cooking juices, pressing down on the vegetables to extract the fullest flavour. Return the liquor to the heat and reduce until you are left with approximately 2 pints (1.1 litres). Allow the liquor and meats to cool, then refrigerate.

THE DAY OF THE PARTY

Remove all the ingredients from the fridge. Remove the skin and bones from the duck legs.

Cut the meat off the bladebone into 2in (5cm) chunks; discard the bone. Cut the meat from the lamb shanks; discard the bones. Remove the skin from the garlic sausage and cut into 1in (2.5cm) rounds. Cut the pork rinds into small dice.

Combine the bean cooking liquor with the meat cooking liquor. Warm the beans through with the belly of pork and the pig's trotter and a little of the liquor. Remove the belly and the trotter; cut the belly into cubes and place in the food processor with the meat and skin from the pig's trotter. When removing the bones from the pig's trotter be very careful as there appear to be hundreds of little bones as well as the toenails. Blend the meats until you have a smooth paste and fold this paste back into the beans. Check seasoning of the liquor.

Take a large earthenware dish (6 quarts/12 pints or 6.75 litres capacity and 6in/15cm deep) and place a layer of beans in the bottom, followed by a ladleful of the cooking liquor, a couple of spoonfuls of diced pork rinds then a few pieces of each of the meats. Cover with beans and liquor and continue to alternate until the casserole is full. Make sure there is plenty of liquid in the casserole.

AT LEAST 2 HOURS BEFORE SIT-DOWN
Preheat the oven to 350°F/180°C/Gas 4. Sprinkle some thyme leaves and breadcrumbs on top of the cassoulet, dot with melted duck fat and place the dish in the oven. As soon as a crust forms, break it and push it into the beans. Add a little more cooking liquor and extra breadcrumbs. Repeat every 25 minutes. After the first addition, reduce the oven temperature to 300°F/150°C/Gas 2 and cook for a further 1½ hours. The juices at the finish should be reduced and thickened by the starches from the beans.

PRESENTATION
Present the bubbling dish as is to your guests and allow them to tuck in. A large bowl of salad is all that is needed.

CHICORY AND WATERCRESS SALAD
Pick over 2 bunches of watercress, removing the tough stalks. Take 2 heads of dandelion, remove root end and rip the leaves into smaller pieces. Pull the leaves off 4 heads of chicory or Belgian endive and break into smaller pieces. Wash and dry the leaves thoroughly. Simply toss the leaves with 2fl oz (60ml) extra virgin olive oil and 1 tablespoon aged sherry vinegar. Season with salt and freshly ground black pepper.

LEMON GRANITA WITH CITRUS BISCUITS

1¼ lb (550g) caster sugar

24fl oz (700ml) water

24fl oz (700ml) fresh lemon juice

Make a syrup by heating the sugar with the water. Simmer for approximately 15 minutes and allow to cool. Mix with the lemon juice, pour into a shallow tray and freeze. After 1 hour, scrape the sides and the bottom of the tray and combine all the solid icy parts. Repeat every half hour, mashing the ice until you have a flaky light frozen mixture. Serve with the citrus biscuits.

CITRUS BISCUITS

Preheat the oven to 350°F/180°C/Gas 4. Combine 4oz (100g) plain flour with a pinch of salt and 2¾oz (75g) powdered almonds. In a saucepan combine 5¼oz (160g) light soft brown sugar, 6oz (175g) golden syrup and 4oz (100g) unsalted butter. Stir until the mixture has blended together and has come to the boil. Remove from the heat and fold in the flour mixture along with 2 tablespoons lemon juice and the grated zest of 2 oranges.

Prepare a baking tray and drop teaspoonfuls of the batter on to the tray about 3in (7.5cm) apart. Cook for approximately 12 minutes or until the edges of the biscuits are lightly browned. Allow the biscuits to cool for a few minutes on the tray, then transfer to a wire rack to cool completely.

WINE NOTES

Cassoulet shouts for Madiran, like the excellent Château d'Aydie, or a Côtes de Buzet, both wines from the very home of cassoulet near Toulouse, but not easy to find in the UK, especially with a bit of bottle age. A chance for California therefore, and not just California as in Gallo Brothers, but the very top, from the Napa Valley: Stag's Leap, Beaulieu Vineyard, Clos du Val, Pine

Ridge, and Shafer as producers and Cabernet Sauvignon or Merlot for grape varieties.

And then to follow, another Napa Valley speciality: Joseph Phelp's Late Harvest Johannesberg Riesling. Paired with the natural acidity of the frozen lemon juice, it will make you realise that some of the greatest wines on earth are - sweet.

A Fantasy In Black

Black Velvet

Black Pudding with Pickled Walnuts

Sevruga Caviar with Black Bread

Foie Gras Mousse set in Black Truffle Jelly

Risotto Nero with Grated Botargo

Salmis of Woodcock on Field Mushrooms with Molé Sauce

Black Fruits in Cassis and Vodka

Espresso Ristretto with Black Russian

I've always wanted a restaurant with a series of private rooms where you could have theme evenings created by changing the decor to suit your clients' perverse needs. The only problem is that there are not many customers who can afford to change the decorations just for one evening, and even if they could afford it then you'd have difficulty getting good decorators at short notice. You just can't get the staff any more.

One of my fantasies, and I won't mention the rest, was inspired by a scene in J. K. Huysmans' book *A Rebours* (*Against Nature*), where the main-man, Des Esseintes, an eccentric, made his reputation entertaining the literati to weird and wonderful dinners. One of these was a *black dinner*, at which, not suprisingly, everything was black. It was designed as a funeral banquet in memory of his virility which had recently expired. Luckily, I don't have that problem, yet, but I would still like to create an equivalent event. In essence, I suppose I must have a little of Des Esseintes' macabre sense of humour.

His dining room was draped in black - velvet or silk, I guess, would be the order of the day, but he omits to tell his readers the material he used. I would want something billowing,

similar to parachute material, which would move with the draughts each time the door was opened. This would be back-lit with uplighters. The rest of the room would be painted in matt and lacquer, black, of course. The chairs would be black, as would the table linen; and there would be black candles in black cast candelabras (the only other form of lighting save the uplighters). The flower arrangements would be black tulips, if available - violets if not. Whereas Des Esseintes must have had his dinner in summer, mine would be in winter, as there are more black ingredients available at that time of year. (Shame about the tulips, but you never know, it's marvellous what the Dutch can produce.)

As with Des Esseintes, there would be a hidden orchestra playing funeral marches - and some Leonard Cohen. I remember at school being almost suicidal having to listen to my study mate constantly playing Cohen, not very uplifting. Des Esseintes has negresses wearing only slippers and stockings serving the dinner; nice idea, but I'm not so sure Hillingdon council would approve. Maybe Whitney Houston and Grace Jones would agree to do a celebrity stint as floor staff. I'd be willing to train them.

On to the food. Des Esseintes enjoyed turtle soup, Russian rye bread, ripe black olives, caviar, mullet botargo, black puddings, game 'served in sauces the colour of liquorice and boot polish', truffle jellies, chocolate creams, plum puddings, pears in grape juice, mulberries and black-heart cherries, a fair mixture of seasons but a great dinner nevertheless. My extravaganza would start with Champagne and Guinness (Black Velvet): the Champagne (apologies to Moët and Chandon) would be Dom Perignon - a sexy Champagne, a sexy bottle and fitting well into my black theme. The mixture with Guinness would not be my first choice, as I prefer Murphy's, but availability over this side of the water is not so great. (I wish Guinness would spend more on their product over here, and less on smoothie-chops advertising the product.)

With the Black Velvet would come a mouthful of pan-fried black pudding on a mash of puréed black beans, with a scattering of diced pickled walnuts. To follow, a large tin of Sevruga caviar, Beluga if you must, set in a large block of frozen Quink black ink (I'm assuming it freezes) which would be served with black bread. An inter-course could be a mousse of *foie gras* encapsulated in a dark wild mushroom jelly lined with truffle slices. The fish course would follow: a small portion of the risotto nero with some delicious grated botargo on top. (Botargo is the dried and salted roe of the grey mullet.) For the meat course, following Des Esseintes' route, I would serve game - a woodcock salmis, served with a Mexican-inspired sauce, molé, which uses chocolate to intensify and add silkiness to the texture. A little braised cavolo nero, the Italian black cabbage, would accompany the bird. After that blow-out, a few dark berries collected over the season and macerated in vodka and Cassis - mulberries, blackcurrants, blueberries and blackberries. All the food would, of course, be served on black china, and the liquid substance in dark-tinted glasses. Naff, I know, but they go with the theme.

For this fantasy dinner, guests would assemble in front of the black marble surround of a roaring log fire, all dressed in black, of course. I might have trouble in persuading one or two of them to wear black, especially the oldies, but my fantasy guests would have, for once, to do as they were told. My seven guests would be Kim Philby, Sinead O'Connor, Lord Montgomery, Barbara Cartland, Jack Nicholson, Cher and Jodie Foster, chosen to create a night of controversy and uproar. Philby and Montgomery were my distant cousins, on different sides of the Park, I assume. (I would be fascinated to see what they thought of each other, would it be pistols at dawn?) From all accounts from spending many hours listening at the feet of my grandfather, Montgomery was a very difficult man, a real prima donna, contrasting with Philby who was a real charmer, apparently. I have pictures of him as a child playing games with my mother and uncle.

Barbara Cartland would be appalled by the company, I'm sure, but it would be interesting to see her in black instead of one of her bright pink numbers. Her powder-puff, candyfloss complexion and extended eyelashes would be kind of spooky in the sombre surroundings. (I would love to see her face when the naked negresses started serving dinner.) If she passed the first course, there would be voracious debate between her, Jack Nicholson and Cher. Sinead O'Connor would have a healthy input, especially when it came to religion, as we hold similar views. I get the feeling she's the type of girl who won't take no for an answer. Cher would be the perfect witch for the occasion and, with her blatant sexuality, offer a stark contrast to the almost innocent aura of Jodie Foster. Jodie Foster is the one person on the guest list whom I would love to meet and get to know. During the evening when debates were at their loudest, I would sneak away and give her a quick cookery lesson or something. I think she's the most brilliant young woman of our times.

It would certainly be a lively evening. Whether there would be any guests remaining by the time coffee was served is another story.

Serves 8

BLACK VELVET

For each glass, pour 5fl oz (150ml) stout into a half pint glass and fill with Champagne. Do this very carefully so that the stout and Champagne don't mix.

BLACK PUDDING WITH PICKLED WALNUTS

1oz (25g) dripping or butter
8 x ¾in (2cm) slices black pudding (preferably a soft variety)
2 shallots, peeled and finely chopped
2fl oz (60ml) walnut oil
1fl oz (30ml) corn oil
1 apple, peeled, cored and cut into ¼in (5mm) dice
4 pickled walnuts, cut into ¼in (5mm) dice
4 tablespoons chopped parsley
1 fl oz (30ml) cider vinegar
salt and freshly ground black pepper
8oz (225g) Black Bean Purée (see below)

Heat the dripping or butter in a large frying pan. Place the black pudding slices in the pan, not overlapping (cook in two batches, if necessary). Cook over a medium heat for 2 minutes each side. The slices should be slightly crusty. Remove and set aside, discarding any tough skin.

In the same pan add the shallots and oils, and cook until soft but not brown. Add the apple, cook for a further 2 minutes, then add the walnuts and the parsley. Pour in the cider vinegar and amalgamate with the other ingredients. Season to taste with salt and black pepper.

Warm through the black bean purée and place a spoonful on each of eight warmed plates. Top with a slice of black pudding and garnish with the warm walnut vinaigrette. Serve immediately.

BLACK BEAN PURÉE

Soak 1lb (450g) black turtle beans overnight in cold water. Place the beans in a large pan with a roughly chopped onion, a carrot and a celery stalk, 3 teaspoons chopped garlic, 4oz (100g) roughly chopped ham, 1 clove, 1 sprig thyme and 1 bay leaf. Cover with cold water or chicken stock, bring to the boil and simmer until the beans are soft (approximately 2 hours), adding more stock if necessary to keep the beans covered. Drain the beans and remove the clove, thyme and bay leaf. Put the beans through a medium fine food mill. Mix the resulting purée with 1 tablespoon ground cumin and ½ tablespoon chilli powder. Return the purée to the heat and add 5fl oz (150ml) soured cream. Season with salt and black pepper to taste.

SEVRUGA CAVIAR WITH BLACK BREAD

See the Valentine's Day menu on page 18. Serve an 18oz (500g) tin of Sevruga set in a block of frozen black Quink ink with black bread. Give each guest a bone spoon to serve themselves.

FOIE GRAS MOUSSE SET IN BLACK TRUFFLE JELLY

1lb (450g) duck foie gras or duck livers, gall bladder removed, cut into ½in (1cm) cubes
4oz (100g) unsalted butter
1 onion, peeled and finely chopped
2 cloves garlic, peeled and finely chopped
½ teaspoon soft thyme leaves
2¼ pints (1.3 litres) cèpe broth (see page 50)
5fl oz (150ml) sweet wine, such as Sauternes or Muscat de Beaumes de Venise
2 tablespoons small capers
4 anchovy fillets
salt and freshly ground black pepper
14 leaves gelatine
3 x 2oz (50g) black truffles, peeled and thinly sliced
chives to garnish

Heat the butter in a frying pan and over a medium heat, cook the onion, garlic and thyme until soft but not brown. Tip the mixture including butter into the bowl of a processor. Place the same pan over a high heat and add the *foie gras*. Cook for 2 minutes, turning regularly (7 minutes if duck liver). Place the *foie gras* and any discharged fats in the food processor. Deglaze the frying pan with 5fl oz (150ml) of *cèpe* broth and the sweet wine, scraping any grungy bits from the bottom. Over a high heat reduce the juices until you are left with approximately ⅙ pint (100ml). Pour this liquid into the food processor. Add the capers and the anchovies and purée the mixture until almost smooth. Season to taste with salt and black pepper. You shouldn't need much salt because of the inclusion of anchovies in the recipe.

SETTING THE MOUSSE IN JELLY

Allow the leaves of gelatine to bloom in cold water (the leaves will swell up and become soft without melting). Whilst the leaves are softening (this takes about half an hour) heat the remaining *cèpe* broth. Add the gelatine to the broth and stir well to blend into the stock. Take 8 dariole moulds and set them in crushed ice in a tray. Pour in the stock until it comes up to the rim. Place the tray of moulds in the fridge and chill for 15 minutes. At the end of this time there should be a ¼in (5mm) layer of jelly set on the walls of each mould. Pour out the remainder of the liquid in the moulds and discard or use for another recipe. Line the interior of the jelly with slices of truffle so that the jelly is totally covered with truffle. If this extravagance means an extra bank loan, place truffle slices only on the bottom of the mould. (Adjust the ingredient quantities accordingly.) Spoon the soft mousse into the moulds, filling them to the top. Smooth the top with a knife or palette knife. Tap the moulds lightly on a hard surface to remove any air bubbles. Refrigerate overnight.

FINAL PREPARATION AND PRESENTATION

Dip each mould briefly in hot water to loosen the jelly. Turn the moulds out onto eight cold black plates. Garnish each plate with a criss-cross of whole chives and serve with Crostini (see page 166) made with black instead of French bread.

RISOTTO NERO WITH GRATED BOTARGO

4oz (100g) unsalted butter, cut in small cubes
6 shallots, peeled and finely chopped
1 clove garlic, peeled and finely chopped
1 teaspoon soft thyme leaves
1lb (450g) Arborio or risotto rice
½ bottle dry white wine
1 dessertspoon tomato purée
3½ pints (2 litres) light Fish Stock (see page 131) or water, heated
6 sachets cuttlefish ink
salt and freshly ground black pepper
lemon juice
8oz (225g) botargo (dried grey mullet roe), grated (optional)

Heat half the butter in a deep heavy-based saucepan. Add the shallots, garlic and thyme leaves and cook over a medium heat until soft but not brown. Add the rice, toss with the shallot mix and cook until the rice becomes opaque and pearly and smells slightly nutty. Add the white wine in one hit and stir to emulsify with the rice. When the rice has absorbed the majority of the liquid, add the tomato purée and a ladleful of the boiling stock or water; allow the liquid to be absorbed, and repeat ladle by ladle until the rice is nearly cooked (about 20 minutes). Add the sachets of squid ink and stir thoroughly. During the cooking process, stir continually, making sure the rice does not catch on the bottom of the pan. Season to taste with salt, black pepper and lemon juice. Fold in the remaining butter and scatter the top of the risotto evenly with grated botargo. (A nice idea, but as most of you won't be able to find botargo, I suggest thin strips of pan-fried squid as an alternative.)

Serve immediately in eight hot black bowls.

SALMIS OF WOODCOCK ON FIELD MUSHROOMS WITH MOLE SAUCE

8 woodcock, uneviscerated, wrapped in thin sheets of pork fat, 3in (7.5cm) square, or streaky bacon
3oz (75g) unsalted butter
8 large field mushrooms
Braised Cavolo Nero (see below)
2 tablespoons chopped parsley
1 tablespoon grated orange zest

Molé Sauce

2 carrots, peeled and roughly chopped
2 onions, peeled and roughly chopped
3 cloves garlic, peeled and smashed
1 celery stalk, roughly chopped
2 bay leaves
2 red chillies, seeded and chopped
1 sprig thyme
1 teaspoon ground black peppercorns
3 cloves
½ cinnamon stick
1 teaspoon toasted coriander seeds
½ teaspoon toasted cumin seeds
1oz (25g) unsalted butter
1oz (25g) plain flour mixed with ½oz (15g) cocoa powder
2fl oz (60ml) brandy
18fl oz (500ml) gutsy red wine, such as Cahors or Zinfandel
1 pint (600ml) Chicken Stock (see page 91)
1oz (25g) dark chocolate
salt and freshly ground black pepper

Preheat the oven to 400°F/200°C/Gas 6. Roast the woodcocks for 12 minutes on a rack. Allow to cool and then cut off the legs and breasts; remove the thighs by cutting between the thigh and drumstick. Eviscerate the birds and remove the livers. Set aside the livers, the breasts and the thighs.

For the sauce, chop the remaining carcass and innards and return to the roasting pan with the carrots, onions, garlic, celery, bay leaves, chillies, thyme, black peppercorns, cloves, cinnamon, coriander seeds, cumin seeds and the butter. Sprinkle the ingredients with the flour and cocoa mix. Return to the oven and roast for 30 minutes or until nicely browned. Deglaze with the brandy and ignite. Put it all, along with any juices, into a medium saucepan. Deglaze the roasting tray with the red wine, scraping up any coagulated matter. Pour the resulting juices into the saucepan with the other ingredients. Add the stock to this pan and bring to the boil over a medium heat. When it boils, reduce the heat and simmer for 1 hour. Pass the mixture through a food mill or fine sieve, rubbing through all the ingredients to get the best of the flavours. The resulting liquid should be reasonably thick. The sauce can be made ahead to this point.

About 30 minutes before you are ready to serve, reheat the sauce and add the dark chocolate. Do not re-boil, simply stir until the chocolate has blended into the sauce. Season to taste. Remove from the heat and pop in the woodcock breasts and thighs.

Meanwhile cook the mushrooms and the cavolo nero. For the mushrooms, heat a large frying pan, add the remaining butter and pop in the mushrooms, gill-side down. Season with salt and black pepper, cover and cook over a medium heat for 10 minutes. Remove the cover and turn the mushrooms, season again and repeat the cooking procedure for a further 10 minutes. Keep the mushrooms warm.

PRESENTATION

Place a mushroom on each of eight black plates and top each with 2 woodcock breasts and thighs. Sprinkle with parsley and orange zest.

Braised Cavolo Nero

2½lb (1.1kg) cavolo nero or Savoy cabbage
3 tablespoons extra virgin olive oil
2 cloves garlic, peeled and finely chopped
1 shallot, peeled and finely chopped
1 red chilli, seeded and finely chopped
1 teaspoon soft thyme leaves
salt and freshly ground black pepper

Remove any damaged leaves and thick stalks from the cabbage. Cut the leaves into thin strips. Blanch the leaves in plenty of boiling salted water for 4 minutes. Drain well pushing out any excess water.

Heat the olive oil in a saucepan over a medium heat and add the garlic, shallot, chilli and thyme and cook until soft but not brown. Add the cabbage and stir to combine. Cook for a further 5 minutes and season to taste with pepper. Serve separately.

BLACK FRUITS IN CASSIS AND VODKA

3lb (1.4kg) each of mulberries (if you find them), blackcurrants, blueberries and blackberries
2 pints (1.1 litres) vodka
1 pint (600ml) Cassis
caster sugar

This mixture takes all summer and autumn to prepare and any fruit can be used, including the above, as well as peaches, pears, nectarines and oranges, etc.

Use a large earthenware crock and pour vodka and Cassis into the bottom. After removing the stems, add fruits as they come into season; they should be washed and dried. Add their weights in caster sugar each time.

Keep the crock covered and give it a good stir every other day. The fruit will start to ferment, giving out a strong heady aroma. When all the fruits have been prepared, pour them with their juices into Kilner jars and seal. They will keep for at least a year.

ESPRESSO RISTRETTO WITH BLACK RUSSIAN

Make some very strong coffee and serve everyone about 1oz (25ml) each in tiny coffee cups. Accompany with a Black Russian - two-thirds vodka, one-third Kahlua built into an ice-filled, Old-Fashioned glass.

WINE NOTES

Black wine? Cahors was once described as such, but since the wines needed all of fifty years to become drinkable, the producers changed grape varieties and vinification. 1988 Château Eugénie is the best of the new kind, but black it ain't.

Barbaresco by Angelo Gaja might fit the bill, dark wine, black and white label. His Sori Tildin or Sori San Lorenzo would certainly be the perfect wine for risotto and the salmis of woodcock.

But black is Russian and although Moldavia has since seceded from the old USSR, Moldavia has the right wine: Negru de Purkar. Black wine,

with an extraordinary label as way out as this kinky dinner. The 1978 can be bought from Avery's in Bristol or from André Simon shops in London.

Back to the beginning: Black Velvet made with Dom Perignon should take you through the black pudding. Then vodka (with ink?) for the caviar, followed by some more Dom Perignon with the foie gras, but this time with Crème de Mûres instead of Guinness. This should give a slight sweetness, which will do well with the goose liver, and then Negru de Purkar. After that, black Alka-Seltzer, if you can find it ...

INGREDIENT GLOSSARY

There will be some of you who are unfamiliar with some of the ingredients I have listed. Below are a few which may be a problem, with substitutes where possible.

ORIENTAL INGREDIENTS

Bok Choy: A member of the cabbage family, originating from China, and looking similar to spring greens, with bright green stems and spinach-type leaves. Good blanched and chargrilled. As a substitute, spring greens or, if you wish to use the stems mainly, broccoli.

Dashi: A clear soup made from dried bonito flakes and seaweed (kelp). Instant *dashi* is available from Japanese stores. It is an essential part of Japanese cooking for as well as being served as a soup it doubles up as a stock base, and is an integral part of many of their sauces. I have explained how to make *dashi* on page 43, but the powdered version is very acceptable.

Dried Bonito Flakes: Fillets of bonito, a member of the mackerel family, are dried and then shaved. Packaged dried bonito is called *hana-katsuo*, and is available in Japanese food shops.

Hoisin Sauce: A sweet, spicy, reddish-brownish thick sauce often served with crispy duck, spring onions, cucumber and pancakes in your local Chinese restaurant. It is made from soy beans, garlic and spices. It is a difficult ingredient to substitute, but under pressure I would go for a Chinese plum sauce.

Katchap Manis: A sauce which has nothing to do with tomato ketchup. It is a milder, sweeter form of soy sauce from Indonesia, and is now available from several branches of Sainsbury's. As a substitute I suggest regular soy with a little honey.

Kelp (Kombu): A Japanese seaweed available dried from health shops in broad greyish-green strips. It's used in a variety of Japanese recipes including *dashi* and sushi rice. It keeps forever. If you can't find it, substitute another strong dried seaweed.

Nam Pla: A thin, salty, brown sauce widely used in South-East Asian cooking, commonly known as fish sauce. It is used to highlight flavours in other foods. Made by salting fish in wooden barrels. As the fish dries the salt extracts a clear liquid which is the fish sauce. A substitute can be made by using light soy sauce with grilled shrimp paste. In emergencies a light soy on its own will do.

Nori: The commonest seaweed used by the Japanese, most often for wrapping sushi. A type of laverbread, it comes in greeny-purple sheets approximately 8in (20cm) square. In its dried form, the *nori* should be freshened by toasting over a gas flame or under a grill. This is done by waving the sheet over a flame two or three times. No real substitute, but for the same effect in the scallop dish (see page 44), blanched spinach leaves can be used.

Oyster Sauce: Widely available from most supermarkets, and used to add flavour to various sauces. Made from oysters that have been cooked in soy sauce and brine. There are no real substitutes, but it can be kept indefinitely.

Wakame: A type of seaweed which is sold dry. In its dry state it looks a rather unappealing brown colour, but when soaked turns bright green. It is extremely good for you and can be used with a dressing in salads.

Wasabi Powder: A powerful green horseradish sold in powdered form, and reconstituted like Colman's yellow mustard powder by the addition of cold water. A unique taste, the Japanese use it in its made-up form to accompany sashimi and in constructing their sushi rolls.

Won-ton Wrappers: Small squares of fresh noodle dough available in Asian food stores. As a substitute, but giving a different finish, use filo pastry, and cut it to size.

ITALIAN INGREDIENTS

Mascarpone: This is a rich creamy cheese originating in Lodi in the Lombardy region. Lovely served as a cheese course, it has a sweetened taste and is famously used in *tiramisú*, which is a cream cheese and rum 'trifle' with hints of coffee and chocolate. Mixed together with sugar and alcohol, Mascarpone is often served as a cream or crème fraîche substitute with fruits.

Pancetta: This is the Italian equivalent of our unsmoked streaky bacon, but is it? Pancetta costs a lot more, but it is a much superior product. Mainly used in cooking, it is occasionally seen on *antipasti* tables usually in the guise of speck. It is a speciality of the Piacenza region, and for my money it's well worth paying the extra.

Prosciutto di Parma: Translated as Parma ham, it comes from the Bologna region. Ham is salted and left for a few weeks to allow the natural juices to evaporate. The salt is then washed off and the ham is hung, for up to fifteen months, in a cool dry environment. When buying Parma ham, insist on it being cut paper thin and before cutting make sure the salesman first removes the rind. It is also important that the slices do not overlap as you'll have a nightmare of a task trying to separate each slice.

Sun-dried Tomatoes: One of the by-words for Californian or modern Italian cooking. A trendy ingredient that appears to be surviving the ups and downs of food fashions. Can come in two varieties: totally dried, which need soaking in olive oil; or bottled in olive oil. They are useful products, condensing the sweet flavour of sun-ripened tomatoes. Great in salads or in slow-cooked casseroles, or on *pizzas* and *bruschettas*. Our summer sun is not strong enough to make your own, but there is another method that is widely used. Cut the tomatoes in two horizontally, remove some of the seeds and lightly salt the cavity. Place the tomatoes cut side down on a rack and drain for 30 minutes. Sprinkle the tomatoes with a few Provençal herbs and place on a rack in the oven at the lowest setting. These are cooked for approximately 8 hours, or overnight, until they become shrivelled and most of the liquids have been extracted. Allow to cool, then bottle in good olive oil with a sprig of thyme, a couple of garlic cloves and a chilli. Use as required.

Taleggio Cheese: An Italian cheese from northern Italy. It is soft and creamy when young, and firms up and attains a stronger flavour when older. It retains its lush velvety texture throughout its lifetime, however. It belongs to the class of cheese the Italians call *stracchini*. A very good cheese eaten raw, but equally good in cooking. Substitutes are never the same, but for cooking purposes a Mozzarella or even a Gruyère would do.

CREAMS

I've mentioned Mascarpone, but there are a huge variety of substitutes for our rather boring double, whipping and single creams. While mentioning these products I should point out that these ratings refer to the fat content which is usually 48 per cent for double, 30 per cent for whipping and 18 per cent for single. It's the fat content that makes them rich and moreish: the higher the fat, the more likely you are to take extra helpings. When cooking use double cream, especially if you want to boil or reduce the sauce, as using a cream with a lower fat content can often cause the sauce to split. Other cream substitutes include the following.

Clotted Cream: My favourite, the richest of all creams, and unique to Great Britain, especially the south-west. It's the perfect accompaniment to scones, summer fruits and sticky puddings.

Crème Fraîche: A thick, slightly soured cream originating in France, but now widely available in the UK. Good in cooking, but as many chefs in France import our double cream, I should stick to what you know.

Greek Yogurt: As a child I used to hate plain yogurt, but had I known about this rich creamy variety, I'm sure it would have been a different story. Has increased in popularity enormously over the last few years. It is, however, important to choose your brand carefully, as there are many poor imitations available. A breakfast favourite of mine, especially with sliced banana, honey and a sprinkling of bran.

Soured Cream: Excellent in cooking. Time was when you'd only see it on top of Hungarian goulash, but it's now used in many forms of day-to-day cookery - salads, jacket potatoes, potato skins, smoked salmon and blinis, caviar ... the list goes on.

VINEGARS

The *Nouvelle Cuisine* days brought a fashion for fruit-flavoured vinegars, with raspberry being the most popular. While most of these have now disappeared, this period did introduce us to choice. There was a time when variety was limited, with cider and tarragon vinegars being luxuries. No longer do we have to put up with dull factory-produced red, white and malt, as quality and variety are now available. Most popular in these food-trend times is undoubtedly balsamic vinegar, but like anything else there's good and bad. A good balsamic should be matured for at least ten years, but nowadays a cheap one might be matured for only one or two, and then it might never see a wooden barrel. The best comes from Modena in the Bologna region, where the vinegar is transferred yearly from barrel to barrel, each being made from a different wood; this builds up wonderful aromas, unique to the finer arts of vinegar making. Beware, the price can be silly, with very old vinegars costing more than a better vintage of Château Mouton-Rothschild. Enough said about balsamic, save to say that it's good and a little goes a long way: use in dressings, on fruit, on cooked offal or with poultry.

Another vinegar growing in popularity is sherry vinegar which has similar qualities. Again it's aged in sherry barrels which give it its unique sherry flavouring - very powerful.

In one or two recipes I suggest aged red wine vinegar, which also has a strong depth of flavour. It is difficult to find, so adding a dash of a chunky red wine to normal red wine vinegar isn't quite the same, but it does remove some of the harsh acidity normally associated with cheaper varieties.

Rice vinegar is another variety that gets more mentions in cookery nowadays. Although Asians have been using it for centuries, it has only recently captured the attention of the western public. Buy from an Asian store where possible, otherwise you're quite likely to get ripped off for what in essence is a cheap product. Go for the Japanese variety rather than the Chinese, as it has a much smoother, more mellow, almost sweet taste. Makes excellent dressings especially when combined with sesame oil.

SALAD LEAVES AND HERBS

What happened to the good old days when we had little or no choice - round, Cos or Webbs, quickly followed by iceberg? But they weren't really the good old days, not when there are now so many exciting varieties to choose from. Here follows a quick alphabetical run-down of my favourites.

Arugula: Also known as roquette, rocket, rugula, or rucola. Probably the trendiest of all the restaurant salad leaves, but try buying it in a supermarket and you'll find they're still treating it like a herb: a few paltry leaves wrapped delicately in see-through bags and being sold for silly money. No, what you want is a big bowl of the stuff, dressed simply in your best olive oil with just a squeeze of lemon, enhancing its delicate, spicy, peppery flavour. An essential addition to a *mesclun* or salad of mixed leaves. Easy to grow.

Basil: Don't leave home without it. 'The' herb to impart summer to a dull-grey day, it comes in many varieties, sweet, purple, French and lemon. Excellent with tomatoes, and of course essential to pesto or pistou, words now firmly implanted in the English culinary language.

Belgian Endive: Known to the Brits as chicory and to some foreigners as *witloof* (white leaf). Grown in total darkness to retain a compact head of long, thin, white leaves with pale yellow tips. It has a crunchy texture and a mildly bitter flavour. Never buy when the tips are green: this usually means that it is old and the

greengrocer has exposed it for too long to daylight. Daylight imparts an ever-so-strong, almost inedible bitterness. Also good in cooking.

Borage: A slightly furry herb with beautiful cobalt-blue flowers. Excellent as an addition to a salad as the leaves have a taste reminiscent of cucumber. Older Brits would normally associate this with the jungle that garnishes the top of a Pimms, but nowadays mint tends to have replaced borage. Once it has found its roots in the garden, there is no stopping it, it comes up year after year.

Chervil: A delicate, sweet, aromatic herb with an anise-like flavour - excellent in salads.

Chives: A relative of the onion with grass-like leaves in deep green. Produces beautiful purple and white flowers which have an even more oniony taste than the leaves. Garlic chives are found in Asian shops and as the name suggests have a flavour of garlic. Chives are easy to grow and ideally should be grown in a rose-bed. Roses can't stand their smell, so in order to combat this nuisance, they go out of their way to produce an even stronger scent of their own!

Coriander: Also known as cilantro or Chinese parsley, this is another 'in' herb, usually associated with Asian cooking. Use sparingly as it has a really kick-ass flavour. Also used in Mexican cooking in dishes like the famous *ceviche*, a salad of raw marinated fish.

Dandelion: Also known as *piss-en-lit*, familiar to most Brits as a weed with incredibly long roots. Excellent on its own as a salad with lardons and croûtons. It has a prominent bitter taste which is even stronger in the dark green variety; I prefer the pale yellow, or bleached leaves. Excellent source of vitamins and minerals, especially iron.

Dill: A herb with a feathery, blue-green foliage similar to fennel, with a strong anise flavour. Excellent in salads, but widely known for its use in flavouring *gravadlax*, the marinated salmon of Scandinavia.

Edible Flowers: I'm not a great fan of flowers in salads, but a few stand out as acceptable: arugula, borage, nasturtium and chive. But as for pansies and violets, they are far more suited to a vase, or woven into someone's hair ... that's the ageing hippie in me.

Escarole: Not widely found, but sometimes known as Batavian endive. Similar in flavour to chicory, or curly leaf endive. A good-flavoured salad leaf.

Fiddlehead Ferns: Rarely, if ever, seen in the UK, but if you get the opportunity to eat them, you'll enjoy the experience. Widely available in season in the USA, they are the newest growth fronds on the centre of ferns. Can be eaten raw with a vinaigrette or steamed with hollandaise. A nutty taste, similar in texture to asparagus.

Greens: More associated with USA, but have recently become popular in the menu phraseology 'Wilted Greens'. Can be eaten raw in salads, but tend to need blanching to remove the bitterness. They include beet greens, mustard greens, rape, chard, carrot tops, turnip and radish greens.

Lollo Rosso: Definitely not a favourite - yuk, is all I can say - a tasteless designer leaf, far more suitable in a flower arrangement than to be seen socialising with some of the user-friendly leaves. AWT restaurants are definitely lollo rosso-free zones.

Lovage: A herb tasting of celery. Use young leaves for salads, but once old, their flavour becomes too strong, so only use sparingly in soups, stocks and stews.

Mâche: Also known as corn salad or lamb's lettuce. A small, deep-green round to oval leaf with a mild flavour. Boring on its own but useful as a component for a leaf salad. Widely used in *Nouvelle Cuisine* days for its uniform shape to circle plates - a discipline of the 80s, but a waste of time in the 90s. Wash well, as it tends to be very sandy.

Marjoram: A more refined cousin of oregano, it has a small grey-green leaf with a sweet pungent flavour. Use sparingly in salads or salsas.

Mint: A tart in a vicar's world, probably on a par with parsley as the most widely used herb. When you think how many different products it flavours then it's probably the No. 1 (toothpaste, chocolates, chewing gum, ice creams, etc.). Over forty different varieties - no need to say more.

Nasturtium Leaves: Young leaves are excellent in salads, giving hints of pepper. Easy to grow, hard to buy.

Parsley: A herb with a variety of uses, most widely found in the curly variety, but the flat leaf has a better flavour. Very rich in Vitamins A and C, excellent for removing garlic breath and, I've read, a good cure for baldness. Now I can't be eating enough ...

Radicchio: Also known as red chicory. A compact cabbage-like head of red leaves with a bitter taste; used in all modern leaf salads, but also excellent grilled with olive oil and a little balsamic vinegar.

Salad Burnet: A herb with a taste of cucumber. It's funny how everyone says cucumber tastes of nothing but here we have at least two herbs tasting of cucumber ... strange. Good in salads, easy to grow, but hard to find in the shops.

Sorrel: A similar leaf shape to spinach but a totally different taste - more acidic and lemony. When cooked, while spinach keeps its shape and colouring, sorrel breaks down quickly to a purée. Use sparingly as the taste can be very overpowering. Rich in Vitamin C.

Spinach: Use baby spinach in salads as the larger variety tends to be tough in its raw state. If cooking, I prefer the New Zealand variety which has a higher proportion of leaf to stalk; wash well as it seems to grow in muddy conditions. Rich in iron.

Watercress: One of my favourite salad leaves: it's excellent for health, as well as having a delicious peppery taste. Available all year, but when buying make sure the leaves are bright green as it deteriorates quickly. Normally stored in cardboard cartons packed in ice.

OILS

Olive oil plays a large part in the Mediterranean style of cooking served in some of our restaurants. I've even named a restaurant dell'Ugo after the famous oil made by Amici Grosso, but apart from olive oil, there are many other oils that play a part in cookery as a whole. Here are a selection that I regularly use.

Chilli Oil: Also called red pepper oil, it is made from an infusion of spicy hot red peppers in either vegetable or sesame oil. The best is one made from sesame oil called Aji Oil from Japan which, as well as being very hot, has a certain fragrance and elegance. Chilli oil keeps indefinitely when stored in the dark and away from the heat. You can also make excellent chilli oil at home (see page 123).

Corn Oil: A bland oil used when you don't want any flavour to permeate the food. Ultimately you should buy a cold-pressed 100 per cent corn oil. A good oil for frying and for making blander mayonnaise-based sauces.

Grapeseed Oil: A lightweight, very pale oil favoured by the French for cooking purposes. It has a mild nutty flavour, and makes a pleasant salad dressing.

Hazelnut Oil: Similar in style to walnut oil, and not to be used neat. When mixed with milder oil or an olive oil, it makes a good dressing to accompany bitter greens. It has a short life-span so buy small quantities and keep refrigerated.

Herb Oils: These flavoured oils can be produced at home. You can use olive oil, or a milder variety. Mix 1 pint (600ml) oil with 4 tablespoons chopped herbs of your choice. Allow the flavours to infuse for fourteen days, turning the jar from time to time. After this period of time strain the oil into another bottle. The flavoured oil will keep for about two months.

Olive Oil: There are so many varieties on the market that it is up to you to discover one to your liking. As a general rule you do not need an expensive first pressing oil for cooking, a good second or third pressing will do. Extra virgin olive oil should be reserved for dressings or for finishing off dishes in the same way as you might use butter. My favourite extra virgin olive oil is undoubtedly dell'Ugo, which has a peppery rustic roughness about it, with a mysterious cloudy, pond-green disposition. I often drink a spoonful of it without any attachments ... strange how one falls in love with certain produce.

Safflower Oil: A very healthy, but not a slimming oil. High in polyunsaturates, it's supposed to break down cholesterol; it is very pale and very bland. Good for cooking, but it is also capable of making very light salad dressings.

Sesame Oil: Two varieties are available, a light and mild oil made from raw white sesame seeds, and the dark Asian variety made from toasted sesame seeds. The dark variety can be overpowering and should be mixed with milder oils for dressings, but can be very effective in cooked dishes.

Walnut Oil: In a similar vein to hazelnut oil, this is a wonderfully extravagant oil with a highly potent taste and perfume. Excellent for salad dressings although, as with hazelnut, I prefer to mix it with milder oils. Does not keep well.

White Truffle Oil: An unbelievable oil at an unbelievable price, mortgage stuff this one, but it is magic: a few drops added to mashed potatoes or a risotto sends one into seventh heaven. But beware, there are versions on the market which are often flavoured with chemicals. It's a highly perfumed number, worth paying the extra for.

MISCELLANEOUS INGREDIENTS

Agen Prunes: These are the best, other brands just will not do. They come from the Garonne valley in south-west France, and the town of Agen is the chief distribution area. They are of course just dried plums, but what plums! These are the *crème de la crème* of plums, grown on a special tree called *prunier d'ente*. To use the prunes they have to be rehydrated, and traditionally the French would do this in an infusion of dried lime blossom (*tilleul*), but if you don't own a lime tree than soak them in tea.

Botargo: This is the dried roe of grey mullet, very popular in Portugal and Spain. It has a very hard texture which makes it easy to grate over a salad or risotto. It would be quite difficult to substitute for botargo: although there are a few hard roe alternatives, they haven't quite got the same luxurious taste.

Cavolo Nero: An Italian 'black' cabbage. Can be grown easily in the UK, but rarely found in the shops. As an alternative I would suggest the simple old Savoy cabbage, John Major's favourite vegetable.

Cuttlefish Ink: One of the 'in' dishes of recent times has been risotto nero (see page 179), which uses cuttlefish ink to give it a potent fishy taste and its distinctive black colour. You will find this ink in a little pouch inside the body. Be very careful in trying to remove the sac intact, because if it bursts you've got a nightmare on your hands, and everywhere else for that matter. Far easier is to locate a fishmonger, or more likely Harrods, who will sell you ink separately in man-made pouches; unfortunately there is no real substitute.

Goat's Cheese: I use two varieties of goat's cheese in the text. A harder Crottin de Chavignol and a soft goat's cheese log. *Crottin* means dung, not a fair description, but Crottin de Chavignol is a local French term for a fully ripened goat's cheese. Unfortunately many that one can buy nowadays are very young. Crottin de Chavignol was hardly ever found in England until the *Nouvelle Cuisine* era when it became popular as part of a warm salad.

When I need a softer goat's cheese I turn to my favourite, Gedi, which is made on a small farm in Britain, not far from London. The boss of this farm is a giant of a man with long grey hair and an even longer grey beard. They do say that humans end up looking like their pets, in this case, very appropriate ... If you can't find Gedi, then choose another soft goat's cheese which you like.

Harissa: This is to Morocco and Algeria what tomato purée is to western souls. It is a strong chilli paste imported from Tunisia, and its only substitute is *sambal oelek* from Indonesia. I suppose under pressure you could add chilli oil or Tabasco to a tomato purée, but the effect wouldn't be quite the same. However, the good news is that you can make it at home. Take 2oz (50g) dried red chilli peppers and soak them in hot water for 1 hour. Drain them and cut them into small pieces. Pound them in a mortar with 2 peeled garlic cloves until you have a purée. Sprinkle with a little salt, then bottle and cover with a layer of oil. Refrigerated, it will keep for a few months.

Lentilles du Puy: Not just any old lentils, by now you'll have understood that where possible I only use the best. These are tiny lentils, again from France, which are sometimes called blue lentils. They are, in fact, in their dried state more of a speckled browny-green, but catch them in the right light with a certain amount of imagination, and I suppose they could be blue. Apart from their petiteness, the good thing about Puy lentils is that they don't fall apart when cooked. For substitutes, if you must, then the brown or green standard lentils will do, but be careful, because turn your attention away at the wrong time during the cooking process, and you could end up with a mushy mess.

Liquid Smoke: A strange one this ... and American product widely used over there when they want to simulate barbecued food. It is available from Harrods or from a new American shop called, surprisingly, The American Shop in New King's Road, London. Only a few drops are required for a pretty good interpretation of an authentic taste.

Plum Tomatoes: I regularly spout off about my dislike for hot-house Canary or Dutch tomatoes. They were created to satisfy the alleged customer demand for perfectly shaped tomatoes. Unfortunately, unless sun gets to tomatoes and ripens them naturally, they end up with little or no taste. A well-bred tomato has a sweet powerful flavour. I and many other chefs resorted to using Italian plum tomatoes in our search for quality. When we started buying them they were craggy, odd shapes with warts and all sorts of imperfections, but we knew they were going to taste wonderful. We could make flavourful sauces without having to resort to the tin - purée, that is. Unfortunately, as fashions catch on, so standards tend to slip, and now the Californians produce these perfect plum tomatoes that, surprise, surprise, have very little flavour. So what's the answer? Grow your own I suppose, given that we occasionally have a summer, or insist on the Italian variety or those from the South of France.

The good news, however, is that supermarkets are catching on to your new taste requirements, and are now insisting that growers find them varieties that have some depth of flavour.

Swiss Chard: Also called chard, leaf beet, sea kale beet, silver beet, white beet and spinach beet. Poor thing, it must be terribly insecure having all those names. If you like spinach, then you'll love Swiss chard. It has large green leaves and fleshy stalks which resemble flattened celery. The leaves and the stalks are generally cooked separately. It doesn't keep well so make sure you only buy the freshest available. Pan-frying is often the best way to cook it as it tends to retain its flavour. Excellent as a vegetable or as a cooked salad served with a little lemon juice, olive oil, pine nuts, garlic and a few raisins. In France they cook the stems in stock which is thickened with a roux and seasoned with garlic and anchovies.

Chard needs washing well as it tends to be very gritty, and unless the stalks are very small they need the strings removed in a similar vein to celery. More benefits follow: it is very low in calories and is a good source of Vitamin A, potassium, iron, Vitamin C, calcium and fibre ... an excellent vegetable all round.

INDEX